D0585984

Community Informat...

AN IMMODEST VIOLET

AN IMMODEST VIOLET

The Life of Violet Hunt

by JOAN HARDWICK

ANDRE DEUTSCH

First published in Great Britain 1990
by André Deutsch Limited
105-106 Great Russell Street London WC1B 3LJ

Copyright © 1990 by Joan Hardwick
All rights reserved

ISBN 0 233 98639 1

Printed in Great Britain by the
St Edmundsbury Press, Bury St Edmunds, Suffolk

HERTFORDSHIRE
LIBRARY SERVICE

No.

Class

Supplier	Price	Date
JMLS	14.99	2/2

For Keith

Contents

For permission to quote I should like to thank the following: Laurence Pollinger Ltd and the Estate of Mrs Frieda Lawrence Ravagli, *The Letters of D.H. Lawrence, Vol.1*, edited by James Boulton (Cambridge University Press); The Bodley Head, *The Wife of Rossetti*; The University of Victoria Press and Robert and Marie Secor, *The Return of the Good Soldier* and *John Ruskin and Alfred Hunt. New Letters and the Record of a Friendship*; William Heinemann, *My Friends When Young, White Rose of Weary Leaf, More Tales of the Uneasy*; Macmillan Inc, *In the Days of My Youth*; Constable, *South Lodge*; Random Century, *Their Lives, Their Hearts*.

My work has been greatly assisted by the help of the librarians of the following libraries: Special Collections and Inter-Library Loans, The University of British Columbia; Vancouver Public Library; Lichfield Library. I would like to give special thanks to John Hamp of the Local Studies Department of the Central Library, Royal Borough of Kensington and Chelsea, Chris Hays of Birmingham Central Library, Lynne Farrington of Cornell University Library and Alex Kidson of the Walker Art Gallery, Liverpool

Alan Judd very kindly let me read his fine biography of Ford Madox Ford while it was still in proof stage and he has assisted with illustrations. Dr Philip Sinanan gave me advice about syphilis and its long-term effects.

I would like to thank Jeremy Lewis for his patience and his careful attention to the early stages of this book. To Esther Whitby, my editor at André Deutsch, I give my warmest thanks for all she has done from the moment of acceptance until publication.

Finally I want to thank those friends whose encouragement in difficult times was invaluable: Frances Gordon, Brigid Smedley and Karen Gelmon. I thank my son Benjamin for his patience and interest and my daughter Miranda Alldritt for all her willing help.

To my husband, Keith Alldritt, without whose support this book would never have been written, I owe a debt of gratitude beyond words.

Illustrations are by kind permission of Cornell University Library except where indicated

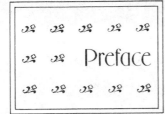

Preface

In his introduction to his mother's memoirs, *My Friends When Young*, written in 1968, Derek Patmore said of Violet Hunt:

> It seems to me that literary biographers have woefully underestimated the role which Violet Hunt played in the literary world at this period. She was the first hostess to recognise the genius of Ezra Pound, gifts of rising writers like Rebecca West and Norman Douglas, and, through her love affair with Ford Madox Hueffer, the rare talents of such unrecognised men as D.H. Lawrence.

In the twenty years that have gone by since these comments were published Violet Hunt has continued to be largely neglected. It is difficult to understand why. For not only was she an important catalyst for much of the new talent of her time, but she was also a considerable writer herself.

Robert and Marie Secor have done some invaluable work in publishing parts of Violet Hunt's voluminous diaries, her unpublished memoir of Oscar Wilde and many of the Hunt family letters to such distinguished men as John Ruskin and Robert Browning.

But to date there has been no book-length study of Violet Hunt's life or her writing. I see this book, therefore, not as a definitive biography or critical work, but as the first step in bringing Violet Hunt once more to the forefront. There is much more to be said about her life, and certainly more to be written about her novels and other writings. It is my hope that this book will serve the purpose of interesting readers in Violet Hunt and encouraging that necessary further work.

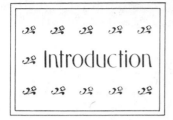

Introduction

When Violet Hunt died in 1942 she was a forgotten old woman of seventy-nine. Her house, which had been the centre for two generations of artists, poets, politicians, men of letters, was now only infrequently visited by a few loyal friends. What remained of her colourful and dynamic past were all those letters and diaries she had preserved with meticulous care over the years. There was still the desk at which Christina Rossetti had written her poetry and there was the chair in which Oscar Wilde had sat as he pursued his courtship of Violet. There were still the paintings by her father, Alfred William Hunt, and by Ford Madox Ford's grandfather, Ford Madox Brown, hung on the walls. There were the portraits of Conrad, Henry James and Robert Browning. And, of course, there were the books she had written.

But the people were all gone. Her mother's generation was, of course, long since dead. Her own generation was scattered. They no longer shared that intense life of the mind and of the eye which had distinguished the gatherings at her house, South Lodge, 80 Campden Hill Road, Kensington.

Ezra Pound was in Italy, soon to be imprisoned at Pisa and then in St Elizabeth's Hospital; Ford Madox Ford was dead; Joseph Conrad was dead; Wyndham Lewis was in Canada; T.S. Eliot, though in London, never visited; James Joyce was dead; D.H. Lawrence was dead; even the young Henri Gaudier-Brzeska was dead.

Of her two closest friends who had stuck by her through all her vicissitudes, Ethel Colburn Mayne and May Sinclair, the former was dead and the latter had been rendered helpless by Parkinson's disease.

Violet's 'flurried years', when she had been in her forties, had been strongly affected by the onset of the First World War. The Second World War had been the background for her last years.

So much had happened in the period between the two wars. Women had gained the vote; they had shown themselves capable of work previously done only by men. The two wars had made middle-class morality less hypocritical and less based on double standards than in the days when Violet had been ostracised for her affair with Ford Madox Ford. The generation of women coming to maturity in the Second World War was less sensitive to the experience of the preceding generation than are women today. They did not appear to remember the hardship experienced by the women who had fought for the freedoms they enjoyed. To Violet Hunt it seemed that no one was aware of what courage it had taken to live life as she had done.

As she always said of herself, she was born at the wrong time, too late to be able to accept comfortably the restrictions upon women that her mother found natural, and too soon to be truly the New Woman of the next generation.

She had ended up, as she had dreaded, without a husband, a child or anyone very close to her. And yet the life she had lived had been a full one. And although she herself did not benefit from it, she was one of those women who led the way out of Victorian times into a new age.

Her own writing stands as evidence for this. As a novelist she had broken new ground for a woman with her middle-class background. As a result, unlike much of the fiction of her contemporaries, Violet Hunt's novels are very relevant today. Because much of her writing has a strong autobiographical component, she has left a vivid record of what it was like to grow up at the turn of the century. She unhesitatingly exposes the hypocrisies and confusions of her society. Her heroines are all independent-minded, strong-willed women like herself. These women do not always succeed in their efforts to make their wills prevail, but their courageous and energetic attempts to do so are impressive, as is the unflinching honesty of their creator.

In Violet Hunt's life, as in her novels, it is her determination not to accept a predetermined role which engages our attention.

She told Trimmer that she had heard that Mr and Mrs Radmall's had been a regular love match; they had only known each other a week when Miss Bowman threw over the man she had been engaged to for years and ran away with the young painter.

Orinthia knew it wasn't quite that. Mamma's Papa had been very much against it because Papa was an artist, and they had had to wait until he died to get married. They must have been awfully fond of each other to wait five years, till Mamma was thirty, but they never called each other pet names or kissed — too old perhaps.

In the fictional account of her parents' marriage which we find in her autobiographical novel, *Their Hearts*, written when she was fifty-eight, Violet Hunt asserts, as she was to do throughout her life, sometimes with some bitterness and envy, that her parents' marriage had been a striking example of a love match. Indeed it must have been so, for husband and wife came from very different backgrounds.

The Raines, who lived at Crook Hall near Durham, were a family with very strong ties to the Church. James Raine, Violet's grandfather, had been ordained a priest in 1818; he had become the librarian to the Dean and Chapter of Durham Cathedral and held the living of St Mary's in Durham. In addition he was passionately interested in the history of Durham and Northumberland, and wrote an impressive number of books on the subject. His delight in the history and archaeology of the North was to surface later in his grand-daughter's work.

Not only was Margaret Raine's father a priest, but her mother's father was the Reverend Thomas Peacock, her uncle was the reforming Dean of Ely Cathedral, and her only brother was also to go into the Church.

So it is not surprising that James Raine was disappointed when his daughter — the toast of Durham, with many eligible suitors including William Greenwell, later Canon Greenwell — did not wish to marry someone from their own circle but a landscape painter. Violet describes the situation in *Their Lives*, the novel which,

1

together with *Their Hearts*, constitutes a fictional autobiography up to the death of her father: 'Her father, the Dean, had never quite approved of her betrothal to a nice fellow with, however, no fixed income, and he had died before she had consummated the sacrifice, as she laughingly called it, of a clerical virgin to the monster of pre-Raphaelitism.'

The Dean might have seen the likelihood of this eventuality when Margaret first began to take a close interest in the art world. She was twenty when she began to take drawing lessons in Durham from William Bell Scott, who held a Mastership at the Newcastle School of Design.

William Bell Scott, who had been born in Edinburgh in 1811, was a poet as well as a painter. He had already been approached for his advice as a poet by the nineteen-year-old Dante Gabriel Rossetti in 1847. When the Pre-Raphaelite Brotherhood was formed in 1848 he was fully conversant with its activities. Through Rossetti, Bell Scott became acquainted with William Holman Hunt and with Ford Madox Brown, whose pupil Rossetti became for a while. It was thus through William Bell Scott that Margaret first heard of that group of painters and poets who were to play such an important part in her life.

'The nice fellow', — Henry Radmall in the novel, Alfred William Hunt in reality — had been born in 1830 in Liverpool, a year earlier than Margaret Raine. His father, Andrew Hunt from Erdington near Birmingham, was also a landscape painter. After his marriage Andrew Hunt had gone to Liverpool, where he became one of the leading members of the Liverpool Academy.

He had taught his son and his daughters to paint at an early age, so that by the time he was twelve Alfred was sufficiently advanced to be able to exhibit a painting at the Old Water-Colour Society. Although the prime focus of Andrew Hunt's household was painting, his son's formal education was not neglected. Alfred Hunt attended Liverpool Collegiate School, and from there he won a scholarship to Corpus Christi College in Oxford. At this time he was destined for the Church. Had he pursued this calling he might have been more acceptable to James Raine, though not to his daughter Margaret.

The young painter had some success at Oxford, where he made a name for himself as a public speaker. He also distinguished himself by following in John Ruskin's footsteps and winning the Newdigate Prize for poetry in 1851. However, his first love remained landscape painting, and he decided against taking orders. The College took the unusual step of making him a fellow despite this.

When, in 1871, Margaret Hunt published her first novel, *Magdalen Wynyard, or The Provocations of a Pre-Raphaelite*, she included a thumbnail sketch of her husband, thinly disguised as the painter Bernard Longley:

> He intended Bernard for the Church but let him join his sketching excursions during his school and college vacations, and lounge about the studios (which were freely open to him for his father's sake) when in town. . . . Bernard had coquetted with art all the time he had been at university; and though he worked steadily enough to gain honours, his heart was with painting, and his mind full of the desire to reproduce on paper some of the beauty which he saw in the world around him. He said to do anything good in art, a man must give his whole life to it; and, as a clergyman, he could not do that, for he had a conscience.

Hunt's career as a painter began in earnest when James Wyatt, who sold paintings in his shop on the High Street in Oxford, bought some of his paintings and commissioned him to go to Wales and bring back as many paintings as possible.

It was at this time that Hunt began to be aware of the Pre-Raphaelite Brotherhood. His father was a member of the Liverpool Academy when it awarded William Holman Hunt a fifty-pound prize in 1851 for his painting 'Valentine Rescuing Sylvia'. The two young men, who were to become such good friends, were of a similar age — Alfred being just three years younger. But their backgrounds were very different. Whilst Alfred had been brought up on painting and had been encouraged by his father, Holman Hunt had met with opposition to his ambition to paint from his father, a warehouse manager in the City of London. His art education had been supported by odd jobs until he had begun to make a small income from portrait painting.

Despite the difference in backgrounds, the two young men had similar views about art. Both had been greatly influenced by the two volumes of *Modern Painters* published by John Ruskin in 1843 and 1846. David Barrie's comments on the influence of these two volumes on Holman Hunt could be applied equally well to Alfred Hunt: 'Ruskin's enthusiasm for the minuteness of handling and complete naturalism reached out through him to the other Pre-Raphaelites and beyond, as did his conviction that great art ought to serve a high moral or spiritual purpose.'[1] Through Ruskin both men had come to appreciate the works of J.M.W. Turner.

Although Alfred Hunt never became a member of the Pre-Raphaelite Brotherhood — indeed the group itself had become a very loose association by 1855 — he always shared with them notions derived from Ruskin. Holman Hunt's description of his own methods and aims is an apt description of those of Alfred Hunt. Both were in search of 'an out-of-door picture, with a foreground and background, abjuring altogether brown foliage, smoky clouds, and dark corners, painting the whole out of doors, direct on the canvas itself, with every detail I can see, and with the sunlight brightness of the day itself.'[2]

In the matter of colour Alfred Hunt differed from the Pre-Raphaelites, for his paintings do not have their vivid brightness. He steadfastly painted from nature and took little interest in the human form. For this reason he never painted such self-consciously literary paintings as those done by the Brotherhood.

The influence of the Pre-Raphaelites on the young Liverpool painters was enough to alarm the older members of the Academy, including Andrew Hunt. Alfred Hunt, on the other hand, was sufficiently sympathetic to the movement to argue on its side and against his father when he became a member of the Liverpool Academy in 1856, going so far as to do what Coventry Patmore had done before him in 1851 and call upon John Ruskin to use his great influence on the side of the maligned painters.

By the time he met Margaret Raine in 1857 — through their common acquaintance, William Bell Scott — he was an established painter. Edward Burne-Jones, who was about to launch on his own career, recollected going into Wyatt's in Oxford with William Morris in 1854, where 'We used to be allowed to *look* at Alfred Hunt passing through the shop — it would have been too great an honour to be allowed to speak to him.'[3]

James Raine continued to object to his daughter's marrying a man whose only source of income was his brush. Magdalen Wynyard's parents are surely expressing the horror of Margaret Raine's own parents when they realised that she was interested in marrying a painter:

> 'An artist!' said Lady Cecilia in a sharp, shrill voice.
> 'Is Bernard Longley mad?'
> 'Something very like it; for it seems to be his fixed intention to
> sell his pictures and live on the proceeds.'

It was not only the great difference in their backgrounds that made the match an unlikely one, but also the different personalities of the couple. Alfred Hunt was modest and self-effacing. He was a handsome man, but his absorption in his work showed in his eyes, which always seemed to be looking into the distance rather than at those in whose company he found himself.

His quiet modesty was a complete contrast to Margaret Raine's confident out-goingness. Her dark, rather severe good looks were accompanied by a sharpness of wit and intelligence. Alfred Hunt said very little, and was always careful not to hurt the feelings of others. Margaret spoke out with a North Country directness, and was often wounding in her forthrightness. Alfred attracted friends and admirers in spite of himself. Margaret Hunt was always seeking out acquaintances, especially if she thought they would be socially helpful to her.

Despite these differences the relationship was a firm one and withstood time and parental opposition. But it was not until 1861, after the deaths of both James Raine and Andrew Hunt, that Alfred Hunt and Margaret Raine were married. Margaret was then thirty and her husband thirty-one. Alfred gave up his fellowship at Corpus Christi, and the newly-married couple settled for a while in rented accommodation in Durham.

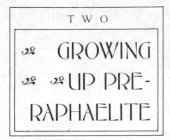

GROWING UP PRE-RAPHAELITE

Margaret Hunt quickly realised what it meant to be the wife of a landscape painter. Soon after their marriage the Hunts set off, in the summer of 1862, on a painting trip into the wilds of Northumberland. Such trips were to punctuate their lives until Alfred Hunt became too ill to withstand the rigours of painting out-of-doors in all weathers.

Their lodgings were dismal. Alfred was totally preoccupied with his work to the exclusion of any concern for his or her creature comforts. The food was inadequate. Margaret felt these discomforts, to which her husband had already become accustomed, all the more keenly because she was pregnant.

Her experiences on this and on other such occasions are described in her first novel: 'Bernard drew a moving picture of artists' miseries — ogresses of landladies, hateful lodgings, wretched food, and complete solitude, all of which must sometimes be endured almost beyond the limits of endurance, for the sake of finishing some piece of work in the place where it was begun.'

As she was to do for the rest of her life, Margaret Hunt put her husband and his painting before anything else. It was only shortly before the baby was due that Alfred Hunt woke up to the necessity of getting his wife back to Durham and more suitable surroundings.

Isobel Violet Hunt was, therefore, born in Durham on 28 September 1862. Canon William Greenwell was chosen as her god-father. This rankled with Violet all her life, for a year later another daughter was born; she was called Venetia Margaret as a compliment to John Ruskin's keen interest in that city, and Ruskin himself was asked to be the god-father.

At the age of fifty-three, Violet remembered how she had felt as a child about this matter of god-fathers through Christina in *Their Lives*: 'A great man went a very long way with Christina. She could not quite forgive her mother for not having realised that Christina was the baby who would have best appreciated the honour in later years.'

In 1865, when Violet was three, the Hunt family left Durham and moved to London. By now Alfred Hunt was a member of the Old Watercolour Society and in 1854 he had become an associate of the

Royal Academy, of which he aspired to become a Member. It is likely that the move to London was intended to further Hunt's career and improve his income now that he had a family to support, since the market for landscape painting was more limited in Durham than in London. The Hunts also hoped that the backing of John Ruskin would be helpful.

A further impetus for the move was the fact that Durham, particularly for those living in close proximity to churchmen and their wives, was far from congenial to an artist and his wife. In *Magdalen Wynyard* Margaret Hunt describes the philistinism and hypocrisy of the Close at that time, with its heavy emphasis on social climbing and the accompanying backbiting.

The family rented 1 Tor Villas in Kensington from their friend William Holman Hunt, who was about to embark on one of his recurrent painting trips to the East.

The house as Violet describes it in *Their Lives* and *Their Hearts* — where it is renamed Davenant Villa — was, like the rest of their lives, designed more for the needs of their father than for the rest of the family.

It was an inconvenient house with never enough warmth or light except in the studio, which occupied the whole of the second storey. This was a high room with the essential northern light obtained through a tall window which was half skylight. In an article about her father written for the Old Watercolour Society, Violet describes the view from the studio and its appropriateness for her father's art: 'The skies to be seen over Holland Park before Airlie Gardens was built and intercepted the view to the west were magnificent.'[1] The studio was heated by a green enamel stove with red fleurs-de-lys embossed on it. This useful item had been left by Holman Hunt. It was in this room, when the girls were old enough, that they were entrusted with washing the less valuable brushes and 'rubbing' colours for their father.

The bedrooms were on the third floor. There was no bathroom and all the hot water for washing had to be carried up from the basement kitchen.

It was in the drawing-room that the family's Pre-Raphaelite connections and tastes were announced. They were unable to do anything much about such fixtures as the ugly chandelier and the Victorian marble fireplace. But the rest of the room was in

7

Pre-Raphaelite style, with heavy, carved chairs and glass cabinets. On the walls was William Morris's 'Daisy' paper and at the windows hung red and green woollen curtains with great scrolls woven in silk and gold. These were also from The Firm, William Morris's company. Margaret Hunt, who was thrifty in many matters, did not count the cost in acquiring these items. The finishing touch was provided by Alfred Hunt's watercolours, which were hung about the room.

Although in later years the rest of the house was decorated in other styles, this room remained dedicated to Pre-Raphaelitism. And long after Alfred Hunt was dead and Margaret and Violet had moved to South Lodge, Margaret still insisted on having the 'Daisy' paper on the drawing-room walls despite the protests of extravagance from the rest of the family and accusations against Violet of encouraging her mother to fritter away her money and their potential inheritance.

At this time the Pre-Raphaelite painters and their families were socially very close. In 1870 William Bell Scott moved to Bellevue House in Chelsea and the Hunts were frequent visitors. Violet describes this emphatically Pre-Raphaelite house in several places, including *Their Lives*:

> The walls were hung with the great Pre-Raphaelite masterpieces whose subjects were the substance of Christina's broodings, but which to all those persons were a splendid commonplace: 'The Blessed Damozel', 'La Belle Dame sans Merci', and 'Mary in the House of John'. There stood the great cupboards, the *armoires* of the Middle Ages, left open, some of them, to show the inside panelling, painted by William Morris and Dante Gabriel Rossetti. In the corner was the portrait of a contemporary poet with his head like a burning bush, as her mother had remarked to the man himself.

The Alma-Tademas, the Ford Madox Browns, the Burne-Joneses, the Millais and Lord Leighton all lived close by and were frequent visitors. Indeed a clay pipe was kept in the house specifically for the visits of Millais.

The children were invited to each other's parties. In her autobiography, *The Flurried Years*, Violet recalls such parties and her first meeting with the man whose wife she later aspired to be: 'I used to go to Pre-Raphaelite children's parties at the Seddons' and Tebbs' to help, and often had to rap the fingers of the two high-spirited Hueffer boys for playing ball with the penny buns.'

There were other parties at which Violet and Venice, as the family had come to call Venetia, competed for the attentions of Philip Burne-Jones, who was just a year older than Violet — though Violet herself appears to have been more interested in his father, Edward.

For such occasions the girls would be dressed in Pre-Raphaelite style — partly, it must be said, because it was cheaper to dress them in this way. We get a glimpse of Margaret Hunt's attitude toward this in *Their Lives*: 'Mrs Radmall found it came cheaper to dress her children artistically. There was a distinct sartorial standard to be adhered to by the children of the members of the Brotherhood.'*

If we look at contemporary fashions, with their elaborate frills, bustles and yards of fabric under which tight corseting was necessary, then we can see that Margaret Hunt had good reason for the style she settled on for her daughters.

It was at such a party that Ellen Terry saw Violet and described her as being 'out of Botticelli by Burne-Jones'.[2] Violet would have appreciated this compliment since she was, as a young girl, a fervent admirer of Burne-Jones and consciously tried to model her appearance on the figures in his paintings.

A photograph of Violet as a young girl shows what a beauty she was. Her auburn hair is fluffy and substantial, pulled back behind her ears but low on her forehead. Her eyebrows are deeply marked, her nose pronounced. Her eyes are beautiful and challenging, her mouth is full and well moulded, her chin is cleft. The photographer has enhanced the exotic in her appearance by emphasising the shadows in her face and by placing behind her a parasol, which gives the curious effect of a peacock headdress.

An important paradox emerges from this photograph. Although all the requirements for Pre-Raphaelite beauty are there, the

---

* Although Violet continued to describe the group of friends as the Brotherhood, the term was not strictly accurate by this time. The original group, which had been formed in 1848, had long ago disbanded. William Holman Hunt, John Everett Millais, Dante Gabriel Rossetti and his brother William Michael Rossetti continued to be regarded as Pre-Raphaelites by the general public. To their number had been added Ford Madox Brown, Edward Burne-Jones and William Morris, largely because of their association with Dante Gabriel Rossetti.

forcefulness of her character, which even at this age is very evident in her expression, goes against what the painters chose to see in their women. She distinctly lacks the proper melancholy and sexual ambiguity of a Burne-Jones model. She had inherited her appearance from her father but her temperament from her mother.

Although Alfred Hunt was so closely associated with the Brotherhood and had even defended their cause in Liverpool when his own father was against them, he was very different from them both in temperament and in his art.

Everyone who knew him agreed that Alfred Hunt was a modest, quiet and kindly man, completely dedicated to his art. He was prepared to spend long hours alone painting in wild places in harsh weather conditions. His favourite haunts were Wales, Northumberland, North Yorkshire and the Lake District. In this he was very like Turner, to whose work his own was often compared. Late in life, when Ezra Pound was recollecting the paintings of Alfred Hunt that Violet had loaned him to furnish his rooms, he wrote: 'Don't think I much appreciated the Hunts at that time. . . . Now I should probably wonder if any école de Turner was as good let alone better.'[3] A contemporary critic, W. Newall, claimed even more for Hunt's art. He wrote: 'He had a keener sense of observation of Nature than Turner but his style was different — his power of work was less but the order of mind with intense appreciation of atmospheric effect was greater than Turner's.'[4]

In Margaret Hunt's novel *The Leaden Casket* several of his paintings are described in detail. The contrast between his work and that of the more fashionable of his associates is vividly demonstrated:

> Olive's eyes strayed away from these garish glories to a smaller picture which was placed just above. A bit of blue sky and an ash bough drooping down to a river bed with quiet grey stones in it, made her wish that the peacock's eyes of this mystical lady's mantle were not so bright, or the red of her hair not so pronounced; for, whether this landscape was well or ill painted, she felt a pleasure in looking at it. The artist had done his best to realise a scene like ever so many that she remembered, with little thought, perhaps, of the fantastic juxtaposition which his work was destined to suffer.

Violet herself said of her father that 'Turner was his master in spirit — David Cox in the flesh.'[5]

His children were very fond of him, but he was a rather absent figure in their lives. He was mostly either away on painting trips or closeted in his studio, where he was not to be disturbed. The portrait of Mr Radmall in *Their Lives* and *Their Hearts* is very closely based on Alfred Hunt: 'It was Mamma's business to amuse the children, nurse, scold, do everything for them; Papa only loved them, and must not be disturbed.'

Margaret Hunt was a very different personality from her husband. She was confident, outgoing, witty, with a gift for biting sarcasm. Violet portrays her as Mrs Radmall:

> The wife of Henry Radmall had by inheritance and acquirement high standards of conduct. She lived up to them, but having more wit than heart, she could not help taking a low view of human motives and ideals. She was generous and cynical; always inclined to think the worst, and then forgive it.

Elsewhere in the novels Violet says that 'To Mrs Radmall's own family her tongue was a matter of painful and daily impact.' In his preface to *The Governess*, Margaret Hunt's novel which Violet edited, added to and published in 1912, Ford Madox Ford gives his perspective on Margaret Hunt:

> She had, moreover, a brilliant social popularity — if that can be called popularity which consisted in having most of the great men of her day constantly in her drawing room and equally constantly afraid of her biting and nimble tongue. From Rossetti to Ruskin, and from Ruskin to my grandfather, Madox Brown, and from Madox Brown to Sir John Gilbert and the artists of the Old Water-Colour Society, and from them to Sir Charles Dilke or Mr Joseph Chamberlain, there was not one that, from the 'seventies to the 'nineties, would not have told you that Mrs Alfred Hunt was the wittiest woman in London.

Although published under the pseudonym of Averil Beaumont, *Magdalen Wynyard* caused a scandal and a sensation such as must have been very painful for her self-effacing husband. In it Margaret Hunt portrays the lives and personalities of those associated with

Durham Cathedral Close, using only thin disguises. It is a far from flattering portrait and offended all those who recognised themselves. She followed this in 1873 with *Thornicroft's Model*, very broadly based on the character of Dante Gabriel Rossetti and his relationship with Elizabeth Siddal. Once again she used her pseudonym, and once again she provoked a controversy with her implied criticism of the selfish attitude of men towards marriage and its ties, and with her depiction of a bigamous marriage.

She was a handsome woman with an upright carriage and an elegant figure of which she was very proud. She wore her long dark hair parted in the middle and pulled back somewhat severely from her face with its high broad forehead. Her eyebrows were well marked and her eyes slightly hooded, giving an expression of reserve and severity. Her nose was very straight, her mouth rather narrow and tight. The strength of her character is clearly visible in her face. In the portrait of her which was published in the periodical *The Throne* in 1912 she appears an arrogant woman.

In 1866 a third child, Silvia, was born. As the girls grew up she was always the odd one out, the least assertive and, as a child, the least attractive. Margaret Hunt did not welcome this addition to her family. In her novels Violet conveys Silvia's feeling of being the odd member of the family by repeatedly using the image of the changeling with reference to Orinthia, Silvia's fictional counterpart.

The three sisters were brought up in a rather haphazard manner. Not only was their father too preoccupied with his painting to pay them much attention, but their mother, who was theoretically responsible for their upbringing, was often unavailable because she gave so much time to her writing. By the time Violet was sixteen her mother had already published six novels and she was to go on to write more. In one of them, *The Leaden Casket*, Margaret Hunt shows some awareness of what her novel-writing cost her family, but she justifies this by having Mrs Brooke, who is largely based on herself, quote Plato in her own defence: 'The education of the children of great men is often neglected; if people are to be great, they can only attend to their own development.'

For much of the time the girls were cared for by a succession of nurse-maids and governesses who spoke a variety of languages. Both Alfred and Margaret Hunt were interested in Germany. They had visited the country together before they were married, and took their children there when they were young; and Margaret had worked with Andrew Lang on his versions of *Grimms' Fairy Tales*. The children were encouraged to follow this interest of their parents, and one of the first books to be given to them was Grimm. So it is not surprising that a German nursemaid was hired to look after them. Violet describes her influence in her book about Germany, *The Desirable Alien*, and again in *The Flurried Years*: 'My German nurse, Milly, from Paderborn, the home of folk-lore and superstition, had for the time made me and my sisters into such little Germans that it was useless to give us an order or scold us in any other tongue. French nurses at eight years old made an end to that.'

The French nurses were Catherine and Reine Dausoigne, two sisters from Corsica. The manner in which they came to have a place in the Hunt household tells us much about how the girls were being brought up.

In 1869, when Violet was just seven, the Hunts accepted an invitation from the wealthy industrialist and art patron Sidney Courtauld to go on a nine-month cruise in the Mediterranean. While their mother and father were away the girls were sent to stay with relatives in Cambridge.

In 1866 Margaret Hunt had reviewed *Edward Lear in Corsica: The Journal of a Landscape Painter*. She had been particularly struck by his description of two sisters living above an inn in the mountain village of Gratte di Vivario, so when the party landed at Ajaccio she took the opportunity to drive into the mountains to see the two sisters for herself. She found the inn just as dirty and uncomfortable as Lear had described it. There were no stairs to the upper floor, only a ladder. At the top of the ladder, in an elegant parlour, were the two sisters. They had been educated in a French convent and could no longer even speak the local patois. Their convent education had enabled them to perform the accomplishments of the drawing-room. They were skilled in embroidery and drawing and had thoroughly elegant manners. It was rumoured that their father was not their mother's husband, who had been the innkeeper, but the Marquis de St Brie.

Margaret was struck by the beauty and the accomplishments of the two girls whom they had found in such unlikely surroundings. It was her belief that the girls need only make an appearance in society to achieve the good matches which would provide them with appropriate settings in which to shine.

So the two girls were taken back to England and made a part of the Hunt household. They taught the girls French and how to make beautiful clothes for their Parisian doll.

But, despite the interest shown in the girls as models by the Pre-Raphaelite painters and by the photographer Julia Margaret Cameron, and despite Sidney Courtauld's short-lived passion for Catherine and Holman Hunt's passing fancy for Reine, they received no proposals of marriage. Eventually they returned to Corsica. They made subsequent visits to England and stayed with the Hunt family, but no husbands were found for them. Their sad life after this excursion into the larger world is depicted in Violet's story, 'The Corsican Sisters'.

The upbringing of the Hunt girls may have been haphazard but it was certainly not bohemian. They may have been the daughters of an artist, but the family was basically middle-class, and the structured lives of the three young girls reflected this. For the most part they were in the company of nurse-maids and governesses. They had lessons in the morning, simple food at midday and then walks in nearby Kensington Gardens with one of the maids. It was here that the German nurse-maid, Milly, liked to stop and watch the royal children playing in the gardens of Kensington Palace while she chatted with their nurse-maid.

In the evening the family might gather together in the drawing-room. If she was in a good mood Margaret Hunt would help her daughters select cards to be pasted into a scrapbook, while Alfred Hunt sat somewhat apart and read. The two younger girls would be sent to bed early while Violet cherished her privilege as the eldest one of being allowed to stay up an extra half hour in which she might read.

As Violet and her sisters grew older they became increasingly quarrelsome. Most of the trouble was the result of the hostility between Violet and Venice. The two girls were very close to each other in age but Violet was always distinguished as the oldest child and given little privileges and they were both conscious of the difference in the way they were treated. Violet was proud of her status while Venice was, understandably, resentful. For many years, for example, it was Violet who had all the new clothes which were then passed down in turn to her younger sisters and it was a triumphant day for Venice when she outstripped her older sister in growth and the practice had to be discontinued.

Despite these problems the two girls might have been good company for each other had they not been such very different personalities. Violet was lively and often in trouble; Venice was quieter and more withdrawn, even to the point of being secretive. Their mother began to have difficulty in maintaining the tranquil atmosphere she felt her husband needed for the success of his work. It was for this reason that it was decided to send Violet and Venice to school.

The school chosen for them was the new and progressive Notting Hill High School, within walking distance of the house at Tor Villas, down Holland Park Road. It was

> the first of its kind planned by Lady Stanley of Alderley, Mrs Russell Gurney and all sorts of bigwigs, for the amalgamation in infancy of the classes and the masses. Miss Mash, the green-grocer's daughter, and Miss Agnes Lane Fox, now Lady Grove, sat on either side of one. Miss Margaret Burne-Jones and Miss May Morris held honoured places in the school.

In this description in *The Flurried Years* Violet does not mention that Catherine Madox Brown, Ford Madox Ford's mother, had also attended the school.

Violet was very impressed by May Morris, whom she described as 'the most beautiful creature I ever saw, cold and unkind to me who adored her from afar'. But it was with May's older sister Alice, whom Violet called Jenny, that she struck up a friendship, and it was Jenny who invited Violet to tea at Kelmscott House. The occasion was a memorable one for a girl brought up on stories of Jane Morris and her relationship with Dante Gabriel Rossetti: 'Rapt, holding my breath with awe, I had tea with her and her father and mother. I can never forget Mrs Morris sitting still, silent and withdrawn, on the high-backed settle with the painted bend-over roof.'[6]

Although she enjoyed the experience of school, Violet considered that she learnt very little in her time there. Her education continued to come from her own extensive reading and from the exchanges she heard at home.

The main beneficiary of the new regime was, as planned, their father, as Violet indicates in *Their Lives*: 'Her father, as usual considering matters from the point of view of the furtherance of art, used to say, laughing, that there was a marked improvement in the conditions of his work since the two eldest had been at school all day. The house was delightfully quiet.'

Violet's formal education was concluded with time spent at the Kensington Art School when she was eighteeen. Georgina Burne-Jones, the wife of Edward, had also been a pupil there. Although Violet proved to be a competent student she did not take her studies or her fellow-students very seriously. She received and refused her first proposal of marriage at this time.

The theatre attracted her, and she considered writing plays. For a while she was obsessed with the actor Henry Irving and took every opportunity to see him perform. The knowledge she gained of the theatre was to be of use to her when she came to write dialogue in her novels and as her background for the plot of her novel *The Celebrity's Daughter*.

Throughout these years all three girls were made aware that the livelihood of the household depended not only upon Alfred Hunt's ability to paint but also to sell his paintings. He was not, however, by nature a man to promote himself or to put commercial considerations before artistic ones. Landscape painting became unfashionable but Hunt persisted with it. He failed to be elected to the Royal Academy but swallowed his disappointment and continued as usual.

Margaret Hunt felt that both problems could be solved if only her husband would be content to produce from time to time the kind of painting that the public wanted. It galled her to see contemporaries of her husband, who were, in her opinion, his inferiors, receiving the money, the acclaim and the public recognition that she felt properly belonged to him.

But Alfred Hunt would not be moved by her arguments. She had to content herself with supplementing the family income by her writing. That this was both distressing and irritating to her husband is revealed in a letter he wrote in November 1873 to John Ruskin: 'Margaret and I are pleased with the *Spectator*'s article upon her novel. What she will write hereafter (after the next) will I hope have a better plan and a moral meaning. It's a fashious thing meddling with art at all.'[7]

Alfred Hunt's worries about money and his disappointment at his

failure to advance in the art world made a deep impression on
Violet. At the age of seventy her opinions were still coloured by her
mother's view of those who had failed to elect him to the Royal
Academy. She writes of them in her biography of Elizabeth Siddal,
The Wife of Rossetti, as 'the Sanhedrin of old, mild but evil men who
had sat down heavily in the High Places of British Art and
persistently stifled all efforts to see things truly and well'.

Of her three daughters Margaret Hunt favoured her eldest.
Perhaps she appreciated in Violet a similar personality. It was, after
all, Violet who aspired to write; it was Violet who enjoyed meeting
people, especially if they were famous in any way; and it was Violet,
with her striking looks and charming manners, who could be relied
upon to do her mother credit on social occasions. As a result, she
was allowed into adult company far more than other girls of her age.
It was on one of these outings, a tea party at the apartment of her
mother's friend Louise Chandler Moulton, that she first met the
naturalist W.H. Hudson. She describes her first meeting with him at
some length in *The Flurried Years*:

> I had met him for the first time at a tea-party, when he was
> married and starving in Southwick Crescent and I was a lively
> child too much brought forward for her age, allowed to 'pour tea'
> for her mother's great friend, Mrs Louise Chandler Moulton. It
> was in one of those sets of furnished apartments where that lady
> entertained her European friends every season. I hope that I gave
> him enough cake. He may have been about forty-five, and his hair
> was already grizzled. His skin was dark, and colour was on his
> high cheekbones, which was not there in the last three years of his
> life. He appeared to my eyes so foreign-looking that I first missed,
> and then almost seemed to see, the earrings in his ears and the
> scimitar in his sash. But he was, in effect, wearing a blue serge
> reefer suit.

He was an old man when, in 1921, Violet dedicated her novel
Their Hearts to him. Although it deals with a period in Violet's life
that Hudson would have remembered, the dedication is puzzling —
for, if he ever read the novel, what would he have made of the severe
portrait of his good friend Margaret Hunt? And how would he have
responded to this exposé of such a seemingly respectable and
respected household?

Violet was fourteen when she first met Henry James in a chemist's shop. She was formally introduced to him shortly after at a party given by George Boughton, the painter.

Henry James was nineteen years older than Violet and very much an *éminence grise* by the time she became aware of him. His career as a novelist had begun with the publication of *Roderick Hudson* in 1875. He had then spent time in Paris where he had met such literary figures as Flaubert and Turgenev before moving to London in 1876.

Violet's memory of James at this time is of a silken-bearded man with 'deep wonderful eyes'. She felt that he too looked as if he might have worn earrings and been an Elizabethan sea captain.

Despite the way in which Margaret Hunt took Violet into society and gave her the opportunity of meeting distinguished people, Violet was always aware that she, like her sisters, came a poor second to her father in her mother's thoughts and considerations. Time and again in her fiction she emphasises her father's centrality to the otherwise female household. Even holidays were organised to meet the painter's needs rather than the children's.

Apart from occasional trips abroad, holidays were mostly taken in the North of England. Margaret Hunt justified taking her children to wet, inhospitable places on the grounds that it was good for them to get out of the city and have an opportunity to run wild. Violet saw through this reasoning, as the following passage from *Their Lives* indicates:

> They went across country to join their father in a place where it always rained because of the mountains. He had warned them, but they did not really know it would be so bad. And they were not really allowed to run wild. It always rained and yet you were not supposed to get wet. They rebelled in all sorts of ways and Mrs Radmall bitterly regretted her experiment.

Because Violet was fond of her father and respected him she was resigned to accepting his special place in the household. She was less able to accept and act upon her mother's attitudes towards sex, morality and the proper female role. A confusion was set up in her young mind which persisted all her life.

In *Their Hearts* she explores the effects of the extreme prudery with which the girls were brought up. It is the day on which Virgilia is to be married, and she is getting washed in the bedroom she shares with her younger sister:

> And Orinthia, according to the formula prescribed since child-hood, buried her face in the sheet, while her sister emptied the jug full of cold water into the basin, dropped her nightgown to the waist, knotted it by the sleeves, and bathed her body, which no one, it was her boast, had ever seen naked, not even the doctor. She would die sooner than permit an operation.

As far as sexual matters were concerned, the girls, almost as a matter of principle, were kept in ignorance. Violet depicts Virgilia on the eve of her wedding as being still unsure of what will happen to her once she is married. Her older sister, when consulted, proves to be just as ignorant. The fact that this was not an unusual situation in Victorian England did not prevent Violet from deploring its consequences.

Even the self-confident and precocious Violet was affected by her mother's attitude:

> Mrs Radmall looked upon sex as a slightly revolting pathological detail and refused to penetrate further than was actually necessary into any such byways of medical science. She vaguely realised and it did not interest her much, that Christina's physical development had not kept pace with her mental progress.

But most puzzling to the three girls growing up must have been the discrepancy between their mother's attitude towards their sexuality and that of the men of their acquaintance. She thought none the worse of Rossetti and Burne-Jones for their well-publicised affairs, nor of Millais for having wooed Effie Ruskin while she was still John Ruskin's wife; nor did she seem to have found anything strange in the elderly Ruskin doting on a schoolgirl.

Much later, in her own fiction and in *The Wife of Rossetti*, Violet was to react against her mother and take a strong position against her double standards.

It is in the relationship Margaret Hunt promoted between her daughters and Ruskin that we can see most clearly the strange morality and sexuality that permeated the household in which Violet grew up.

19

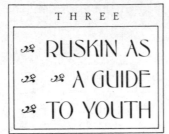
The long friendship between Alfred Hunt and John Ruskin had begun in 1856, when Alfred had exhibited his painting 'The Stream from the Llyn Iwal' at the Royal Academy. Ruskin saw in it the strong influence of Turner, and he approved. In his *Academy Notes* he praised the painting in terms that gave Alfred Hunt the confidence to write to him for support for the Pre-Raphaelites in Liverpool.

Ruskin continued to praise Hunt's work in public, but as the friendship developed he had no hesitation about urging Hunt on to greater efforts to improve his work. It was Ford Madox Ford's contention that Hunt's landscapes would have been better without the improvements suggested by Ruskin.[1]

It was after their marriage that Alfred Hunt introduced Margaret to Ruskin. She was delighted to become acquainted with a man whom she rightly saw as a very influential figure in the art world. Throughout the rest of Ruskin's life Margaret Hunt did all she could to promote and maintain the friendship. While they were still living in Durham Ruskin was their guest on several occasions, and after they had moved to London they were invited to visit the Ruskins.

It was with a view to forming a lasting connection with the great man that Margaret had asked Ruskin to be the god-father of her second child — and this despite her strong Church background and Ruskin's declared views on orthodox religion. Unlike the traditional god-father he was not prepared to hold the baby at the font to be christened — nor indeed would he attend the ceremony. And he could not undertake, as a god-father should, to ensure that his god-daughter was educated in the Anglican faith: rather he would encourage her to know the truth of God through 'the light of heaven and the laws of Earth'.[2] Margaret's determination to form strong ties with Ruskin overcame any religious qualms she might have felt.

The children were occasionally taken to 163 Denmark Hill where Ruskin lived with his parents. Violet's sense of him at this time was of a 'kind wolf with bushy fierce eyebrows'. After lunch they were taken into his study. In her essay 'Ruskin as a Guide to Youth', published in the *Westminster Gazette* in February 1900, Violet recreates one such occasion:

There were glass cases all round the walls and no pictures at all. In these cases reposed Mr Ruskin's famous collection of minerals, most of which he afterwards gave to Sheffield. They were lying, some on shelves lined with delicate pieces of satin and velvet, that served to throw them up, others in neat cardboard boxes with glass lids on them. Mr Ruskin took them down one by one, and showed us the beautiful bits of semi-transparent stone, polished quartz, brown shaggy lamps shot through with 'gems of purest ray', as it seemed a golden spider had spun a web across the dusky ground-work, and one or two bits he gave us for our own. But to the eternal disgrace, perhaps, of utilitarian, materialistic childhood be it told that our hearts were lovingly fixed on those beautifully made cardboard boxes, so sure to be useful in a thousand childish ways.

Whenever Ruskin visted 1 Tor Villas he would take with him gifts of books for the children. The illustrations in these books never met his own high standards and he always felt obliged to apologise for their poor quality, saying that he could, however, find no better to buy.

In his letters to Alfred and Margaret Hunt Ruskin always sent his love to his god-daughter Venice, only rarely mentioning Violet and Silvia. But in 1873, when he was in despair about Rose La Touche, with whom he was hopelessly in love and whom he saw growing increasingly insane as she approached her death, Margaret Hunt decided that Venice would be the very person to comfort him for his loss.* Venice was then only eight years old. Ruskin was enthusiastic about the idea, so arrangements were made. Margaret and Alfred went to Ruskin's house in the Lake District – Brantwood, on Lake Coniston – taking Venice with them, but leaving the other two girls behind. Eventually Alfred Hunt took lodgings on the other side of

---

* Ruskin had first met Rose La Touche when she was only ten years old. By the time she was twelve he was in love with her and remained so until her death. The relationship was for the most part a torment to Ruskin. He was prepared to wait until Rose was old enough to marry him. Her parents took fright at this point and, after consulting Ruskin's first wife Effie, they broke off the relationship. For some years Ruskin alternated between the hope that Rose would eventually marry him and despair that she would not. He was never able to break completely free from the effect she had on him. Rose became progressively more ill in her early twenties. At times only Ruskin seemed able to calm her madness. She died in 1875, aged twenty-seven.

the lake. Margaret returned to London and Venice was left with Ruskin. Margaret had unrealistically high hopes of Ruskin's ability to be a good influence on Venice and of Venice's ability to bring comfort to the fifty-four-year-old man. Her hopes, inevitably, were not realised. Venice was not happy at Brantwood away from her family. Ruskin wrote that she always appeared to be frightened. She did not have much to say to him, and he complained of her reserve.

Ruskin's theories about young girls had much in common with those of the French philosopher, Jean-Jacques Rousseau. He believed in the essential innocence and goodness of children. He was not prepared for Venice who, though shy and quiet in the presence of adults, was assertive, selfish and determined to stand up for her own rights when with other children. Ruskin came to realise this as the result of a particular incident. He asked Venice, along with a neighbour's child, to clear an overgrown path, and Venice bullied the other child into clearing all the holly branches while she undertook less disagreeable work. Although her behaviour was not at all unusual, Ruskin was deeply shocked by it. He felt he had to send for Margaret to take Venice away. In his letters about Venice after the unfortunate visit, Ruskin hints that perhaps the Hunt girls did not get enough loving attention from their parents and that this was responsible for the character flaws he observed in them.

Unlike Venice, Violet already understood that the attention of such a great man as Ruskin was something to strive for. When the family were all settled in Alfred's lodgings on Lake Coniston in the later part of the summer she set about cultivating Ruskin's friendship. He found her precocious manner of conversing very distressing. Her remark to him that she was a 'disreputable baggage' found its way into his diary with the comment 'modern education'. When she remarked to the company that Venice was 'the flower of the flock', Ruskin wrote at length to Margaret Hunt with advice on how she should handle this eleven-year-old who showed no proper modesty and who made such knowing comments.

However, Violet quickly found a way to gain the lasting attention of Ruskin. She knew that he greatly admired the novels of Sir Walter Scott, so she set herself to read them and to talk to Ruskin about them. He was so delighted with her good taste that he arranged for a set of Scott's works to be sent to Violet in London. He followed this with other gifts of books, including the works of Maria Edgeworth.

Violet's evident success with Ruskin is shown in a letter written to her at the end of that summer of 1873:

> My dear Violet,
>   I am obliged to be at Coniston this afternoon myself —
> so if it is fine, I will come about half past two and have a little play
> and talk on the hillside — if it rains, it must be for another day —
> unless you're going away — if so I'll come to say goodbye this
> afternoon rain or fair. Love to Venice and Silvia.
>   Ever affectionately yrs/J. Ruskin

One of these talks was recalled in later years in *I Have This To Say*, the American edition of her autobiography:

> When I was a little girl John Ruskin took me for a long walk in the
> nut woods at Brantwood and, in reply to one of the heart-
> searching, anticipating questions of girlhood — questions that on
> no account can be put to one's parents but only to one's chosen
> mentor as this man was to me and many other children — he told
> me simply — simply, earnestly as if one was grown up though one
> was only eleven and that was why one loved him; – 'Find someone
> you can love and trust and then count no sacrifice too great to
> make in that one's service.'

From then on Violet was mentioned in all the letters from Ruskin to the Hunts.

If Margaret's behaviour in sending Venice to console Ruskin for the loss of Rose La Touche could be considered strange and unhealthy, how much more extravagant was her attitude in 1875. Ruskin had seen his beloved Rose for the last time. She was in such a state of madness that he was deeply upset. Margaret, his confidante in the matter of Rose, and always looking for ways to develop the family's intimacy with him, encouraged the thirteen-year-old Violet to offer herself as a wife to Ruskin in three years' time, when she would be a more suitable age.

Ruskin's letter shows how moved he was by this proposal.

> My dear Margaret,
>   I really think Violets must be nicer than roses after all
> — Another three years to wait — though! What a weary life I have
> of it.

23

Oh me, I don't feel, just now, as if there were three years waiting in me for anything. I wonder if it's pride — or duty that makes me hold on here — I do so long for any place where I could rest and have — Violet, or the like — to manage everything for me — and nurse me — and no one hear of me any more.

Love to Sylvia and Venice and my fiancée (goodness! I don't know which way to put the accent!)

This new intimacy with Violet, evidently encouraged by Margaret, is maintained in a letter written in March: 'I was greatly tempted to beg for a kiss from Violet in bed — but thought that *our* extreme naughtiness was enough for *one* day.'

In 1876 Margaret was still promoting the relationship between Violet and Ruskin. This time she sent him some poems that Violet had written. Ruskin liked the poetry but, perhaps resisting the way Margaret sought to encourage Violet's precociousness, concluded his letter by saying that, 'nor can I in the least measure the quality of work done by children in the hothouse of the modern world.'

It seems that Violet herself took her engagement with some seriousness, for replying in June 1879 to a letter from her we find Ruskin sensibly putting their relationship into perspective and by implication releasing Violet from any bond she might have thought existed:

My dear Violet,

I am very glad of your loving little letter, and I hope you will always love me enough to read with some prejudice in their favour books which you might have otherwise little cared for, and which I am yet sure contain things that will be useful to you. But you must not waste your heart — or your time, in what Papa and Mamma might think only a dutiful and necessary memory of me.

Although in 1878 Margaret had helped to organise the purchase and presentation of a Turner drawing which Ruskin had coveted as a young man, as he became more and more of a recluse, at times overcome by fits of madness, his relationship with the Hunt family became more tenuous. In the 1880s news of Ruskin came largely from his niece, Joan Severn, who had undertaken to look after him. The last time Violet saw him was at a viewing at the Old Watercolour Society. She wrote in her diary: 'Ruskin old and bearded. "Do you know me?" "No — no — unless" a radiant smile — "unless you're Violet?" He is quite mad.'

The deep impression Ruskin made on Violet as a young girl remained with her all her life. He is portrayed with sympathy and respect as the Professor in *Their Lives* and *Their Hearts*. She largely accepted his standards and tastes as far as art and literature were concerned. She remained a loyal supporter of the Pre-Raphaelite painters whom Ruskin had promoted, and in her own writing she tried always to achieve the clear-sighted honesty that Ruskin had preached.

She could not subscribe to his views on women and the place they should occupy in society, though her mother found it possible to do so. However, she came to understand how much of his personal life had been affected by his strange sexuality.* In putting the blame for this on Ruskin's mother, was she commenting also on her own mother and on the generation of middle-class women who had brought up their children to think of sexual relationships as somehow dirty, to be endured rather than enjoyed? Her last portrait of him in *The Wife of Rossetti*, published long after his death, is understanding and sympathetic without in any way trying to disguise his eccentricities.

FOUR

⁂ ⁂ ⁂ THE
⁂ SWEETEST
⁂ ⁂ VIOLET

As an old woman Violet used to point out to visitors the chair in which Oscar Wilde had sat when he proposed to her. Whether he actually went so far as to propose marriage is uncertain and, in view of his circumstances, unlikely. He was fully aware that Alfred Hunt was not a rich man and that he would not improve his own financial position by marrying Hunt's daughter. But there is no doubt that for a time he was very close to the Hunt

---

* Ruskin was unable to love adult women. He was always interested in little girls and he always wanted to keep his relationships with them pure and spiritual. He did not remarry after his marriage to his cousin Effie Gray had been annulled on the grounds that it had never been consummated because of Ruskin's impotence.

family and made a point of singling out Violet for his attentions.

At first Alfred Hunt was the attraction in the household at Tor Villas. Oscar Wilde's mother, Lady Wilde, was a great admirer of Hunt's paintings. Wilde himself must have felt a bond with the painter when, in 1878, he won the Newdigate Prize at Oxford with his poem 'Ravenna', just as Hunt had won it for his poem in 1851.

In her essay 'My Oscar', Violet claims to have first met Oscar Wilde at the home of William Bell Scott in 1880, when Violet was eighteen and Wilde twenty-six.[1] Wilde was already a fashionable and much sought-after young man, so the young Violet was extremely flattered by the attention he bestowed upon her.

Wilde became a regular visitor to Tor Villas, but he was always entertained as part of a larger group or with the whole family present. These visits, and the growing intimacy between Wilde and Violet, are described in *Their Lives*, in which Wilde appears as Philip Wynyard. When she describes Wilde in *The Flurried Years* she used more or less the same words as she had in the novel:

> I remember Oscar, before America, when he was really still a slightly stuttering, slightly lisping, long-limbed boy, sitting in the big armchair at Tor Villa, where we lived then, lounging fatuously, tossing the long black lock on his forehead that America swept away, and talking — talking — happening to talk about maps and other things.

In *Their Lives* Violet suggests that while she was attracted intellectually to Wilde she found him physically distasteful. Mr and Mrs Radmall are made to drop dark hints about the impossibility of marriage between Philip and Christina. It is, however, unlikely that the Hunts would then have known about Wilde's homosexuality, particularly since he was known to have courted Margaret Burne-Jones briefly and was to go on to become engaged to Constance Lloyd in 1883.

Other characters in the novel warn Christina that Philip needs to marry for money, and that he will overcome whatever feelings he has for her in order to find a suitable heiress.

Clearly Violet was attracted to Wilde and enjoyed the attentions he paid her. When she came to fictionalise the relationship, to hide her disappointment she created obstacles in the way of a marriage between Christina and Philip, and makes her heroine feel some physical distaste for her suitor.

The letters between Margaret Hunt and Oscar Wilde collected in Rupert Hart-Davis's edition of Wilde's letters suggest no reservations on her part towards him. On the contrary, she urges him to visit frequently, she takes Violet to tea with him and Lady Wilde, and she accepts invitations for herself and Violet to attend the theatre with him. She even goes so far as to invite him to join the family on their holidays in the North of England. The correspondence makes it quite clear that at this time Margaret Hunt would have found Oscar Wilde a highly desirable match for her daughter. For Violet he had the attraction of a suitable family background combined with a suggestion of excitement and unconventionality.

It is not so easy to judge how seriously interested in Violet Wilde was. He enjoyed flirting with her, but he was almost certainly aware that her veneer of sophistication covered a great sexual and emotional naivety. She had read a great deal about love, but had so far had no real emotional involvements. He calls her 'the sweetest Violet in England', a judgement which he must have voiced aloud, for Violet Wyndham reported the comment with some malice and envy in *The Sphinx and her Circle*, her biography of her mother, Ada Leverson.

Wilde underlined the intimacy of their relationship by sending poems to Violet and by taking a close interest in the poetry she was writing at this time. He sent her his 1881 volume of poems, and Violet responded with fulsome appreciation.

In December that same year Wilde sailed for America. Whatever Violet had expected it was in fact the end of the relationship. Wilde made no attempt to resume his close friendship with the Hunt family when he returned. By 1887, when he was editor of *Woman's World*, he was writing to Margaret Hunt in the most formal terms, as though they were barely acquainted.

The episode with Oscar Wilde left Violet confused. She was to re-examine her relationship with him several times over the years from different points of view and in different forms. What is revealed by all her accounts is that she felt that Wilde had built up her expectations and then dropped her. However much she pretended otherwise, the experience had hurt and bewildered her. Wilde's attentions to her had been so public that she could not fail to feel some humiliation when he proceeded to drop her acquaintance.

She had followed all the rules. She had been courted by a seemingly eligible young man. The courtship had been conducted properly, with her parents' knowledge and apparent approval. She knew that Wilde found her beautiful and intelligent. He had suggested to her that together they would make a formidable partnership, and then he had simply disappeared from her life.

As she brooded over what had happened, she wondered just how wise her parents had been in their attitude towards the relationship. By following their code of conduct she had achieved nothing. It was in a spirit of defiance, therefore, that she launched into a sequence of relationships with men that did not follow the codes of her class. She abandoned her role as the 'sweetest Violet' with such vehemence that her friends quickly found a new nickname for her which was to persist during this next phase of her life. She became known to them as 'Violent Hunt'.

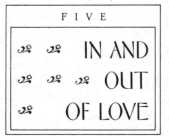

FIVE

IN AND OUT OF LOVE

After Wilde's defection the attentions of the wealthy young Russian Marc-André Rafflovich went some way to soothe Violet's wounded pride.

There was some mystery about this good-natured, highly cultured but very ugly young man. He maintained a luxurious establishment presided over by a lady. No one was too clear what the relationship was between Rafflovich and the woman who acted as hostess at his frequent parties. In her fiction Violet suggests that she was his sister. But in *The Sphinx and her Circle* Violet Wyndham offers another possibility. She relates the legend that Rafflovich's mother 'had been so appalled by his ugliness as a baby that she resolved never to see him again and appointed an English lady to take her place. This was the explanation of the presence of the lady who helped him to entertain his guests in a large house in Mayfair.'

Violet liked Rafflovich very much and enjoyed being taken about by him, chaperoned by the mysterious lady. A strong friendship developed between them, but Violet never took him seriously as a possible husband or lover.

In 1884 Oscar Wilde married Constance Lloyd. That same year, as if in reaction, Violet began to pursue the painter George Boughton. She could hardly have chosen a more unlikely man as the object of her desire. She was twenty-two, and her lover was fifty-one.

George Boughton was a friend of the family. He lived close to them at West House on Campden Hill Road. An unusual house, with rooms linked by stairs in order to make maximum use of the narrow site on which it was built, it had been designed for him by Norman Shaw. Andrew Saint's book *Richard Norman Shaw* includes an account of the painter Whistler's opinion of this particular feature of the house: 'Such an arrangement had its perils. Whistler, in his cups after dining at West House, is said to have tumbled down some steps and cried, "It must have been some damned teetotaller of an architect who designed this house!"'

Born in Norwich in 1833, George Boughton was the same age as Edward Burne-Jones and only three years younger than Alfred Hunt. He had grown up in America and then, like Violet's father, gained a reputation as a landscape painter. In 1863 he moved to London where he had rather more success than Alfred Hunt, for in 1879 he was elected an associate of the Royal Academy and in 1896 he became a full member.

Violet had begun sitting for him as a model in 1882 when she was twenty. At first she was always chaperoned but gradually this convention was dropped. The Hunt family had complete trust in their friend who was, after all, old enough to be Violet's father. It was at this time that Violet learned to become less physically self-conscious and to abandon some of the prudishness inculcated in her by her mother.

She did not pose nude, but she did learn to 'drop her dress to the waist' without embarrassment. It may well have been this experience that gave Violet the idea that George Boughton would make a good lover and help her to overcome the obstacle of her virginity.

That the impetus for the affair came from Violet herself she makes quite clear in *Their Lives*, where she describes how Christina (Violet) laid siege to the artist, making excuses to visit him in his studio alone, waylaying him on walks. Eventually, understandably, he began to respond to the wiles of the attractive young woman. At the same time, like Ruskin before him, he found fault with the way Margaret Hunt had brought up her daughter: 'Although he was at the moment profiting by it he disapproved intensely of what he now learned of Mrs Radmall's irresponsible fashion of dealing with the delicate cattle as marriageable daughters were.'

Violet convinced herself that she was passionately in love, and she greatly enjoyed the sensation: 'She made up her mind then and there in the leaping crescendo of her amorous sensations, that Love was the only thing — that it should be and should remain the only thing in her life, till she was old.'

She was as much in love with love itself, and with all the excitement attending on a secret affair, as with Boughton himself. She took great pleasure in making assignations and in making use of the discreet separate entrance to the studio which had been designed to prevent family and visitors coming into contact with models.

For some time the Hunt family did not see what was happening under their noses. Or, perhaps, they could not believe it was really happening and were unwilling to create any awkwardness with their long-standing friend.

However, in 1887 Boughton married and his wife quickly perceived the situation. She demanded that the affair be brought to an end. By this time Boughton may well have been glad of her intervention and an excuse to bring the relationship to a close. Violet increasingly made her feelings for him apparent in public, and he was embarrassed at the figure he cut through his involvement with such a young woman.

Violet had naively imagined that Boughton's marriage would not affect his attitude towards her, so she was distraught when she was told that the affair must end. Alfred and Margaret Hunt could no longer ignore the situation. Worried that Violet would make a public spectacle of her distress, they at last acted with good sense and determination and packed Violet off to stay with relatives in the quiet seaside village of Robin Hood's Bay, far from the dangers of London and proximity to Boughton.

Their confidence that in this remote place Violet would have no opportunities for mischief proved misplaced. Once at Robin Hood's Bay Violet put Boughton to the back of her mind as her parents had hoped she would. But she could not long remain without excitement of some kind. She quickly entered into a flirtation with Eustace

Strickland, a seventeen-year-old boy who was at home for his school holidays. Strickland was immensely flattered to have the attention of this beautiful and exciting young woman, who had seen so much more of life than he had. After Violet had gone back to London the relationship continued by means of letters, and when Eustace returned to Eton for the school term Violet not only continued to write to him but took to visiting him as well. She was oblivious to the idea that anyone might find her behaviour in any way shocking. But Strickland's parents were scandalised when they learned that Violet was visiting their son at school. They feared for his reputation, and insisted that Violet stopped seeing him.

She never did come to see that there was anything wrong in this relationship. In *White Rose of Weary Leaf* she develops just such a relationship between a boy and a young woman, and justifies the part played by the young woman.

A pleasant diversion in these troubled times was the family's growing friendship with the poet Robert Browning. In 1886 Alfred Hunt had eight pictures on show at an exhibition of the Society of Painters in Watercolours. One of these was entitled 'Childe Roland to the Dark Tower Came', after Browning's poem of the same name. Alfred Hunt sent Browning an invitation to the show, perhaps on the prompting of his wife. Browning visited the exhibition and later, unexpectedly, called on the Hunts. He expressed himself flattered and pleased to have inspired the painting, and was charmed by the modest and gentle man he found Hunt to be.

When Browning met the Hunts he was no longer the *enfant terrible* of the poetic world but a firmly established and eminently respectable man of letters. His wife, Elizabeth Barrett Browning, had died in 1861. For ever after Browning was at the centre of a group of solicitous ladies, of whom Margaret Hunt now became one.

Even during his lifetime a Browning Society had been established, and the Hunts had been asked to join. They were not easy about doing so, as Violet recorded in her 1882 diary:

> Mr Feetham. . . . wants us to go to one of the meetings of the Browning Society, on Friday. There was some talk of M and P joining it when it first started, but it seemed rather absurd, not the object, for we are all great admirers of Browning, but they seemed to be setting about it rather foolishly.

31

After that first meeting, the friendship prospered, even though Browning resolutely refused all invitations to dinner, protesting that he only accepted and gave invitations to tea. Some time before the meeting Margaret Hunt had acquired a photograph of the poet by Rudolph Lehman. She wanted Browning to sign it, so Violet and her mother were invited to tea at his house on the Regent's Canal.

On this occasion there was much conversation about Elizabeth Barrett Browning. What interested and impressed Violet most, however, were Browning's comments on Shelley and Rossetti, two poets who had flouted respectable norms. She had read Browning's preface to his poem *Sordello*, in which he praises Shelley. But now, as an old man, he expressed himself as being disillusioned with the poet because of his behaviour as a man. He was thinking particularly of Shelley's treatment of Harriet Wesbrook. His condemnation of Rossetti was even more emphatic. In *The Wife Of Rossetti*, published some fifty years later, Violet records that visit to Browning: 'Sitting at the round, rickety, unvarnished table in the house on the canal, from which albums were shoved aside for the tea-tray at which Miss Sarianna Browning presided, I heard Browning say in his so loud and guttural voice, "I never can forgive Rossetti!"' A few lines later she says, 'Like Browning, I never can forgive Rossetti.'

This conversation, which took place when Violet was twenty-six, stayed in her mind. It had a peculiar relevance to her own situation. Throughout her life Violet was to hold these two men as puzzling extremes. Browning, the acknowledged poet, even a genius in her eyes, whose private life had been a model of decorum once he had married Elizabeth Barrett Browning, was a reassurance that literary brilliance and respectability were not necessarily mutually exclusive. And, of course, Violet was full of admiration for the fact that his courtship and marriage had been so passionate and so romantic.

On the other hand there was Dante Gabriel Rossetti, the painter and poet to whom even the prudish Margaret was irresistibly drawn — an artist whose charisma and brilliance were accepted as reasons for forgiving a muddled and scandalous personal life.

Whilst Violet spent her life looking for a man like Browning, she seemed fated instead to become involved with men who had Rossetti's fecklessness and inconstancy.

In 1887 Browning left the house on the canal which Violet found so attractive and, with the help of Margaret Hunt, found a house in

Kensington. The new house was in de Vere Gardens, a street in which Henry James was already established. Violet visited him there in 1889 shortly before he went to Venice, where he was to die that same year.

In the meantime Violet's affair with Boughton and her brief infatuation with Eustace Strickland had caused her parents a good deal of alarm. They could no longer ignore the fact that their daughter was not leading the kind of life that her two sisters were prepared to lead, and that she was not following a course which was likely to end in marriage. Of course, they both saw marriage as the ideal culmination of a young woman's life.

With this in mind they began to encourage men whom they regarded as potentially suitable husbands for their wayward daughter. There was, for instance, Dr Albemarle Cholmely, who had wanted to marry Violet for some time. But he was more attractive to her parents than to Violet. She regarded him as a useful admirer to have in the background but she found him physically distasteful and she would not contemplate marrying him.

When Dugald Sutherland MacColl arrived on the scene the Hunts became hopeful. Here was a man who seemed ideally suited to be Violet's husband. Unlike the other men she had shown an interest in, he was close to her in age, being just three years older. He had been born in Glasgow in 1859. Like Margaret Hunt, he came from a church family — his father was the Reverend Dugald MacColl who in 1873 had become the minister at the Kensington Presbyterian Church. Like Alfred Hunt he had been educated at Oxford, and he too had won the Newdigate Prize. He shared the Hunt family's concern for the arts: he was an honorary member of the English and Scottish Royal Watercolour Societies and he lectured in art history at University College, London. What is more he was a writer, becoming art critic for the *Spectator* and the *Saturday Review*. In addition to all this he was handsome and well-off, with a private income inherited from his mother's banking family.

It is not surprising that he was a welcome guest at 1 Tor Villas. But when he proposed to Violet she turned him down. Even though his contemporaries found him 'volcanically energetic', she declared that she found him too cool and self-contained. Violet wanted excitement and passionate love. She did not anticipate either if she married MacColl.

33

Any hopes the Hunts might have entertained that Violet would change her mind and see the advantages of such a marriage were dashed when MacColl left England for two years of travel in Europe. In 1897 he married.

Violet's resumption of her affair with George Boughton looks like an assertion of her refusal to accept a conventional marriage such as her parents wanted for her. She says in her diary of May 1888, 'Si heureuse! George came and our reconciliation was complete.'

Looking back on this affair when she came to write *Their Lives*, Violet conceded the element of perversity in her pursuit of Boughton: 'His queer sunbrowned face, lined and leathery, his twisted humorous smile attracted her. His manners were charming. . . . He was not a romantic figure, it was only the perversity of Christina Radmall which made her lay down her appreciation of him on sentimental lines.'

Despite the resumption of the affair with Boughton, he was no longer so central to her life as he had once been. She was not averse to new romantic attachments, as she proved in September of this year, when she visited Neaune Crag, Albert Fleming's home in Westmorland. Fleming had met the Hunts through Ruskin. He was a lawyer and, like Ruskin, he wanted to see a return to a simpler life. His contribution to this ideal was to re-introduce the spinning-wheel into Westmorland homes. He had corresponded with Margaret Hunt, seeking her advice during periods of Ruskin's insanity when Ruskin had sought his help in disinheriting his niece and her husband, Joan and Arthur Severn.

Also staying with Fleming was an Oxford undergraduate named Harold Chaloner Dowdall, who was similarly destined for the law. He was six years younger than Violet but fell in love with her immediately, quickly proposing marriage. Money was obviously going to be a problem if the couple married before Dowdall graduated. For some inexplicable reason of his own Fleming decided to facilitate the marriage by offering the couple an allowance of £250 a year if Violet's parents would match it.

No sooner were these arrangements agreed upon than the couple quarrelled violently, perhaps as a result of Violet's flirting with Fleming. Once Violet had declared that she would not marry Dowdall, however, Fleming announced his love for her. Violet did not return his feelings. The atmosphere between the three of them was strained by the whole affair, so Violet returned to London. She gives an account of this fiasco in her diary entry for 14 September:

> D offended me with over zeal in some matter. I was angry, he took to his bed. At 9 o'clock AF, who cannot help forcing the note, made me grant him an interview in his room, and D gave me up, but I did not understand till after. AF took me aside, *wept* and upbraided me for a flirt — well I did flirt yesterday, but I cured D of his infatuation so AF owned that he loved me. What a kettle of fish!

Margaret did not give up hopes that the marriage might be arranged after all. With this end in view she encouraged Violet to visit Oxford so as to give Dowdall an opportunity to meet her again and repeat his proposal.

It is an irony that Margaret Hunt, who herself had such a loving and stable marriage and who in all her novels matches up her heroines with suitable husbands, should have had so much difficulty in restraining Violet's rackety way of life and in finding her a suitable husband. As long as Violet's good looks and lively personality attracted men to her she was content with the excitement of flirtation. She was not yet ready to settle down to married life.

By November of 1889 Violet's affair with Boughton was once more coming to an end. She says of him in her diary 'George is growing coarse and jovial, while I stand with tears in my eyes. Perhaps though, he laughs that he may not weep.'[1]

However, sexual excitement was not lacking. Walter Herries Pollock, also an older married man, had begun to pursue Violet early in 1889. A poet, author and journalist, he was at this time editor of the *Saturday Review*. Violet had no illusions about his attitude to her: she knew that he simply wanted a sexual conquest. But Violet resisted his attempts. She was sufficiently intrigued by the excitement of the pursuit, however, to maintain some kind of relationship with him and his wife. In December 1890 she was still socialising with them. She wrote in her diary for 21 December, 'I longed to have a reconciliation with him but it is so difficult with a man who can't be in the same room with one alone without wanting to kiss one! A nice habit.'

These disclaimers do not ring altogether true. It is likely that

Pollock's attentions were of some comfort to Violet and an indication of her continuing ability to attract men. For suddenly she had begun to feel that she was no longer the leader, that her younger sisters were leaving her behind.

Venice, who was a year younger, had married William Benson in 1886. But more thought-provoking was the marriage in this same year, 1890, of her youngest sister Silvia to a country gentleman from Durham, John Walton Fogg Elliot. Violet now found herself the only daughter left in the parental home.

Violet expressed disapproval of both marriages. She had some justice on her side in the case of Silvia's marriage, for her husband proved blatantly and cruelly unfaithful. Shortly after their marriage he began an affair with their maid. When this came to an end and he had turned his attentions elsewhere, he saw no reason why his new mistress should not also live in the same house as his wife.

Violet's objection to William Benson as being 'in trade' suggests a certain jealousy on her part as well as snobbishness. William Benson was an architect and a metalwork designer. He came of a good Hampshire family and had been educated at Winchester and New College, Oxford. His business in Bond Street was of a special kind and his affiliations with the Arts and Crafts Movement endeared him to Alfred and Margaret Hunt. Indeed at one point Margaret Hunt was prepared to lend him money to invest in his business.

Both these marriages pleased the older Hunts as being good matches. Violet had had her chances to make similarly good marriages but she had turned them down. Even now the faithful Dr Cholmely would have married her. Violet clung to her hopes for a grand passion. But on her twenty-eighth birthday she began to take stock of her situation and wonder where her hectic relationships with men were leading to. She made this entry in her diary: 'Tomorrow is my birthday and 28, and it is rather a dreary prospect. At present I am happy enough. I have plenty of lovers, of a sort, enough to amuse me but looks, such as they are, cannot last for ever, and then, where am I?'

Her concern for her looks led her to take arsenic. Like many other women of the time, she knew that arsenic in the right amount would help to make her youthful looks last by making her eyes brighter and her complexion clearer. She also knew that once she started taking it she would be unable to stop. But she felt that the immediate resulting improvement in her appearance justified the long-term disadvantages.

The desire to maintain a youthful appearance is just one aspect of Violet's attitude to life at this time. In many ways she was reluctant to grow up, to stop being the beautiful lively young woman with so much potential. For as yet she had little to show for her twenty-eight years, apart from a string of affairs. She knew a great number of people in the literary world; she continued to write poems. She wrote occasionally for the editors to whom her mother introduced her. But she had written nothing substantial so far, while her mother had been producing novels steadily year after year. She was still financially dependent on her parents and she still lived in their house. Only recently had she been trusted with a key to the door — before then it had been the maid's job to stay up to let her in if she were out at all late.

She was ripe for a change in her life, for something — a relationship or an occupation — which would give some substance and meaning to her rather frivolous existence.

It was at this moment that Oswald Crawfurd appeared on the scene.

Like George Boughton he was much older than Violet. When he first showed an interest in her in the summer of 1890 he was fifty-six to her twenty-eight. And, like Boughton, he was already married. He was a very handsome man, dark-skinned and looking like 'an Italian bandit', Violet thought. He had been educated at Eton and Merton College, Oxford. His father had been a diplomat and he too became British Consul at Oporto. Despite this position he was able to spend six months of every year in London, where he had a flat in Queen Anne's Mansions. It was here that he had something of a salon where literary men and handsome women were entertained. When he came to show an interest in Violet she was fully aware of his reputation as a womaniser, for several of her friends had already had affairs with him.

He was very interested in the arts. He wrote novels, and edited *The Novel Magazine* and the review *Black and White*. Violet found him a fascinating and dangerous character. He talked to her of 'free love' and 'exceedingly delicate matters'. For a while she tried to keep the relationship on the basis of an intense flirtation. She wrote in her diary of this time that she felt 'there would be something very ridiculous in my being engaged for the second time in an intrigue with a married man.' Crawfurd, however, was not to be resisted. He did not want a mere flirtation. The frustration and confusion he engendered in her emerges in her diary: 'I have never been so prevented from having my own way in my whole life! I mean as flirtation goes. . . . Sometimes I desperately want OC out of sheer *ennui* — as well as a great liking for him.' They became lovers in 1892. Their affair was to last for the next six years.

By now Alfred Hunt had begun to give his family cause for concern. He was in ill health and his failing eyesight prevented him from painting. This was a profound misery to a man whose whole life had been dedicated to his art. He was also worried about money since his income still depended upon his ability to sell paintings. In 1890 he wrote to his wife 'I am . . . always afraid that if one does not work hard and successfully for that, or takes too much relaxation, the stream which makes for poverty will prove itself the stronger after all.' He sent her an even sadder letter in August 1892. 'Dearest devoted wife — I do so wish that I could give you fortune and comfort and all nice things and could stop my own career old-age-ward.'[2]

Without his painting Alfred Hunt had little left to live for, and in 1896 he died of apoplexy. The Hunts had purchased a grave in Woking, and it was there that he was buried. At the funeral Violet was painfully aware that her two sisters were accompanied and supported by their husbands while she was conspicuously alone, left to attend to her mother. Her relationship with Crawfurd was such that he could give her no public support on this painful occasion even if he had been inclined to do so.

Only now did Violet begin to consider the advantages of being a married woman. She saw how profoundly affected Margaret Hunt was by the death of her husband and she realised fully the strength of her parents' love for each other. She began to hope that Crawfurd would eventually marry her. His wife, Margaret, was an invalid and had been so for some years. She was not expected to outlive her husband. But the relationship between Violet and Crawfurd was never a happy one, however much she tried to deceive herself to the contrary. Crawfurd would blow hot and cold, while on her side Violet caused him much embarrassment and annoyance by her indiscretion in discussing the affair freely and through her public possessiveness.

In 1904 Violet published her novel *Sooner or Later: The Story Of An Ingenious Ingenue*. She made no secret of the fact that it was based on her affair with Crawfurd. She does, however, give the relationship a glamour and even an element of tragedy by altering the ages of the central characters in the drama. Robert Assheton is much younger than the fifty-six-year-old Crawfurd, whilst Rosette is barely more than a schoolgirl. The way in which Assheton coldly and calculatingly works up the girl to the point where she is ready to be seduced has little to do with the progress of the affair between Crawfurd and Violet. At twenty-eight, with a succession of affairs behind her, Violet knew very well what she was about.

A less romantic and more accurate picture of the Crawfurd-Violet relationship appears in *Their Hearts*. By the time this was published in 1921 Violet was able to see more clearly the nature of the affair she had been involved in. She acknowledges the great physical attraction Crawfurd had for her, as the following description shows:

> This man wasn't a poet; he looked as if he were in diplomacy. He was very tall; Philip Wynyard, also a big man, looked short beside him. His eyes alone remained in Orinthia's mental mirror, not so much because they were beautiful as perturbing. They were dark brown, with a kind of smothered, almost blue light in them; the eyelids had a bulldog droop at the corners. . . . His hair was black, with some iridescent lights in it.

She is fully aware of their different attitudes:

> How he always headed off thoughts of marriage! Mrs Balfame's recovery did put it, automatically, out of his power to marry her even if he had wanted to, which he didn't. . . . He liked the adventure, the savour of forbidden fruit. But what she wanted was just to be domestic with him, to have the ordering of his dinners, to cosset him if he was ill (which Sheila didn't), and have a wife's right to be there and order everyone else out of the room if he was dying!

The misery of the lies and deceptions she was reduced to, and the loss of her self-respect when Crawfurd left her, all emerge with painful clarity in *Their Lives*.

39

Crawfurd went to Paris to put a distance between himself and Violet. She pursued him there, ostensibly to seek the advice of an old school friend, who had married an American dentist and now lived in Paris. When Violet returned to England she made excuses to visit friends in Queen Anne's Mansions, hoping to catch a glimpse of him. She wept bitterly and complained to her friends about his neglect of her and of his unkindness. If the beginning of the affair had been public, the end was even more so.

Then, in 1899, Crawfurd's wife died. But Crawfurd had had enough of Violet. He did not want the tempestuous life he knew he would lead with her. Shortly after his wife's death he put an end to any hopes that Violet might still have had by marrying someone else.

For many years Violet cherished the memory of her love for him. She built the relationship up in her mind as a grand passion. She kept in touch with his wife so that she would know what he was doing.

Throughout the affair she had tried to speak of Crawfurd to Henry James. But not only did James dislike Crawfurd, he hated being a party to anyone's emotional entanglements. In 1898 James had left de Vere Gardens in Kensington and moved to Lamb House in Rye. Violet was a frequent visitor. On one such visit, which she recorded in her diary, she was unwell and appeared in the evening in the drawing-room in her white Chinese silk dressing-gown. She attempted to drift about seductively whilst relating the misery she felt about Crawfurd. James would not listen. He showed great concern for her health and then turned the conversation away from Violet's emotional life to the steadying topic of the novels of Mrs Humphrey Ward.

It was always one of Violet's complaints about James that, although he loved her to tell him all the London gossip, he drew back old-maidishly if he felt he might in the smallest degree be touched by scandal.

Violet, however, took her revenge for Henry James's refusal to listen to the story of her affair with Crawfurd. When in 1904 she published her novel *Sooner Or Later*, an account of some of the sordid emotional details of the relationship, she dedicated the work — which is written in a deliberately Jamesian style — to Henry James himself.

It was not until 1905 that Violet discovered that Crawfurd had left a lasting mark on her life: he had given her syphilis.* Even now the discovery of the disease would come as a devastating shock to any woman, but at that time the disease was incurable. Moreover it was considered a shameful disease and for a woman of Violet's background and upbringing it was a terrible moment when she felt that the doctor she was consulting looked upon her 'with disgust and loathing'.

Something of the contemporary attitude towards venereal disease can be gauged from the publication in 1913 of a book entitled *The Great Scourge and How to End It*, written by a friend of Violet's, Christabel Pankhurst. Although Christabel Pankhurst was doing a courageous thing and performing a necessary act in refusing to pretend that venereal disease did not exist, her attitude towards sufferers was far from sympathetic. Reviewing the book in *The Clarion* of 26 September 1913, Rebecca West gives a very clear picture of the situation:

> But this scolding attitude of Miss Pankhurst is not only ununderstanding, it is also a positive incentive to keep these diseases the secret, spreading things they are. Doctors who were studying this matter long before Miss Pankhurst or I were born have complained bitterly that their efforts will come to nothing so long as sufferers are intimidated by a hostile social atmosphere into being afraid to acknowledge the nature of their illness and thus to seek advice as to the best way of treatment. As the great Duclaux said: 'The struggle against syphilis is only possible if we agree to regard its victims as unfortunate and not as guilty. . . .'[3]

Rebecca West's enlightened view was most unusual for the time, as she was very well aware.

---

* Violet discovered that she had syphilis because of the spots on her face and her wrists. By then she was in the second stage of the disease. It was not unusual for a woman to fail to detect the onset of the disease as there are not necessarily any outwardly visible signs. In addition Violet would not have known what any signs meant because of an ignorance typical in a woman of her class at that time.

The disease is no longer infectious from about two years after its onset, except at times when it recurs, as when Violet suffered from spots. This is why her doctor advised her to leave England for a while — he assumed that once the spots had disappeared, Violet would be unlikely to infect anyone else.

Even when Douglas Goldring, who had been a close associate of Ford and Violet, published his volume of character sketches, *Life Interests*, long after Violet was dead and he had had access to all her papers, he could not bring himself to name her illness, simply describing it as the 'disgraceful illness'. He was fully aware that Violet had had syphilis, and that she had contracted it from Crawfurd, but he would not be more explicit than to say that Crawfurd 'did her an injury from which she suffered until the end of her life'.

Matters were made worse for Violet by her own ignorance and the refusal of those who did have information to do other than to talk to her in veiled and ambiguous terms. The first person to suggest to her that she might have a serious illness was Archie Probert, a doctor friend she had come to know through her friends the Monds. He had been close to Violet for some time and she was beginning to feel that he might ask her to marry him. Once he realised the nature of the illness Violet was suffering from he put their relationship onto a new footing. He made it clear that he was no longer thinking in terms of marriage, only of friendship.

Eventually the admirer she had for so long kept in the background, Dr Cholmely, felt that he had to tell her that he thought it likely that she had a 'disgraceful illness', which was the cause of the unpleasant spots on her face and wrists. He sent her to consult a Dr Stephen Paget, who confirmed Cholmely's suspicions. His obvious revulsion was greatly upsetting to Violet. He advised her to leave town for a while, and she went off to Schwalbach in Germany.

Dr Paget failed to tell Violet enough about the nature and the likely course of her illness. Once she had overcome the initial shock of his diagnosis she began to persuade herself that it was wrong. Her view of the matter was confirmed when she consulted another doctor who did not mention syphilis but suggested that the spots on her face were caused by her hair. For some years Violet persuaded herself that there was nothing seriously wrong with her. She told no one of Paget's diagnosis, not even her lovers. It was not until some years later, when she had trouble with serious nose bleeds, that she was forced to acknowledge the true nature of the disease and to accept that it was running its slow but dreadful course.

SIX

❧ THE FIRST ❧ FRUITS OF EXPERIENCE

The years when so much of Violet's time and thought was devoted to Oswald Crawfurd were not entirely wasted. She now began to take her own writing seriously and to write pieces more substantial than reviews and Birthday Albums.* Her first full sexual experience gave her the maturity she had lacked and a better understanding of the position of women who were her contemporaries.

'Every book is an experiment,' wrote Violet in *I Have This To Say*, published in 1926. Her statement is a good summary of her own career as a writer. She wrote not only novels but poetry, reviews, essays, plays, short stories, a travel book, a book about cats, some translations, an autobiography and a biography.

As a novelist she proved to have inherited her mother's eye for precise detail, her accurate ear for dialogue, her sharp wit and her confidence in the importance of the arts.

It was only when she discovered that she could put these talents to different use than her mother had done in her novels that she began to develop as a writer.

Crawfurd's influence in causing her to take this step forward is suggested by the fact that her first serious pieces were published in 1894 in a volume entitled *Dialogues of the Day*, edited by Crawfurd himself.

May Sinclair points out in an article on Violet published in the *English Review* in February 1922 that in Violet's best work her dialogue is 'always brilliant, vigorous and natural'. Although her early works do not measure up to the standards she was to achieve later, this aspect of her writing is immediately apparent. Her skill with dialogue was the result of Violet's inherent delight in witty conversation and her passion for the theatre.

Her first novel, *The Maiden's Progress*, was published in 1894, when Violet was thirty-two. Subtitled 'A Novel in Dialogue', it has many deficiencies as a novel — it lacks a substantial or credible plot, the characters are static and do not develop and they lack psycho-

---

* Birthday Albums were the Edwardian equivalent of 'coffee table books' and contained pleasing poems and passages of prose. They were not intended as serious reading.

logical depth. It certainly does not, however, fit the category of 'bad romantic novels' which one critic has arbitrarily used to characterise all her novels.[1]

What is interesting about it is the way in which many issues this novel touches upon are dealt with in greater depth and more seriously in *Their Lives*. Like almost everything Violet wrote, it has strong autobiographical elements. The central character, Moderna — who, like Violet, is 'scatterbrained', 'reckless, and erratic, and tiresome' — finds herself in many situations which were based on Violet's experiences, in particular her relationships with men.

Like Violet, she is torn between the desire for the position afforded by marriage and the need for independence. In response to her fiancé's comment that 'You have been reading Ibsen — if women would only be content to stay in the niche that Providence intended for them,' she says 'You don't seem to see that a woman has a soul to save as well as a man; a personality she ought to develop, a life to live.'

One of the suitors in the novel is Gontram Vere, who — like Philip Wynyard in *Their Lives* and *Their Hearts* — is based on Oscar Wilde. In this, her first novel, Wilde is more than a character: he is also present as a strong influence. For one of the characteristics of this novel, as of most of the early novels, is a recognisably Wildean tone, such as in this self-description by Vere: 'A small volume of Poems, a large stock of cynicism is as necessary to the equipment of a man of the world as a visiting card.' A similar tone is apparent in the way he is described by Moderna's mother, a character evidently based on Mrs Hunt, who says 'I don't like my daughter's Bohemian friends. . . . They may have superlative genius — but they haven't ordinary manners.'

At this stage in her writing this wit is decoration rather than an indication of any real desire to turn society topsy-turvy. For, despite the fact that because of her views Moderna finds marriageable men dull and stifling, and although the men to whom she is attracted, such as Gontram Vere, are men who live on their wits and cannot afford the luxury of a wife who is not rich, she does not choose the path of spinsterhood. The conclusion of this novel, as of many which follow, is not influenced by Wilde but by Jane Austen. For Moderna, like Emma, comes to see that after all the ideal man has been waiting there all the time until she was sufficiently educated to accept that a good marriage is not based on passion but on respect, esteem and affection.

The pattern established in *The Maiden's Progress* is repeated in the next novel, *A Hard Woman*, subtitled 'A Story in Scenes'. Once again the emphasis is on dialogue and on such cynical comments as 'Men hate to find a woman's husband sitting about when they call.' And once again marriage versus independence is a central issue. However, this second novel is something of an advance on the first in several ways. Although the emphasis is on dialogue, Violet has developed a framework which gives her more opportunities in which to consider her characters and their relationships than the earlier restricted form. This framework also allows her to discuss the conventions of the novel itself. Her narrator, who observes the action rather than actively participating in it, says that 'Many conversations, which it was my privilege to hold with the lady herself, I have literally transcribed; but I mean likewise to assume the novelist's prerogative, and set down, with equal confidence, scenes and conversations in which I personally had no part.'

The central character of this novel, Lydia, is not a heroine in the normal sense of the word. She is typical of many of Violet's central characters in that much of what she does and professes is unacceptable to the reader, but for several reasons we are never in a position whole-heartedly to condemn her. Most importantly, she is the logical product of the society in which she lives. She is simply honest about motivations which are equally strong in determining the actions of others, but which they would prefer to pass over in silence. In this she bears some resemblance to Lydia in *Pride and Prejudice*. For example, she is outspoken about her attitude to marriage. She shocks us when she asserts that 'a woman's life is an utter failure if she isn't married,' but this is clearly the unspoken principle on which her society works. When Hester Nevill, who has ambitions to be an artist, contradicts her view she voices opinions which many would perhaps like to hold but are afraid to live by because they go contrary to establish norms: 'There are not husbands enough to go round — statistics prove it. Then why can't a certain number of women be allowed to stand out, and not be despised, because they have chosen that line, and mean to abide by it?'

The novel ends inconclusively. Lydia has her husband, but both she and he are aware that he is in love with Hester Nevill. At this point in her writing career Violet has the courage to introduce material into her novels which her mother would not have dreamt of, but she still does not have the confidence to pursue her implications to their conclusions.

A characteristic of all these early novels is the way in which they are responses to Margaret Hunt's fiction. As yet Violet is sufficiently conditioned by her upbringing to need to make this response before moving on to entirely new ground.

A recurrent figure in the fiction written for and by Victorian women is the governess or the companion. Margaret Hunt was no exception in choosing such a figure for her heroine, as we can see in *Thornicroft's Model* and *The Governess*. Violet takes up this figure and transforms her.

In *Unkist, Unkind* the central character and narrator describes herself as 'only the companion — poor, plain, and ill connected'. But this realistic assessment of herself gives her a confidence and a courage something like that of Jane Eyre. She does not allow her strength of character to be diminished by her position, and she does not respond in a saintly way like poor Helen Morris in *Thornicroft's Model*. For while Margaret Hunt depicts the real misery of a governess in a household, she does not give a convincing picture of how such a life would really affect a young woman. Violet's governesses and companions fight back and try to determine their own fate. However lovely and lovable, Margaret Hunt's are victims whose only hope in life lies in escape through marriage.

Given the life she led, it is not surprising that most of Margaret Hunt's novels focus on artists and their work. Even her first novel, despite its title, *Magdalen Wynyard*, is better characterised by its subtitle, 'The Provocations of a Pre-Raphaelite', since it is much more about the artist Bernard Longley than the young girl of the title. There are many scenes in the novel set in the North of England, especially close to the River Greta. Most of Violet's novel *The Human Interest* is set in the same locations, and again the central character is a landscape painter. In this novel, as in all her novels and all Margaret Hunt's novels, Turner and Ruskin are discussed and used as touchstones by which to judge all art. The big difference between the novels by mother and daughter lies in their conclusions.

Despite difficulties, misunderstandings and the actions of malicious characters, in the end Bernard finds happiness in marriage, as does Magdalen. *The Human Interest*, however, does not end with satisfactory marriages. In the first place the central female character is already married. She runs away from home to be with the artist, Edmund Rivers. Her husband conveniently dies during the course of the novel, leaving the way clear for her to put her relationship with Rivers on a respectable footing. But Violet has already established the incompatibility of the dedicated artist with a regular married life. Its very subtitle 'A Study In Incompatibilities', leaves us in no doubt from the outset that this novel will not end 'happily ever after'.

Already Violet knew a truth about herself and the men who attracted her that she was as yet unable to apply to her own life.

SEVEN

SOUTH LODGE

The last years of the century brought several changes to Violet's life. Three men who had been important to her in her younger days died. Robert Browning died in 1889. Violet attended his memorial service in Westminster Abbey. The occasion brought other memories to her mind as George Boughton was also present. Oscar Wilde died in Paris, a broken and disgraced man. News of his death reminded Violet of the days when she had been close to him and he had been a rising star. Such an end could not have been predicted for him then.

Similarly reduced from his former position as the acknowledged leader of the art world was John Ruskin, who died at Brantwood in 1900, aged eighty-one. Who could have foreseen that he would outlive his younger friend Alfred Hunt by five years, and that his last days would be spent as a recluse, tormented by fits of madness?

Since she was three years old, home for Violet had been 1 Tor Villas, but in 1900 she and her mother left that house and moved the short distance to South Lodge, from where they could still see their former home.

It was to be in this house that Violet would establish herself as a hostess and a member of London's literary society quite independent of her mother. Margaret Hunt made her presence felt in their new home by insisting that the drawing-room should have the same William Morris 'Daisy' wall-paper as Tor Villas. The curtains also had a Pre-Raphaelite look, though they were not from The Firm but had been embroidered by Violet, using a William Morris design.

Otherwise Margaret Hunt was a spent force. She had published her last novel, *Mrs Juliet*, in 1892. She had come to realise that the publishing world was changing and that she could not change with it. Three-decker novels of the kind she was accustomed to write were no longer wanted, and the financial rewards she could expect were much reduced. She had begun another novel, *The Governess*, but was too discouraged to finish it.* At sixty-nine years old she began to live on the fringes of her daughter's life, thus reversing their earlier roles. Her mental health now began to deteriorate.

The effects of Violet's entanglement with Crawfurd continued to surface. In 1900 her first collection of short stories, *Affairs of the Heart*, was published. As its title suggests, the stories are linked together by their focus on love relationships. These relationships, however, are not happy ones. In each case there is some kind of imbalance or cruelty. There are no happy endings here either, and it is generally the women who are the losers. Either they are like Anne Elliot in *Persuasion*, whom Violet regarded as 'the type of all the abject loving women of the world', or they are struggling to maintain some kind of independence which proves incompatible with marriage. For example, in 'A Matter of Opinion', when a lady journalist is asked if she is married she replies, 'No. I earn my living.' And in 'An Impossible Situation' the narrator is told that 'Emancipated women are all very well — they make good friends — but a wife is a different thing.'

When Violet went to Paris after Crawfurd had left her, she had tried to overcome her distress by working with her friend Agnes Farley on *The Memoirs of Jacques Casanova de Seingalt*. Violet had begun the translation while her father was still alive. He had objected to the project involving, as it did, a man whom he considered grossly

---

* *The Governess* was to have an odd history. Unable to complete it herself, Margaret gave Violet permission to do what she wanted with the manuscript and her daughter later finished the novel taking care to write in the same style as her mother. For instance, she gave it the kind of ending she felt her mother would have written rather than the kind she favoured in her own novels.

immoral. He did not want a daughter of his associated with such a person. In 1902, however, with neither parent any longer in a position to object, Violet published the book with an introduction by her and notes by Agnes Farley. Neither woman signed her name to the work. In 1903 Chapman Hall, who had commissioned the *Memoirs*, published a further translation from the French by Violet — *The Heart of Ruby* by Berthe Tosti.

That same year, Violet made the acquaintance of Somerset Maugham when she published her story 'The Gem and its Setting' in a short-lived review, *The Venture, An Annual of Art and Literature*, which he edited with Laurence Housman. This story foreshadows the kind of 'nastiness' of tone which both Maugham and Violet were to bring increasingly into their fiction. In it Violet fictionalises her relationship with Albemarle Cholmely and exposes the distaste he occasioned in her.

Now that she was launched on her career as a novelist she continued a steady output of work. In 1904 she published *The Celebrity at Home*, but this was overshadowed by the first of her major novels, *Sooner or Later*, published in the same year.

Before Violet dedicated *Sooner or Later* to Henry James she asked his permission to do so. He replied with a 'fervid telegram' of acceptance. Violet sent him a copy of the published book which he did not trouble to read. He was, therefore, taken aback when a friend wrote to him that 'Violet Hunt has gone and written a novel weltering with sex, and dedicated it to you!'

Violet did not deny this description of her work. But not everyone found the subject matter dismaying. Somerset Maugham read the book in manuscript form, and wrote encouragingly:

> I liked your novel because it explored undiscovered country; I do not think, in English at least, that the relationship between a married man and his mistress, a *jeune fille*, has ever been analyzed before. I think you have done it with very great skill. I confess I should have liked a little more 'obscenity', because Appleton's charm is obviously sexual, but I recognise that this was impossible ... of course the work has an autobiographical ring about it and you must expect to hear a good deal of disagreeable things — however what does it matter?[1]

The points raised by Maugham in this letter are very pertinent to a discussion of the novel. Violet is certainly exploring new ground and she is following the French tradition with which she was familiar. Two English novelists, however, do come to mind — Richardson and Jane Austen. The relationship of this novel to *Clarissa* is established early on when the well-read Rosette, who is more familiar with the relationship of the sexes from literature than life, says, 'Dear, clever Lovelace! . . . I think Clarissa was quite horrid to him.'

Like *Clarissa, Sooner Or Later* tells the story of the seduction of a young virgin by an experienced roué. However, many of the values of the earlier novel are turned on their heads in *Sooner or Later*, as the quotation above suggests they will be. Rosette is indeed a virgin, but she is avid for experience of every kind, including the sexual. Unlike Clarissa she is not dismayed by her lover's reputation for his numerous affairs — rather she is piqued by it. She becomes his mistress with a full awareness of the implications of her position. It is her attitude towards this socially unacceptable relationship which breaks new ground in English fiction, especially that written by women. And the reader is invited to question whether being a mistress is after all such a bad thing given the legal marriages we are allowed to observe — such as that of Montagu de Warenne, who is also Assheton's mistress and who marries Rosette's guardian for reasons of expediency rather than love, compatibility or attachment. She is aware that she has reached a certain age and achieved a degree of notoriety which will lead to her being a social outcast unless she marries. She confesses frankly to herself: 'the patient public has a way of turning at a given moment like the proverbial worm, and, as every woman is aware, there is a tide in the affairs of scandal, which if not taken at the flood leads straight to perdition.' The man she marries gives as his reason for marrying her that 'there are things that a man, and a man only, can do for a woman, but only if he is married to her'.

Throughout the novel it is made clear that women urgently need marriage for the position in society it gives them, and for the protection and financial security it affords them. In return for this men expect to be able to regard their wives as more or less valuable property. Montagu acknowledges this when she says of Assheton, 'No watch-dog like a roving husband. Set a thief to catch a thief.'

Within the society of this novel basic attitudes to marriage have changed little since Jane Austen's time; what is new is the frank cynicism and hypocrisy about the relationship between the sexes.

At the end of the novel Rosette has been made an honest woman by her seducer. But her marriage does not afford the reader the satisfaction and sense of rightness and completion provided by marriages in earlier fiction. On the contrary, the comment of Lady Newall seems more appropriate, when she says, 'Of all the absurd fetishes which society has set up, that notion of tying two criminals together and letting them drown in company is the most absurd. If a man has acted without faith, without consideration before marriage, what will he do after?'

After the frank outspokenness of *Sooner Or Later*, Violet's next novel, *The Workaday Woman*, published in 1906, is something of a surprise. Its title suggests that it will be a reaction against the conventional depiction of women in literature. In the early part of the book this expectation is met as the positions of men and women are very nearly reversed. Jehane Bruce 'is one of those women who ought to have been a man — a well known and puzzling breed. She lives alone in a flat and pays its rent and supports herself on regular journalism and occasional fiction.' In the society in which this young woman moves the men are 'decorous black-coated figures who were less to be regarded in the light of fellow bread-winners than in that of playmates.' She can say quite seriously, 'Well, well, women must work and men must play, I suppose. It's the rule all the world over, and what are women, that we should complain of it?'

However, even in this novel, some regret is expressed that the life of the working woman leaves little room for love, and one of the heroines finds herself disappointed, in spite of herself, when the man she thinks she loves marries someone else for her money.

Amongst the many women writers of Violet's acquaintance was Marguerite Radclyffe Hall. The two women had been friends for some time, but it is unlikely that Violet realised that her friend was a lesbian. She was forced to acknowledge this when, quite unexpectedly, Marguerite decided that she wanted a closer relationship with Violet. While the two of them were spending a weekend with mutual friends, Marguerite declared her love. It was a new experience for Violet to find herself desired by another woman, and for a while she was flattered and intrigued. She enjoyed being treated

51

as the beloved and given gifts. But when she visited Marguerite at her home in Malvern Violet realised that she was not ready to enter into a sexual relationship with her friend. There was inevitably some initial coolness after this rejection, but before long they entered into a less fevered and intimate relationship which was to prove long-lasting. When Marguerite published her lesbian novel *The Well Of Loneliness*, Violet was quick to defend her against her attackers.

The year 1907 was an important one in Violet's life. On 21 March she was a dinner guest at the home of John Galsworthy. A fellow-Kensingtonian, five years Violet's junior, he had already begun to make a name for himself with his novel *Man of Property* and his play *The Silver Box*, both of which were published in 1906.

Ford Madox Ford was a fellow-guest at dinner. When it was time to leave Galsworthy suggested that Ford might escort Violet home as they lived quite close to each other. Walking up Campden Hill Road together the two rediscovered their common Pre-Raphaelite background. By coincidence, it was shortly after this that Violet first met Douglas Goldring, who was later to become Ford's editorial assistant, at a luncheon party. But for a while she saw little more of either man, since she was preoccupied with other new friendships.

Somerset Maugham was living in Paris when Violet made one of her regular visits in the summer of 1907. The two of them spent a good deal of time together and for a short time were lovers. Maugham was an ideal companion in Paris, since he knew all the literary and artistic expatriates. He had been born in Paris in the British Embassy and had lived there, speaking only French, until he was ten. When Violet first knew him he was beginning to have some success with his novel *Liza of Lambeth* and his play *A Man of Honour*, but it was not until October 1907, when his brief affair with Violet was over, that he became a celebrity and a rich man with the production of his play *Lady Frederick*.

Maugham was twelve years younger than Violet: was his portrayal of the ageing Lady Frederick, pursued by a man much younger than herself, based on his affair with Violet? In a letter to Ted Morgan, Maugham's biographer, Rebecca West wrote that Violet had confided in her 'the painful tale' of her seduction of the younger man. However painful the affair may have been, it left neither party with bad feelings. On the contrary, they saw each other regularly and maintained a steady and affectionate correspondence. Maugham confided in Violet about his affairs and gave her detailed accounts of the places he visited and the people he met. Most importantly, the two writers exchanged comments and criticisms of each other's work. As they were both breaking similarly new ground they had a special sympathy for each other's endeavours. Violet dedicated her best novel, *White Rose Of Weary Leaf*, to Maugham. He in his turn dedicated his travel book about Spain to Violet. Apparently she was not altogether pleased about this, as Maugham related in a letter to Edward Marsh. He said that Violet was put out 'chiefly, I think, because it is called *The Land of The Blessed Virgin* and she could not imagine what the hell would be her business in such a country.'[2]

One day whilst Violet was walking along a Paris street with Maugham he spotted an acquaintance on the other side. The meeting was to be a fruitful one for Violet. As she said in her essay 'Arnold Bennett in Paris', 'That little excursion of Somerset Maugham's across the crowded boulevard to catch "Enoch Arnold", as he persisted in calling him, was the very beginning of my long friendship with Arnold Bennett.'[3]

When Maugham left Paris Arnold Bennett took over his role as escort, showing Violet a side of Paris she might not otherwise have seen:

> There was not a place of amusement or a restaurant about which he did not know, and together we sampled those on both banks — not of course the very expensive ones. Our dinners — he didn't want wine but I made him drink it — used to cost for the two of us not more than six or eight francs, and he loyally permitted me to pay my share. . . . Afterwards he would take me somewhere, perhaps to the Moulin Rouge — under protest, for it was the kind of place patronised only by international trippers. . . . The dancing hall at Montmartre was better. Quietly, like two bourgeois, we would sit at a little rickety table with iron legs, order our bocks, and watch the dancers. . . . Often as not after dining we would go straight to the Rue de Calais, up steep uncarpeted stairs, all the way to his flat, where he would put some milk on to boil, sit down to the piano, and pound out Chopin.[4]

Another friend arrived in Paris — Edward Heron Allen. Once again Violet visited the Moulin Rouge and was fascinated by the spectacle of half-naked girls dressed in glittering openwork net garments. She was surprised when Heron Allen made sexual advances on her, and laughed at him. Her rejection of him was to have long-term consequences, and was to a large extent responsible for his subsequent treatment of Ford Madox Ford.

It is a little surprising that Violet did not take him more seriously than she did. He was a handsome man, a successful lawyer with an amazingly wide range of interests and abilities. He was a bibliophile, a conchologist, a Fellow of the Royal Society and an expert on the manufacture of violins.

Back in England Violet was briefly attracted to H.G. Wells. He was by this time a successful writer with a reputation as a compulsive womaniser. Violet managed to get herself invited to Wells's home in Sandygate by his second wife, Jane. She was there in 1908 when Wells brought home from London the newly published *Old Wives' Tale* by Arnold Bennett — the book which Wells accurately prophesied would be the making of Bennett's career.

Once again, however, the interest was stronger on Violet's side than on Wells's — she was one of the few women who did not succeed in becoming Wells's mistress. But he took an interest in Violet's literary career, and it was with his encouragement that she renewed her acquaintance with Ford Hermann Hueffer by giving him some of her short stories for publication in *The English Review*, of which he was then the editor. Thus began the most important relationship in Violet's life.

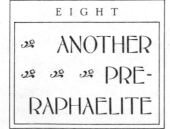

EIGHT

ᕆ ANOTHER ᕆ ᕆ ᕆ PRE- RAPHAELITE

Violet had known Ford Hermann Hueffer* as a child, for both families moved in Pre-Raphaelite circles. But she was eleven years his senior, so there had been no friendship or intimacy between them when they were young.

There is a remarkable similarity between their childhoods. Like Violet, Ford grew up in a household where the belief was 'that to be an artist

---

* Ford Hermann Hueffer and Ford Madox Ford are one and the same person. He changed his name from Hueffer to Ford in June 1919.

was to be the most august thing in life'. He too was dressed in Pre-Raphaelite style with a suit of greenish-yellow corduroy velveteen with gold buttons and two stockings, one red and one green. He wore his blonde hair in a page-boy bob. The portrait of him by his grandfather as William Tell's son gives some idea of his appearance at this time.

Unlike Violet, however, he did not enjoy wearing such a costume, nor did he enjoy as a boy the close intimacy of the families of the Brotherhood. He felt very intimidated by his precocious Rossetti cousins.

Ford had been born in 1873. His father was the musicologist Franz Carl Christoph Johannes Hüffer, who came from a prosperous Catholic family in Münster. Hüffer was an atheist and felt out of place in his devout family. He moved to London where he felt free from family pressures.

It was there, in 1872, that he married Catherine Madox Brown. She was the daughter of the painter Ford Madox Brown by his second marriage to the fifteen-year-old Emma Hill, the daughter of a farmer. Her older half-sister Lucy had married William Michael Rossetti.

The relationship between the Rossettis and the Browns had begun in 1848 when the young Dante Gabriel Rossetti had sought out the older man and asked if he might become his pupil. Brown was at first suspicious of Rossetti, and could not gauge the seriousness of his request. Eventually, however, he agreed to the arrangement and from then on, despite Rossetti's shifts in loyalty and his general fecklessness, Brown took an almost parental responsibility for the younger man.

William Michael Rossetti, the painter's brother, was one of the founding members of the Pre-Raphaelite Brotherhood. He had neither the artistic talents nor the artistic temperament of his sister Christina or his brother Dante Gabriel; he was even-tempered, sensible, conscientious and steady, and it fell to him to hold the Brotherhood together and to curb some of their excesses.

Like Violet, Ford was sent to an enlightened school run along principles which were very advanced for the time. It was while he was at this boarding school — run by Dr Albert Praetorius and his wife — that he first met his future wife, Elsie Martindale, and his future mistress, her sister Mary.

55

There was a sudden change in the fortunes of the family when, in 1889, Franz Hüffer died and left his widow and three children penniless. Ford Madox Brown took his daughter Catherine and her two sons Ford and Oliver into his already chaotic household at 1 St Edmund's Terrace, while Juliet was sent to live two doors away with Lucy and William Michael Rossetti.

Ford's memories of what it was like to live in the painter's household closely resemble Violet's recollections of her experiences of the Pre-Raphaelites quoted earlier:

> I would sit there on the other side of the rustling fire, listening, and he would revive the splendid ghosts of the Pre-Raphaelites, going back to Cornelius and Overbeck and to Baron Leys and Baron Wappers, who taught him first to paint in the romantic, grand manner. He would talk on. Then Mr William Rossetti would come in from next door but one, and they would begin to talk of Shelley and Browning and Mazzarin and Napoleon III.[1]

Ford Madox Brown could not afford to keep his grandsons at boarding school, and they were sent instead to University College School in Gower Street. One of the advantages of this, as far as Ford was concerned, was that it gave him the opportunity to roam freely about the streets of London and to get to know the city intimately. This gave him a love of London life which never left him.

By now his admiration for his grandfather had overcome some of his earlier hostility to Pre-Raphaelitism. His change of heart could be clearly seen in the way he dressed. For now, as part of his unconventional costume, he wore proudly a dramatic black coat with a cape over the shoulders which had belonged to Dante Gabriel Rossetti. He also had a German forester's jacket and an old linen shirt, both of which had been his grandfather's. The ensemble was completed by a red satin tie. He looked the complete Pre-Raphaelite.

Although he had left Alfred Praetorius's school he had not lost contact with some of the pupils he had known there. In 1892, when he was eighteen, he began to court the fifteen-year-old Elsie Martindale. Elsie's parents objected to this on several grounds, including Elsie's youth and her delicate health. Nor were they sure how reliable Ford and his family were. Their doubts were not without grounds. Although Ford Madox Brown worked hard and was held in some esteem, he was not at all businesslike, and his difficulties were compounded by the fact that he was extremely generous. Even when in dire straits himself he would always share what he had with fellow-painters. As a result his affairs were always in a muddle. Dr Martindale feared that the grandson would be similarly poor at managing his money. The fact that Ford's younger brother, Oliver, had at the age of seventeen become hopelessly embroiled in debt did not make Dr Martindale look more favourably on the match. A further important factor in the attitude of Elsie's parents was that they knew, as Elsie did not, that their other daughter, Mary, was also in love with Ford. They feared trouble from her if Elsie was allowed to become engaged to Ford.

Their violent opposition to the match, which even led them to lock Elsie up to prevent her from meeting Ford, proved unwise. The two young people became determined to defy Elsie's parents and their unreasonable behaviour. First Elsie ran away from home. And then, because her parents would still not relent and at least agree to her meeting Ford, Elsie and Ford felt that the only course open to them was to marry. So in 1894, with the knowledge of Ford Madox Brown, who was sympathetic to their situation, they were married in Gloucester — claiming, falsely, that Elsie did not need her parents' consent because she was twenty-one.

When Ford was hauled into court — the first of many occasions on which he would find himself there on Elsie's account — he fared rather better than he would in the future. The marriage was declared valid despite the false declaration, and the couple were free to set up house together.

Dr Martindale's worst fears were realised. Ford could not earn enough to support two people, nor could he manage effectively the little money he had. The situation was only saved when Ford inherited £3000 from his rich uncle Leopold, his father's brother.

For a while the couple were happy. Ford was proud of his dark-haired handsome wife who dressed in William Morris style in richly coloured unconventional garments and not only helped him with the biography of his grandfather Ford Madox Brown which he had undertaken to write but was also writing on her own account.*

Then there were the two children — Christina, born in 1897, and

---

* She wrote two novels, *Ellen Slingsby* and *Margaret Hever*. The latter was published in 1909.

Katherine, born in 1900. The birth of the second child undermined Elsie's delicate health. She became something of an invalid and remained so throughout the rest of the marriage. Inevitably this, together with the presence of the children with their demands upon their mother, interrupted the close companionship and the sharing of work and ideas that Ford had valued in the relationship. He had warned Elsie that he did not believe that an enlightened marriage such as theirs was should bind him to be faithful. It is unlikely that Elsie took this idea too seriously at first, so the marriage was seriously undermined when Ford began an affair with his sister-in-law, Mary Martindale. Mary was a tall, vivacious, red-haired woman, very different to Elsie both in appearance and temperament. Ford's vanity was appeased by her willingness to give him her undivided attention. But the lovers were careless, and Elsie quickly found out about the affair. She was unable to stop it, however, and the two were lovers intermittently until Violet appeared on the scene.

Ford began to weary of family life in the country. He longed for the excitement and the new possibilities that he felt sure London would bring, so he was eager to accept when, in 1903, his brother Oliver, who was now married, offered him the use of his house at 10 Airlie Gardens on Campden Hill in Kensington. Ford believed that Kensington was the place to be for anyone involved in the arts — a view later shared by Ezra Pound who, when asked to co-operate on a book called 'Pound's London', would only do so if the book were called 'Pound's Kensington'.

The move to London gave Ford some of the close contact with other writers that he had craved. The Conrads had also left the country for a while and were living close by. He was also able to socialise with Henry James and John Galsworthy.

But in every other respect the move to London was disastrous. A virulent 'flu virus was flourishing in London and the whole family fell victim to it and were miserably ill. Then Christina managed to set her hair on fire. Elsie blamed these mishaps on London, and she persuaded her reluctant husband to move back to the country for the sake of the family.

The taste of London literary life had made Ford restless. On the one hand he did not enjoy country life with his wife and children as much as he used to. But, on the other hand, now as always he did not enjoy being alone. Having worked himself up into a neurasthenic state, he went off to Germany, without Elsie and the children, to visit his father's relatives and to recover his health. He stayed away six months.

When he returned to England the loan of William Michael Rossetti's house enabled him to be in London once more. After Christmas his family joined him there. Once again Elsie was ill — more seriously than anyone, including her doctors, would acknowledge. She had tuberculosis of the kidney, but this was not diagnosed correctly until three years later. She was fretful and unhappy in London, but Ford could not tolerate the idea of living permanently in the country.

A compromise was reached whereby Elsie moved back to the country with the children while Ford remained in London. He was to visit the family at weekends, with Elsie occasionally visiting him in London. The marriage was now under great strain. When Ford rented a flat at 84 Holland Park Avenue in 1907 it reached breaking-point.

Their finances were as precarious as ever. Even the money for Elsie's kidney operation had to be borrowed. In an attempt to salvage the relationship Elsie gave London one more try. But she could not abide it. There were quarrels and the marriage seemed to become less rather than more stable. Elsie left once more for the country. Ford's visits to her at Hurst Cottage in Aldington became increasingly infrequent and irregular.

Ford had met Violet at the Galsworthys' in 1907 and she was invited to 84 Holland Park Avenue while Elsie was still living there. She noted in her diary that the two were on bad terms and had quarrelled in front of their guests. She invited the couple to her annual garden party in July, noting that Ford attended without his wife.

But it was not until 1908 that Violet's relationship with Ford began to develop. By chance Violet met Ford shortly after the publication of her novel *White Rose of Weary Leaf*. By now he was the editor of *The English Review*, a journal which was held in high regard. She asked him to see that she got a good review. Then, in October, taking up Wells's suggestion that she should show some of her stories to Ford to see if he would be interested in publishing them, she went to *The English Review* offices.

Ford looked at the stories with interest and agreed to publish 'The

59

Coach'. It was over tea that day at 84 Holland Park Avenue that the relationship moved to a closer, more intimate footing.

NINE

❧ ❧ ❧ LOVE ❧ ❧ ❧ AND LITERATURE

What kind of a man was Ford Madox Ford that he could sweep Violet off her feet and remain from this point on the most important man in her life? There are several contemporary descriptions of him. The young Rebecca West did not find him physically attractive. She described him as 'stout, gangling, albinoish', and said that to be embraced by him was 'like being the toast under a poached egg'.[1] David Garnett was similarly unflattering in his portrait of Ford: 'He was arranged in a magnificent fur coat; — wore a glossy topper; drove about in hired carriages; and his fresh features, the colour of raw veal, his prominently blue eyes and rabbit teeth smiled benevolently and patronisingly upon all gatherings of literary lions.'[2]

Of the younger generation, D.H. Lawrence, who first met Ford in 1909, was more favourably impressed, at least initially. Writing to Jessie Chambers, he describes Hueffer as 'fairish, fat, about forty, and the kindest man on earth'.[3] And at the end of the year, in a letter to Blanche Jennings, he again speaks kindly of Ford: 'He is really a fine man, in that he is so generous, so understanding, and in that he keeps the doors of his soul open, and you may walk in.'[4]

Douglas Goldring, who was to work closely with Ford on *The English Review*, also noted his first impressions of Ford when he met him in 1908. He described him as:

> a tall thin man with fair hair and a blonde moustache which imperfectly concealed defective front teeth. He wore a grey-blue swallow-tail coat of uncertain cut, carried a leather despatch case of the kind the French call a *serviette* and had an important manner which in some ways suggested an Under-Secretary of State.[5]

Stella Bowen, who was to become Ford's mistress after he left Violet, gives some idea of what attracted women to him:

The stiff rather charming exterior, and the conventional omnisci-
ent manner, concealed a highly complicated emotional machinery.
It produced an effect of tragic vulnerability; tragic because the
scope of his understanding and the breadth of his imagination
had produced a great edifice which was plainly in need of much
more support than was inherent in the structure itself. A walking
temptation to any woman, had I but known it![6]

It is quite easy to see why Ford was attracted to Violet despite
the difference in their ages. She shared a common background
with him, she shared his passion for literature, and she was an
established figure in London literary life. Indeed Ford is reported
as having said, 'Of course, at the beginning, Violet was a feather
in my cap.'[7] Goldring felt that one attraction Violet offered Ford
was that 'she appeared to open the door to what, for him, was a
new kind of social world.'[8]

Violet was in her prime when she met Ford. She had already
written several moderately successful novels but in 1908 she published *White Rose of Weary Leaf*, which she considered her best
work to date. Written when she was actively involved in the suffragette movement and before she became involved with Ford, it
is the least autobiographical of her novels though, in an uncanny
way, some of the events in the novel foreshadow those in Violet's
relationship with Ford.

Violet takes for her heroine that familiar character in Victorian
fiction, the governess. Her deliberate challenge to Victorian notions
is established in her use within the novel – ironically and in a slightly
modified form – of the title of a well-known and representative sentimental genre painting of the period: 'The maiden knew that men
must work and women may, if they like, weep, and remember the
palmy days of courtship.'[9] The title of the painting is 'Men must
work while women must weep'.

From the outset it is clear that this governess is a very different
woman from her fictional predecessors. There is no attempt to
make her into a Cinderella-type figure whose tender sensibilities
are injured by her menial position. Amy is described as being 'a
common person's child'. No great claims are made for her beauty,
her sensitivity or even her character. Her horizons are limited. She
professes that 'Art was nothing to her.' She saw 'more beauty in a

new blouse.' The best that can be said for her is that she is efficient.

If Amy is unpromising as a heroine, the same can be said for the 'hero' of the novel, Jeremy Dand, who 'was a large lazy man, supposed to be clever, known to be cool, savage and cross-grained'. May Sinclair described him as 'the one entirely successful male figure that Violet Hunt has created'.[10] She attributes the success to the fact that Violet had 'abandone ! the fallacy of the ruling passion and presented him as he is, with all his inconsistencies; selfish and unselfish, generous and mean, faithful and faithless'.

When, after a series of contretemps, including an affair with a schoolboy, Amy is hired by Jeremy Dand to be his daughter's companion and the two begin one of the strangest love affairs in fiction. What Jeremy Dand appreciates in Amy is her practical common sense and her ability to make his household of oddly assorted women run smoothly. Initially she is not very attracted to him as a potential lover, but she appreciates the material advantages and comparative security she acquires by working for him. She enjoys his company not as a lover but as a man with broader horizons and contacts with the outside world which the women of the household lack.

Jeremy Dand sums up the relationship when he says 'Anybody can be a man's mistress, but companions don't grow on every tree.' Against this comparatively honest if unromantic relationship is set Jeremy Dand's marriage. On the surface it is romantic: Mrs Dand is young and beautiful, and claims to be deeply in love with her husband and to put him at the centre of her life. But under this surface lie the harsh facts of the marriage. Both sides have contracted to a bargain, the bare bones of which are unhesitatingly and matter-of-factly exposed by the widows in the house, Jeremy's mother and mother-in-law. When Mrs Dand baulks at having a baby, saying 'Why should I bother and suffer and endanger my looks, I should like to know, all to bear an heir to the house of Dand,' her mother-in-law replies with complete confidence:

> You have no right to want to get out of it. It's indecent – unfeminine. You have simply got to go down good-temperedly into the arena of discomfort and fight, once you let a man lead you there for your pleasure. It is the duty we women owe to Nature, when we are put under an obligation to her.

Once that heir is produced, the dutiful wife is rewarded with a pearl necklace 'to pay for the baby'.

Dulcie, Dand's daughter by a previous marriage, who is not at all attractive to men, falls in love. Her prospective bridegroom will only marry her if a suitable sum of money is part of the contract. For a while father and fiancé haggle over what the father should have to pay for the satisfaction of having his daughter safely married and off his hands. It is commonsensical Amy who finally persuades Jeremy Dand to put his daughter out of her misery by paying up.

Halfway through the novel all the principal characters are involved in a train crash, the description of which vividly calls to mind an almost identical train crash in Margaret Hunt's novel *Thornicroft's Model*. What happens in each novel after the crash marks the very different kind of fiction Violet was writing. In Margaret Hunt's novel the hero, Stephen Thornicroft, comes to his senses after the accident and realises for the first time the full virtue of Helen, his neglected wife – but Helen is dead, leaving only a beautiful memory. In Violet's novel Dand takes advantage of the general confusion, Amy's delirious condition and his wife's being near to death to complete his seduction of Amy. From now on she is his mistress. Dand's wife does not die, and it becomes necessary for Amy to resume her duties in the Dand household. When she discovers that she is pregnant she is amazed, but she does not collapse in shock and horror, nor does she blame her seducer. She takes matters into her own hands and determines to have her baby without the support, moral or otherwise, of the child's father.

Violet intended to end the novel with the death of Amy and her unborn child, but this proved too strong an ending for her publishers and had to be modified. In the end Amy dies but not the child. There is, however, no sense of the fallen woman having met a deservedly unhappy ending. Amy is praised by all those who meet her in the last stages of her pregnancy and are with her when she dies. And for once the hero does not get away scot-free. His distress at Amy's departure has led him further and further into drunkenness, and when he learns of Amy's death he kills himself: a conclusion which would have been unthinkable to Margaret Hunt.

Violet's knowledge that she had written a good and innovative novel gave her a new confidence in herself. This made her particularly attractive to Ford when he met her outside the office of her publishers, Heinemann, in May 1908.

She was made even more interesting to him by Elsie's declared dislike of the woman who by now had a reputation in London literary circles for being 'very French and fast' and for being 'a fashionable and faintly vicious blue-stocking'.[11]

There are many descriptions of Violet at that time. She made a strong impression on everyone she met, whether for good or for ill. David Garnett described her as 'a thin viperish-looking beauty with a long pointed chin and deep-set burning brown eyes under hooded lids'.[12] D.H. Lawrence gave his impression to Grace Crawford in a letter written after a party at *The English Review* office. 'She was tremendous in a lace gown and a hat writhed with blue feathers as if with some python. Indeed she looked very handsome.' But Lawrence also found her at this time a somewhat intimidating figure. 'When I was coming away, Miss Hunt was talking. She wouldn't look at me: I dare not for my life interrupt her. I fled. Was that criminal? I think I am quite out of favour with Miss Hunt. I'm sorry. I wish she liked me.'[13]

Derek Patmore was similarly intimidated, as he explained in the preface to his mother's autobiography: 'Personally, I was always rather frightened of Violet Hunt. Rather like a handsome witch, she was brilliant and caustic.'[14] Violet had decidedly inherited her mother's sharp tongue.

The most detailed picture of her is drawn by Brigit Patmore, who became very fond of her and was sympathetic to her later problems:*

In what has been written about Violet Hunt, much has been made of her malice, wit and cleverness, but very little of her

---

*Brigit Patmore was born in Dublin in 1883. She was extremely beautiful and was described by Ezra Pound as 'one of the charming people on this planet'. When she met Violet she was a wealthy woman as a consequence of her marriage to John Deighton Patmore, the grandson of the Victorian poet with strong Pre-Raphaelite connections, Coventry Patmore. She had two sons, one of whom, Derek, was responsible for the publications of her memoirs. The Patmores lived in Kensington, but the marriage was unhappy and broke up in 1924. From 1931 to 1941 Brigit Patmore lived with Richard Aldington. In 1941 he left her for a younger woman.

good looks and strange pathos . . . What struck me at once was the startling beauty of her eyes, for it was almost painful; their clear, curious green colour and the perfect leaf-shape of the lids round them were lovely . . . Her pointed chin and sparrow-brown hair, plummy and softly drifting as her head moved, added to the impression of feyness.[15]

It was uncharacteristic of Violet to begin a relationship with a man who attracted her and then to see little or nothing of him for almost two years. During that time she was busily engaged in a pursuit which was also in many ways uncharacteristic of her. For the most part the larger world of politics concerned her very little. She was interested in the politicians who visited her mother more as famous and powerful men, social catches, than as shapers of history. Douglas Goldring described her as 'preferring personal politics to public questions'.[16] His assessment is borne out by the fact that Violet's autobiography barely mentions what was happening in the world during the time of her 'flurried years'. Instead the passing of time is marked by events in the lives of her friends and acquaintances, and by her publication dates.

But in the years 1907-9 Violet did become involved in a political cause into which she put such time, energy and enthusiasm that for a while she put aside her interest in Ford.

It was almost certainly through May Sinclair that Violet became actively involved in the suffragette movement. May Sinclair had joined the group of writers living in Kensington when she had moved to a house at 13 Pembroke Gardens in 1905. By coincidence she became acquainted with Ford through the Garnetts in the same year that her friendship with Violet began.

The two women had much in common. They were both single, and to each of them had fallen the lot of looking after a widowed mother. They both knew what it meant to struggle to make a living by writing.

May Sinclair was just a year younger than Violet – she had been born in Cheshire in 1863. She did not have Violet's secure artistic background. Her father, a shipowner, had gone bankrupt and become an alcoholic. Like Violet, she was an avid reader and gained much of her education that way until at eighteen she went as a pupil teacher to Cheltenham Ladies' College, where Dorothea Beale was the headmistress.

She published her first novel, *Audrey Craven*, in 1897. Like those that were to follow, and like Violet's, it was concerned with women trying to make a living and achieve some degree of independence.

In temperament and appearance May Sinclair was very different from Violet. She gave the appearance of being rather prim and quiet. But she had great strength of character and unswerving loyalty to her friends; and, mindful of her own impoverished youth, she was extremely generous to those younger writers who came her way.

She had become a member of the Women's Freedom League and the Women's Suffrage League, so it was entirely appropriate that she should introduce Violet to those organisations.

Together with May Sinclair, Violet took part in the self-denial week organised to raise funds for the Women's Social and Political Union. A more public declaration of her support came when she and May Sinclair were 'drafted off to hold collecting boxes for three whole days in High Street Station'. The station was on Kensington High Street, close to where both women lived and where they might expect to encounter people they knew. The wooden collecting boxes were to be picked up at a stay shop. The obliging owner of the shop was unwilling to have her part in the affair known on the High Street. Violet describes the situation in *The Flurried Years*: 'She was very anxious for us to shut the door, hide the boxes under our cloaks, and keep them there until we got out of the shop, lest she lost custom through her favouring of the suffragettes.'

Neither of the two essentially middle-class women found it easy to support the movement in this way. It was one thing to write articles in support of women's suffrage and even, as Violet did, allow her house to be used as a meeting place for the women involved, but it was quite a different matter to stand in the public street taking all the jibes, innuendoes and even threats from unsympathetic passers-by. Violet describes how she felt 'suddenly stripped naked'.

Her awareness of the violent hostility of the government towards the suffrage movement was increased when she went with Alice Meynell and Lucy Masterman to a meeting in the Albert Hall. On this occasion, as on each occasion when such meetings were held, the women left the Hall to make their protest in Westminster, where there were violent confrontations with the police. The brutality with which the police treated the women came as a great shock to Violet, as to so many middle-class women who had until then respected the police as symbols of authority and law. She recalls the meeting vividly in *The Flurried Years*:

> Later on came the terrible Albert Hall meeting, when a girl near me suddenly slashed out with a whip and cut the face of the steward, and that of one of my friends who was trying to silence her or carry her out. Mrs Meynell, Mrs C.F.G. Masterman and I, all three ardent for the Cause, sat in a box and wept to see our friends so mauled in the arena below – Miss Evelyn Sharp hustled, and Mr Henry Nevinson carried out by three stewards as stiff as if he was being levitated, while Mr Lloyd George, friendly too, dabbing his eternal handkerchief to his mouth, was on principle not permitted to speak.

Although, inevitably, Violet spent much of her time with women in the suffrage movement during these two years, she was not hostile to men in the way some of the militants were. And when she resumed her relationship with Ford their pleasure in each other's company was reinforced by the fact that Ford also backed the suffrage movement – though it must be said that his treatment of all the women who were close to him makes it clear that he was far from being a feminist.

After the tea party at 84 Holland Park Avenue on 16 October 1908, Ford and Violet began to see each other regularly. At this time anyone close to Ford was inevitably drawn into *The English Review* circle, for it was at the centre of Ford's life. It could hardly be otherwise, since the *Review* was produced and edited in his home, with Douglas Goldring as his assistant, and the 'extremely decorative and highly efficient Miss Thomas' as his secretary.

Douglas Goldring had already met Violet at a dinner party and then at a 'very odd dance in a Regent Street picture gallery' at which Violet was chaperoning her niece Rosamond, the daughter of her youngest sister, Silvia. He was to remain close to Violet all her life. In *South Lodge* he gives a detailed description of Ford's home and office, in a building which has since been demolished. Ford occupied three floors above a poulterer's and fishmonger's shop. His premises were reached through a side door which gave onto a dark flight of stairs. Everyone who visited Ford was struck by the particular smell of the place. Goldring describes it as the 'sickly depraved smell of chickens'. On the first floor was a long L-shaped room, and at the top of the house was a small dining-room which served also as a place in which to correct proofs.

The furniture was a strange assortment. There was a Spanish inlaid cabinet and a writing desk which had belonged to Christina Rossetti. Above the latter hung a competent watercolour, 'Notting Dale Mean Street,' done by Ford himself. There was a black grand piano, what Violet described as a 'hideous red plush Victorian arm chair' and a chaise-longue which Elsie had used in the days when she spent some time there.

Ford held more or less open house in this establishment. There is a story of his interviewing Wyndham Lewis whilst he took a bath. Visitors were so frequent that the only way that Ford could accomplish the business of the *Review* was to go with Goldring to the second house at the Shepherd's Bush Empire and do the work there.

Violet was both attracted to, and repelled by, the kind of life Ford was leading. She speaks of his 'miserable household' where disorder, confusion, discomfort and waste abounded. For although there was much in common in their backgrounds, there were also differences which were apparent even at the early stages of their relationship. Ford's household at 84 Holland Park Avenue was temporary. He had never owned a house, nor had he settled in any one place for very long, whereas since Violet was three years old she had lived all her life in the same part of Kensington. She and her mother had been tenants at South Lodge until 1908, when the lease came up for sale. There was an auction at which Violet, with the help of Alfred Mond, who stood as surety, succeeded in buying it.

She was, as a result, firmly and securely established in her own circle. Her house, like Ford's, was the centre of literary gatherings; and when she first became close to Ford those who attended her parties had, like herself, already made a name for themselves.

Brigit Patmore's description of South Lodge and the parties given there shows clearly the differences between the two households:

The drawing room of South Lodge on Campden Hill had a frozen quality, or rather, dreamed gently into a flowery green-and-white garland of William Morris. The wallpaper was cream with very discreet, self-effacing pink and blue flowers and delicate foliage; there was much white painted woodwork and chairs covered with chintz with the same kind of flowers on it. For curtains Violet had embroidered a curious climbing plant design of Morris's on coarse white cloth. Most of the pictures were small gloomy landscapes by her father . . . A large window jutted out into the front garden. It had a broad window-seat, from which one looked across the road to a lawned garden where Violet gave tennis parties. Another small room had obviously been incorporated into the larger one, and it also had a wide window. It was all light and almost gay, but something Victorian kept it sober and as if it could not be changed.

It was good background for Violet's crowded parties of writers – novelists, poets, essayists, historians – and fashionable people who liked a dash of ink with their tea or to pick a bright brain for dinner. During these afternoons you were offered tea or coffee by a devoted old housemaid. Violet also had a pretty niece, whom she was taking out socially and she used to give luncheons for her at the Reform Club, where her guests would often be the Alfred Monds, W.H. Hudson, who was the sour-saddest writer I have ever seen, and H.G. Wells, already a rising star in the literary firmament. But her real heart was with the novelists, who flocked around her – May Sinclair, Ethel Colburn Mayne, W.L. George.[17]

For a while Violet and Ford remained just close friends. Their exchanges at this time still have a certain formality. In the spring of 1909 Ford introduced into his household a young girl named Gertrud Schlablowsky. He had seen her as being in desperate need of a home, he claimed. The presence of this girl under Ford's roof piqued Violet, as the poem she submitted to *The English Review* under the pseudonym of George Angel reveals. Violet chose a suitably Browningesque style to express her ironic view of the situation:

> Stir up the fire, draw out your chair:
> Kick off the shoes: let down the hair:
> Your white kimono, now . . .
> Then snuggle down and let us doze . . .

And both with a most ancient work to do,
You selling worthless love: I modern rhyme,
Sitting beside your hearth in wintertime
Cheer on, I know, each other. Yes I know . . .

But she was not ungenerous in her treatment of the girl. She describes her in *The Flurried Years* as being 'gentle, shy, faint . . . innocuous, like a flake of tarnished snow; her white, heavy, moon-face, with its short Calmuck nose, wide red mouth, and loops of black hair falling over a rather brutish forehead, spoke of her Tartar descent'.

She was even prepared to lend dresses to the girl for parties at the *Review*, although she was a little annoyed when May Sinclair took Gertrud in Violet's finery to be a 'beautiful, pale, Russian princess'.

By this time Violet and Ford were openly going about together. From Violet's point of view Gertrud provided something of a smoke-screen and a focus for Elsie Martindale's increasing jealousy. For, despite their growing intimacy, this was not a very happy time for Ford and Violet. In January of 1909 Oswald Crawfurd had died. The notice of his death brought back to Violet memories of her unhappy affair with him. Ford was having both business and domestic problems. He was desperately short of money. He borrowed from his German relatives, but still relied on the financial backing given to the *Review* by his partner Arthur Marwood. So he was in a difficult position when Elsie began to complain that Marwood had been making improper overtures to her. He made the best of the situation by taking the opportunity to suggest that he needed to see a great deal of Violet Hunt as, with her connections, she might raise new financial backing for the *Review*. In the event a consortium was formed to keep the *Review* alive with Ford's brother-in-law, the Russian David Soskice, as business manager. Ford retained the editorship but with diminished powers.

Ford was bitterly hurt by the turn of events. He went off to see Elsie at Aldington and after a miserable wet weekend in the country he asked Elsie for a divorce.

Although she knew that the marriage was no longer a happy one, Elsie did not like the idea of a divorce. She was convinced that if only Ford would leave London they might patch up their life together.

Ford, however, had already declared his love for Violet and at the end of May he followed her to the cottage – the Knapp, in Selsey – which she rented from Edward Heron Allen. It was here that he made his far from romantic proposal 'in a dead level tone, as if he had simply been saying, "Have some more," at the luncheon table among crumbled bread and smoking Irish stew'. Violet describes the occasion and her feelings about it as follows:

'Will you marry me if ever I am a divorced man?'
It was an essay in Pre-Raphaelite crudity of expression, as if a Madox Brown heavy oil painting or an early Elizabeth Siddal water-colour had been suddenly turned into speech.

Was Violet really as astonished by the proposal as she claimed, saying that it was 'an astounding, romantic, nonsensical proposition'? She certainly did not rush to respond and thus, perhaps, precipitated a truly melodramatic scene. Once again, Violet presents the occasion in a determinedly anti-romantic fashion. She writes of Ford as being 'white like a stick of asparagus grown in a cellar; at any rate, rather pasty. He smoked incessantly, and it made his teeth black. His cuffs wanted trimming.' They had spent the evening together and had a dinner in which 'the cutlets were burnt and the meringues too sweet'.

Ford was very depressed and on this as on other occasions he hinted at suicide. Violet did not know whether to take him seriously or not. She was torn between trying to do something to help him and simply going home in the hope that it was empty talk. She made to leave and put her hand on his lapel whilst her other hand 'stole to the loose, open pocket of the brown velvet jacket that Rossetti had once worn. It fished out a dark, fluted bottle, inscribed in Futurist colours of danger POISON.'

The occasion provided the crisis that they both perhaps needed to advance their affair, and on that night of 9 June 1909 they became lovers. For Violet, at least, there was now no turning back. A few days later she was consulting her solicitor as to how best Ford could proceed in the matter of a divorce, and entertaining Ford with his two daughters to tea at South Lodge.

June was an eventful month for the *Review* also. It was then that Jessie Chambers sent in under a pseudonym some verses by

71

her friend D.H. Lawrence. Violet read them and liked them immediately. Ford also thought that they were very good, and he not only decided to print them in *The English Review* but invited Lawrence to London to meet him at the *Review* offices in September. It was November before Lawrence, with Jessie Chambers, found himself having lunch at South Lodge with Ford and Violet. It was evidently a successful occasion as later in November Lawrence was invited to one of Violet's 'at homes' at the Reform Club. Lawrence seems to have been uncertain about Violet's attitude towards him at this early point in their acquaintance. Violet, however, was unreservedly enthusiastic about both the man and his work. She describes her response to the poetry and her first meeting with Lawrence in *The Flurried Years*:

> They [the poems] were perfectly wonderful . . . Letters were exchanged, and the young poet, bored and weary of his life, teaching at Addiscombe, called at the office. He was very like a board-school boy grown to man's estate. He had the head of a child – the yellow hair with a 'feather' at the back, much as if a school-mate had been having a game with it. His eyes, if I mistake not, were very blue, his lips very red, and his face very white – sinisterly so, for he looked consumptive.
>
> His manner was gentle, modest and tender in a way I did not associate with his upbringing.

At both the luncheon and the 'at home' Ezra Pound was present. He had been introduced to Ernest Rhys* by the bookseller and publisher Elkin Mathews. In his turn Ernest Rhys had introduced the young American poet to May Sinclair. He made a very favourable impression on her, and in the hope of helping to forward his career May Sinclair introduced him to Violet and Ford early in 1909, for it was well known that it could only do a young artist good to be known at South Lodge. By the time that Lawrence came to South Lodge Ezra Pound was already an established figure there.

These young people must have been very much aware of the difference between the occasions at South Lodge and the rowdy and often childish parties to which they were invited by Ford, at which they were required to play such games as 'Clumps, Honeypots,

---

*Ernest Rhys had been an engineer, but at this time he was editor of the Everyman Library classics.

not stopping short at Hunt the Slipper'. And there were, of course, Ford's famous *bouts-rimes* parties.*

They were a far cry from the elegant and formal occasions over which Violet presided. But by November 1909 she had begun to exercise some influence over some of Ford's parties at the *Review* offices. Lawrence records his amazement when summoned to such a party: 'What was my dismay, on running up the stairs, to be received open-armed by a waiter. I was so astonished that I could neither find him a card nor tell him my name. At last he bawled my announcement, and I found myself in what seemed like a bargain sale.'[18]

Whilst all this literary activity was taking place, events had also moved forward in Violet's and Ford's love affair. At first Ford tried to persuade Elsie to divorce him in return for an allowance of £400 a year. Violet must have had a hand in this offer, because Ford was in no position to make any such payment. But Elsie, influenced by her brother Harri Martindale and the Catholic Hüffers in Münster, refused to be involved in a divorce. She was especially fearful about how this would affect the status of her two daughters and about whether Ford would automatically gain custody of them.

So Ford and Violet concocted a plan to obtain the divorce. In July Violet took her niece Rosamond to Aldeburgh. She had been taking her about for some time, introducing her into the kind of society that she felt life in Bedburne would not provide. She saw clearly that there was no possibility of Rosamond ever seeking independence, so she was determined to have a hand in the marriage which she saw as inevitable. Douglas Goldring, who had met Rosamond earlier in the year, describes that meeting in South Lodge and gives a good sense of exactly what kind of young girl she was:

---

*This was a game at which Ford was particularly adept. At one time or another he persuaded all his friends to play. He even introduces the game into *No More Parades* where its rules are explained:

'Do you know what a sonnet is? Give me the rhymes for a sonnet. That's the plan of it.'
MacKenzie grumbled:
'Of course I know what a sonnet is. What's your game?'
Tietjens said:
'Give me the fourteen end-rhymes of a sonnet and I'll write the lines. In under two minutes and a half.'

Violet ... Summoned me to dance with her niece, Rosamond, who was then being chaperoned through her first London season. She was a fresh and innocent North Country girl, rather 'dumb' as we should say nowadays, and with an odd little habit of gasping in the middle of her not over-bright remarks. Violet was possessed by a devouring maternal affection for her which was almost painful to witness.[19]

Photos of Rosamond justify the name of 'Beauty' which Violet uses for her throughout *The Flurried Years*.

Once aunt and niece were settled in Aldeburgh, Ford arrived in the company of Gertrud, whom he described to anyone who showed interest as his secretary. The scandal that he had hoped to provoke was forthcoming. It was generally assumed that Ford was flaunting his relationship with his mistress. In this way he established the basis for the next step of the plot he and Violet had dreamed up.

Ford wrote a letter to Elsie telling her in some detail about Gertrud and emphasising the fact that Gertrud was living with him at 84 Holland Park Avenue. He hoped that the letter would make Elsie so angry that she would want a divorce. His letter's implications of adultery would provide her with grounds while keeping Violet clear of any scandal.

The letter was conveyed on 19 July via Edmée Van der Noot, the nursery maid for the two Hueffer girls and Elsie's close companion. Elsie's first response was all that Violet and Ford could have hoped for. She rushed to London to seek the advice of Robert Garnett. This solicitor, the brother of the publisher Edward Garnett, was a close family friend. He had been accustomed to advising both Elsie and Ford on legal and financial matters. On this occasion he felt that to advise Elsie would be to take sides in the marital dispute, so he sent her to consult another lawyer, William Sturges.

Sturges told Elsie that the first thing to do was to send a letter to her husband demanding 'restitution of conjugal rights' – which was supposed to be a formal first step towards seeking a divorce. When it arrived Violet and Ford were hopeful that it would be only six to eight months before the divorce went ahead and left them free to marry. Time was to prove how very misplaced their hopes were.

The legal document brought home to Ford for the first time that he would not only be divorced from Elsie but that he would almost certainly be estranged from his daughters. To recompense him for this loss Violet made every effort to make him feel much more a part of her family.

Her mother, who had never really recovered from the death of her husband, could no longer be left alone. Although she could remember the past with great clarity, she had no short-term memory at all. It was necessary for her to have a companion when she made her annual visit to Silvia at Bedburne. Violet proposed that Ford should be that companion. Mrs Hunt raised no objections.

As it turned out, neither the Fogg Elliotts nor Ford was pleased with the visit. Rosamond was partly responsible for this. During the time that she had been staying with Violet in London she had seen a good deal of Ford and had become infatuated with him as both Violet and Ford recognised. Violet had told her niece that there was no possibility of Ford reciprocating her feelings and as long as Rosamond could see for herself that it was Violet that Ford cared for she had accepted the situation.

By the time Ford visited Bedburne Rosamond was back at home with her parents. His presence in her home revived the feelings she had experienced in London. Her parents quickly became aware of how much she was attracted to Ford, who was not the kind of man to remain unflattered for long by the devotion of a young and beautiful girl. He did not give any signs of discouraging her, and so alienated her parents.

Both Silvia and her husband had assumed that this visit, making as it did a public declaration of some kind of close liaison between Ford and Violet, meant that Ford was already divorced. Violet had not been quite honest in her dealings with her sister on this matter. Although fully aware of her own husband's adultery, Silvia was scandalised by her sister's conduct. Both she and her husband expressed their distress that their daughter might be involved with such a scandalous couple.

What really made the visit the complete disaster it turned out to be was that Ford made no attempt to make it a success. There are many accounts of his ability to charm when he chose to do so. On this occasion he made no effort at all. He was terribly bored by Violet's sister and brother-in-law, and he showed it. He hated the

North, and he showed that too. He was fully aware that the visit had not helped Violet's efforts to integrate him into her family. He wrote to her saying 'it really was a mistake my coming here . . . And I fancy I have made your sister dislike me.' In retrospect Violet was to feel that she had 'thrown pearls before swine, in the more recondite sense of the word, and . . . that the pearl had been lazy.'

While Ford was in Bedburne Violet was staying with her friends Alfred and Violet Mond. She was already trying to persuade Alfred Mond to buy *The English Review* and thus solve Ford's financial problems and make his position as editor more secure.

It seemed on the surface a good idea, and Ford was eager for Violet to succeed. Alfred Mond, later to become Lord Melchett, was already a rich man. He was a director of the chemical firm set up by his father, Brunner, Mond and Company, which was to become Imperial Chemical Industries. In 1906 he had been elected Liberal member for Chester. He had married Violet Florence Mabel Goetze in 1894. The two Violets were very close friends. Although his outward manner could be very offputting, no one disputed his great strength of character, energy, organisational abilities and love of the arts. He seemed an ideal person to become the owner of *The English Review*. Once again, however, Violet's plans were to prove less successful than she had anticipated. When she returned to London matters were still not settled.

It is not surprising that once they were back in London Ford and Violet found themselves the object of much attention and gossip. Strangely enough Violet minded this. She had set her heart upon becoming a respectably married woman, and now felt the need to keep up appearances. At first the couple tried to keep their meetings a secret by renting a room in John Street. This did not prove to be a satisfactory arrangement. They tried spending alternate nights at Holland Park Avenue and South Lodge. Neither place afforded the privacy they desired. Ford had to get up and leave Violet before her household stirred. It was not her mother they were afraid of but the maid, Annie Child, who had made Ford promise that his intentions were honourable. When they were in Ford's establishment there was always the danger of being intruded upon by one of the contributors to the *Review*, who had long become accustomed to Ford's habit of holding open house. And, of course, Gertrud was still in residence and Violet could never be sure that Ford was simply Gertrud's protector as he claimed at this time.

The relationship was, thus, under some stress and this was to be increased by the fact that Elsie had not proceeded with the divorce as expected. Once again the Catholics in Münster were advising her not to act and seek a divorce, but to regard Ford's affair with Violet as a mere peccadillo, one in a series and, therefore, not seriously threatening to the marriage.

Ford, as was his wont, became ill with the stress of his domestic troubles coupled with the incessant quarrelling at *The English Review*. The last straw was when Edward Heron Allen advised Violet that, as a result of her petition, Elsie was in a position to seize all the furniture in Ford's establishment. In a panic Violet had all Ford's belongings appraised and then deposited the money to that amount in Ford's bank account. She went further and persuaded Mrs Hueffer, Ford's mother, to write a letter in which she confirmed that most of the furniture at 84 Holland Park Avenue now belonged to Violet.

It was to escape all this and to have some time together that Violet and Ford decided to leave London and go to France. They set off via Southampton and Le Havre to the summer cottage of Violet's long standing friend Agnes Farley at Beaumont-le-Roger in Normandy. While they were there Violet had her forty-seventh birthday. She recorded that it was the 'happiest birthday ever'. Ford's health improved and he was able to do some work. It was altogether an idyllic time, as Violet's account in *The Flurried Years* makes clear:

> In the afternoons we walked in the woods . . . Or we would take a rickety calèche and visit Lisieux Cathedral or some old mediaeval chateau ruined by the Revolution, where on the ground floor, old black-robed peasant women pattered about among dressers covered with bowls of pale primrose-coloured cream . . . Or we would walk among high hedges, across marshes, by straggling, forgotten paths, to this or that ruined *manoir* that would not let.

It was in fact the happiest time Ford and Violet were ever to enjoy. For back at home in London trouble was brewing up for them which would have a long-lasting impact on their lives.

TEN

A CHAPTER ✍ ✍ ✍ ✍OF ✍ ACCIDENTS

As on so many other distressing occasions in Violet's life, there was an element of comedy involved.

The couple had gone to considerable trouble to cover their tracks when they left London. Indeed Ford had been so successful that his brother-in-law, David Soskice, assumed that he had left England for good. But their happy and relaxed time at Beaumont-le-Roger had lulled them into a false sense of security. Forgetting that their whereabouts and the fact that they were together was supposed to be a closely-guarded secret, Violet wrote from Paris to Miss Thomas, the *Review*'s secretary. Absurdly enough, this letter which was to cause so much trouble concerned a pair of stays. Violet had promised to find Miss Thomas a pair similar to those she had bought for herself in Paris. But she had forgotten to take the garment with her and wrote to Miss Thomas to tell her so.

By an unfortunate coincidence, 14 October was the day Elsie, her lawyer William Sturges and the governess/confidante Edmée, chose to visit 84 Holland Park Avenue to find out exactly what Ford was up to. It was also the very day that Violet and Ford had chosen to travel back to London.

As a result of Violet's letter the honest Miss Thomas was no longer in a position to deny all knowledge of the whereabouts of Violet. Under further pressure from the trio, and intimidated by the presence of a lawyer, Miss Thomas revealed that she had received a telegram from Ford to tell her that he would be returning home to London from Paris on the train which arrived at Charing Cross at 10.45 pm.

Elsie knew instinctively that Violet would be with Ford. Because she thought she might be recognised at South Lodge and, therefore, given no information or even misleading information, she sent Edmée, who was not then known to the household, to enquire when Violet was expected home. The answers confirmed Elsie's suspicions, for the maid told Edmée that Violet was expected from Paris on the train arriving at Charing Cross at 10.45 pm.

When the happy couple got off the train they found a grim reception committee awaiting them: Elsie, her lawyer and Edmée.

Ford immediately understood what the consequences of their carelessness would be. He knew that this public confirmation of his affair with Violet would provoke Elsie into denying him a divorce.

Violet gives her account of the episode in *The Flurried Years*. She describes how after a bad crossing and a tiring train journey she was in no state for the confrontation and the outburst of anger against the implications of her being with Ford on the train:

> And yet I was, if a drowned, a perfectly respectable rat! Appearances, which after all, on the face of it and in the end, are all we humans have to go by, were against me. For no one on the prosecuting side ever stops to think that for real, intending criminals the easiest thing in the world is to keep the said appearance up. It is no use *being* good.

She quotes Ford as saying 'It's all up, old girl! You will see. There'll be no divorce.'

Ford's worst fears were realised. Elsie now set her face resolutely against a divorce. Rumours about the affair between Ford and Violet abounded, so that when Henry James invited Violet to spend a weekend with him at Lamb House in October both she and Ford felt it necessary to write to him and explain and justify their situation. They unwisely told him that Elsie was intending to sue Ford for a divorce. In a manner typical of him, which the couple could have anticipated, James withdrew his invitation to Violet, having no wish to have his name touched by her scandal. Violet was deeply hurt at the implied criticism of her morals. She tried to justify herself by claiming that she was not responsible for the break between the Hueffers but that they had been separated for some time for reasons which had nothing to do with her. She explained that Ford was only willing to go through with the distress of a divorce because he was so eager to marry her. But James was not to be moved, and he blamed Hueffer for putting Violet in a socially untenable position. Violet tried to dismiss James's response. She says in *The Flurried Years*, 'For one knew that the one thing Henry really dreaded was being mixed up with life in any way, or entangled in anything that went on outside the drawing-room.' But it was a blow to her to lose James's esteem.

Henry James's reaction did, however, have the effect of making them more aware of how other people might respond to their relationship, and from this point on they conducted their affair within strictly conventional bounds. Again there is something comic about their belated response to public opinion, and their strict observance of the proprieties at this late stage in an already very public affair.

However, for the next few months Violet avoided the *Review* offices. Ford visited South Lodge most evenings but on these occasions Mrs Hunt was there as a chaperone and Ford generally played piquet with her. He always left the house alone before eleven o'clock.

Looking back at this time, Violet expresses some bitterness at the position she found herself in. 'One had to take, in fact, all the care in the world to prevent one's flopping, feminine, vulnerable character from getting smirched or, at least, needing a new "bind". Marriage?' Her bitterness is compounded by the fact that in later years little would have been thought of the affair: 'Does post-war woman realise the differentiation of the standard of manners that has obtained since 1918?' But this was 1909 and Violet was 'bewildered, worried, and frightened' and she 'would have taken cover – married anyone!'

A further complication troubled their lives at this time. While Ford had been in France David Soskice, who had no idea when, if ever, to expect Ford back, had appointed Galsworthy as the editor of the *Review* to take Hueffer's place. Ford was angry and quarrelled bitterly with Soskice and Galsworthy. In his upset frame of mind he also managed to quarrel with his agent Pinker and with H.G. Wells.

Violet felt that this at least was a situation in which she could take positive action. She redoubled her efforts to interest Alfred Mond in buying the *Review*, which by now had established a reputation for literary excellence. On this occasion she was successful. It seemed as if one part of their troubled lives was being sorted out satisfactorily.

On this matter, as on so many others, Violet, who was normally a shrewd judge of character, allowed her wishful thinking to overcome her common sense. She had known Mond for many years and she knew clearly what kind of man he was. She was also intimate with the affairs of *The English Review* and with Ford's business practices, or rather his lack of them. So she could have anticipated where her success in financing *The English Review* would lead.

Alfred Mond, lover of the arts as he was, was also a successful and energetic businessman known for his organisational skills. He was appalled when he saw the state of *The English Review*'s financial affairs and was confronted by Ford's totally erratic methods of doing business. What Violet had failed to realise was that, as a staunch Liberal, Mond was as much interested in the *Review* because of its political possibilities as its literary merit. For his purposes, therefore, Ford was not the ideal editor. So instead of reinstating him as editor with increased powers, as both he and Violet had assumed he would, Mond appointed Austin Harrison to Ford's position.

This was not only a financial blow to Ford; it was also a severe blow to his pride and self-respect. As editor of *The English Review* he had been a figure of some importance in his own right, and he had enjoyed that position. Now he found himself very much in Violet's shadow, dependent on her financially and socially. In a letter he wrote to R.A. Scott James in January 1910, Ford's distress is apparent:

> The *Review* was then sold in due course, too, to Alfred Mond who undertook to pay the contributors or I should not have continued to edit it. Mr Mond has now ejected me from the editorial chair because he is a Liberal which no one could accuse me of being. (And you might publish the facts in the *Daily News* as one more instance of political terrorism.)[1]

Both Violet and Ford must have felt that their affairs had reached rock-bottom. But there was more to come. On 11 January 1910, Mr Justice Bargrave Deane made a decree for Elsie and against Ford for 'restitution of conjugal rights'. Ford had to comply within fourteen days, and was responsible for costs. Unfortunately the newspapers got hold of the story. As Violet was out shopping in Kensington High Street she was confronted by the newspaper headline: 'Novelist and his Wife. Mr Hueffer Ordered to Return to Her within Fourteen Days.'

Violet's first response was to feel grateful that for once Rosamond, who was once more staying with her, had not accompanied her on this shopping trip but had stayed at home. Her second was concern about how her servants would react when a man who had been headline news in the afternoon came to visit in the evening.

Violet's worries were unnecessary. Ford did not call that evening. Violet was sufficiently upset that she was at this point ready to give him up before matters grew worse: 'if he had come, I was in the mood to say to him: "Why not go back and have done with it?" For Peace – a dreary sort of Peace would certainly come to him that way.'

Of her friends only May Sinclair reacted, and this was in support of Ford and Violet. She wrote to Violet that she was sick 'of the world we live in, of cowardice and hypocrisy, and abominable, poisonous, sham morality'.

It was some months before Ford again showed his face at South Lodge. When he did appear he remained silent about the court order and his unusual absence. During this time Violet continued as though nothing had happened. She made her usual social calls with Rosamond. But being the kind of woman she was, Ford's absence piqued her. Her original decision to let Ford go was forgotten and instead her determination to marry him was strengthened and renewed.

The newspaper publicity alarmed Elsie. She did not pursue the matter further and Ford did not return to her. With Violet's help Ford was already paying Elsie three pounds and ten shillings a week to help support her and the girls, so when he received a court order requiring him to pay money to Elsie he was enraged. In his view the order implied that he had been irresponsible and had not contributed already, voluntarily, to his family's upkeep. On a point of principle and honour, therefore, he refused to comply with the court order. Inevitably the law caught up with him, and at Marylebone Police Court he was sentenced to ten days in Brixton Gaol.

Violet had already reached the conclusion that it was not sensible for Ford to maintain an establishment at 84, Holland Park Avenue. He no longer ran the *Review* from there and as long as he was in residence he was vulnerable to unexpected visits from Elsie and her family. She took the opportunity of Ford's being in Brixton to move him out of his premises and into South Lodge. In this she found an unlikely ally in Mary Martindale, Ford's earlier mistress and Elsie's sister, whose own affair with Ford had petered out when Ford began to live in London. The two women worked hard returning the many books Ford had borrowed and failed to return, selling other books to raise money for Ford when he got out of Brixton and moving those pieces of furniture which definitely belonged to him. It was in this way that Christina Rossetti's desk found its way to South Lodge.

It was typical of Violet's luck in this whole affair that while she and Mary were thus employed Harri Martindale, the brother of Elsie and Mary, should appear on the scene. He was understandably appalled to find his sister Mary abetting Violet, the source of his sister's misery as he saw it. He reported back to Elsie, and from then on she set her face resolutely against a divorce.

Ford came out of gaol much shaken and in a hysterical state. His frame of mind was not improved by news of the death of his rich Tante Laura in Münster, news which Violet had to break to him. Ford had expected a substantial legacy from her. But her will, changed only hours before she died, stated that the legacy was conditional upon Ford's 'good behaviour'. The scandal over his divorce was deemed to violate this condition, so no legacy was forthcoming.

Violet decided that a holiday away from London was necessary to soothe Ford's jangled nerves. She took him along with her mother and Gertrud Schlablowsky to Fordingbridge. Gertrud served as an extra chaperone, but in any event Violet was less threatened by the girl now as she had arranged for her to return to Königsberg. She later decided that this was not far enough and when Gertrud requested money so that she could emigrate to New South Wales, Violet was happy to help her.

Ford's health improved during the time away from London and he was able to resume his writing. He needed every penny he could earn from the publication of his works to support Elsie and the girls.

When they returned to London Violet decided that the only way to deal with rumours and scandal was to follow her instincts and confront them head on. She gave the somewhat irregular household – Ford was by now her mother's paying guest giving her three pounds a week – a greater respectability by having Ford's widowed mother, Mrs Hueffer, and Mary Martindale join them at South Lodge. With such chaperonage she confidently resumed her social life, taking Ford with her everywhere and defying comment.

Meanwhile there was trouble in another quarter. Silvia had already expressed her disapproval of Violet's relationship with Ford on the occasion of Ford's visit to Bedburne. When she discovered that Ford was living at South Lodge she immediately required that her daughter Rosamond terminate her visit and return home. She was perhaps afraid that Rosamond's obvious infatuation with Ford would develop further, and she was anxious to avoid the girl being involved in what she described as 'an ambiguous position'.

Because there was little they could do about Ford's presence at South Lodge once they had expressed their disapproval, Violet's family began to harass her on other matters.

The responsibility for caring for Mrs Hunt was becoming ever more demanding and irksome as her mental state deteriorated. Until Violet's affair with Ford her two sisters and her maiden aunt had apparently been content to let Violet shoulder the responsibility. Suddenly they began to be alarmed that in her weakened mental condition Margaret Hunt could be manipulated by Violet. What they feared most of all was that Mrs Hunt's money was being used to support the Violet-Ford relationship.

Violet's Aunt Jane set the ball rolling, though it is likely that she was egged on by her god-child Silvia. Jane was Margaret's youngest sister, and she had never married. To allow her to be independent Margaret Hunt had made her younger sister a yearly allowance. She had sent her a cheque every three months 'enclosed with a kind letter in her own large dear handwriting', as Violet explains in *The Flurried Years*. This money had always come from her earnings as a novelist and journalist. She had made it a point of honour not to spend Alfred Hunt's hard-earned income on her own family. But Aunt Jane was not satisfied with this, even though Margaret Hunt had long since ceased to earn any money from her writing and was then drawing on her savings to support her sister. Jane, like Violet's sisters, had begun to consider what kind of legacy they could expect when Margaret Hunt died: all of them were jealous of any expenditure of which they felt Violet was the sole beneficiary and which might diminish the capital they hoped to inherit. Violet found their attitude grasping and unsavoury, to say the least. The first complaint was about wallpaper. Aunt Jane wrote that she had 'heard tell of expensive Morris papers at six shillings a yard being put even on the walls of the upstairs rooms'. 'She naturally did not see why, now that there were so many pretty, cheap papers, my mother should persist in getting up her house Pre-Raphaelite.' Elsewhere in her autobiography Violet reports that she and her mother were in the habit of always replacing the 'Daisy' wallpaper by Morris with identical paper.

Further complaints were made about the addition of a bathroom to South Lodge, since the property was Violet's and not her mother's: 'Aunt Jane did not think that I had any right to "beautify my own property at the expense of my mother's income" and those who had a right to expect to inherit from her.'

The family continued to survey South Lodge with great care and objected when Violet added a cloakroom on the ground floor. On this occasion she was able to prove that she had paid for this improvement exclusively from her own earnings, though her mother stood to benefit as much as anyone. All these interferences made Violet aware that her sisters were watching and waiting for her to put a foot wrong in handling her mother's affairs. Although she was accustomed to being at odds with Venice, she had been on loving terms with Silvia until her marriage, and found her youngest sister's hostility especially hard to bear. She stated her objections to the situation in which she had been placed when she came to write her autobiography: 'I do think that the position of such a one requires special protection. Unpaid nurse and caretaker, she can so easily do something to get herself called a rogue, and be proceeded against on some pretext or other.'

Despite all these problems, life at South Lodge was not one of unrelieved gloom. The young Ezra Pound was by now a regular and a lively visitor. He began to introduce his friends to the South Lodge circle. One of these became a close and loyal friend of Violet's – Grace Crawford, later to become Grace Lovat Fraser. Also an American, she was training to be a professional musician. Although she was so much younger than Violet she was not overawed by the older woman as so many of her contemporaries were. Perhaps the fact that she had a wide social experience and was outside the British class system gave her confidence.

It became the practice of the two young Americans to go to tea at South Lodge on Saturdays. Pound and Ford would go off together to discuss literary matters, leaving the two women together. These were occasions Grace Crawford greatly enjoyed, and despite her youth she became Violet's confidante:

When I could get Violet to myself I would spend a happy afternoon, for she was a splendid talker, knew everybody in the literary and artistic worlds and could satisfy my curiosity about the Pre-Raphaelites among whom she had been born and brought up. She was unhappy at this time, for her association with Ford was bedevilled by all sorts of legal and social difficulties and I felt proud of her trust when she told me of these.[2]

Grace was also very aware of the real problems Violet's mother presented, as two incidents she recounts make clear:

Sometimes Violet's old mother – Mrs Alfred Hunt – would sit with us and this would rather spoil the afternoon for me for the old lady was very eccentric and apt to come out with the most surprising and irrelevant remarks which Violet always received with complete calm. Once, on being handed a cup of tea, the old lady sniffed it suspiciously and then in a deep and tragic voice, said: 'What is this, poison? Well never mind, I'll drink it if you like,' downing it all in a single hearty gulp.[3]

The second incident was more embarrassing for Violet, partly because there were more people present and partly because it cast doubts on the credibility of Mrs Hunt as a chaperone while Ford was living at South Lodge:

On one occasion she was more than usually difficult and asked each man in turn who he was and what he did, including Ford whom she saw nearly every day! A rather embarrassed silence ensued which was finally broken by Violet rather tartly saying, 'You know quite well who they are, Mother, and that they are all poets.' Mrs Hunt's only answer was a loud snort; for the rest of the tea she fixed poor Lawrence with a basilisk stare, occasionally muttering under her breath: 'All poets indeed. Ha! All poets indeed. Ha!'[4]

As the weather improved the Saturday tea parties began to be preceded by games of tennis played on the grass court in the communal garden just across the road from South Lodge. The regular players were Ford, Pound, Grace Crawford and Mary Martindale, though they were frequently joined by other friends as players and spectators. Lawrence sometimes kept score and acted as ball boy.

Mrs Hunt, with the malicious mischievousness of a child, did her best to disrupt these occasions. Grace Crawford reports how it was convenient for the tennis players to keep their equipment at South Lodge. Rackets, balls, tennis shoes were left in the cloakroom during the week. When Saturday arrived Grace would invariably find her shoes and racket put out ready for her. But equally invariably Mrs Hunt would have hidden Ford's and Pound's shoes and rackets. Each week she found a different hiding place and the two men had to search exasperatedly for the missing equipment.

Occasionally Ford would play singles with Pound. These games had to be seen to be believed. Brigit Patmore describes watching the two play:

> Ford and Ezra were sharply contrasted in physique – the latter always looked too loosely fitted in his clothes, 'fat Ford,' as a disrespectful disciple dubbed him, was too smoothly tight. Their game of tennis was a curious exhibition. They were crouched-for-action players, readier to spring at each other's throats than the ball, the service of which was very free. It seemed to matter little how often they served fault after fault. They just went on till the ball was where they wanted, then one or other cried 'Game' or 'Hard luck', 'My set' or 'That's love-all' or 'Six sets to me!' It was beyond anyone to umpire or score.[5]

Violet's sisters now hit upon a solution to the problem of their mother and Violet. Since they were themselves unwilling to look after the troublesome old lady, and since they continued to believe that Violet was taking advantage of Mrs Hunt's feeble-mindedness, they proposed that their mother should be put into a home. Violet described the home they had in mind as a 'cheap asylum'. She refused to entertain the proposition. But the only alternative she could come up with was also very painful. In *The Flurried Years*, written so many years later, all the pain and distress and even guilt that the action caused her is still apparent. For Violet had to resort to committing her mother to the Court of Lunacy and having herself made legally her mother's receiver. Mrs Hunt was still sufficiently aware of what was going on around her to understand how she was reduced by this action. As Violet herself said, under this court order 'She had not a penny of her own, or a purse to put one in, not a postage stamp; everything she had was held by the Court for her children.'

By law it was necessary for Mrs Hunt to be officially informed of her new status. The lawyer Mr Lane visited her and read to her the document informing her that she was 'a person who, through mental infirmity arising from age, was incapable of managing her own affairs'.

After Mr Lane's visit Margaret Hunt had wept and wept and reviled her children and her sister for their unkindness and the indignity to which they had subjected her.

Having been told that she was helpless, Mrs Hunt proceeded to become so. There was no more interaction with Violet's younger friends, no more hiding of tennis shoes, no more tea parties. She took to her own rooms, and from then on needed the services of a nurse to look after her.

All this stress took its toll on Violet and Ford. Violet describes their way of life at this time as follows: 'Dressing for dinners and lunches, cabbing thereto, lying awake from excess of fatigue ... I longed to get out of this pretty tinkling, vapid poison-palace and plunge for the last time into an Odyssey-like adventure that might ultimately end in the peace of ancestral halls.' Her longing for an 'Odyssey-like adventure' crystallised itself into a desire to go to Germany. She was not altogether sure how taking on the receivership would affect her life, and so before the position was confirmed she felt she would like a last taste of freedom: 'I was not yet in what the lawyers call "the saddle". And I desired a last flutter.'

There were other advantages to be gained from the proposed journey. They would be away for a while at least from all the legal problems and, since they would be visiting Ford's relatives, he would be able to regain some self-esteem and Violet could work at being accepted into his family.

Because of her sisters' careful scrutiny of all her expenditure, Violet felt that she must ensure that the money for this holiday was visibly hers. She determined, therefore, to sell to the Walker Gallery in Liverpool a painting of her father's which was indubitably her property. It was perhaps a mistake in the light of further events, for this particular painting had been a gift to Violet from her god-father, Canon Greenwell.

There was just one detail to settle and that was the matter of a chaperone. Violet was doubly concerned with the outward appearance of respectability at this time. For now she not only wished to avoid scandal for her own sake but she also felt that she could not give the slightest excuse to her sisters for intervening further in her affairs and those of her mother. It was her fear that 'one little social slip, and for my mother the cheap asylum and for me everlasting remorse'.

With her unerring skill for causing a stir, whom should Violet choose for this sensitive role but the widow of her former lover, Oswald Crawfurd.

ELEVEN

AN INGENIOUS SOLUTION

From Violet's description of Crawfurd's widow we learn why, after his tempestuous and highly emotional affair with Violet, he had chosen to marry their mutual friend, Lita Brown, a woman nearer his own age. Violet describes her as 'an ideal old lady. She had neither temper nor temperament. No initiative; like an easy chair in a room.' She was, in fact, totally unlike Violet.

This model chaperone was to meet Ford and Violet at Tilbury, and from there the trio was to sail to Rotterdam and then go through Holland, down the Rhine and past its castles, and on to Mainz and Heidelberg. It was to be a totally relaxed time with visits to the various towns they stopped at if and when they pleased.

The company on the boat was various and lively, and Violet began to enjoy herself. Ford spent a good deal of his time playing patience and dreaming up plots for future fictions. Gradually their calm progress down the Rhine had the desired effect: 'It all faded out – the stale horror, like beer spilled on public house tables, of Aunt Jane, Regan and Goneril, Brixton and Charing Cross, lawyer's clerks and affidavits, and statements that seemd to state nothing.'

Her pleasure in the holiday was slightly marred by her growing realisation of how different in temperament she and Ford were. At times Ford was the most gregarious of men but he responded to difficulties of any kind by withdrawing from society. His endless games of patience seemed to Violet just such a withdrawal. In contrast, she was inclined to meet problems head on and to seek refuge from them in the company of other people. But she put such doubts aside as they approached their journey's end.

Ford's aunt, Emma Goesen, lived in Boppard in an Italianate villa on the banks of the Rhine. Ford pointed out the house to Violet as they sailed past. They disembarked a little further along the river and took a hotel in Assmanshausen. From there they could visit Aunt Emma and see what kind of reception she was prepared to give them. Ford tidied himself up in order to make a good impression on his wealthy relative, ostentatiously wearing a black armband as a sign of mourning for the dead Aunt Laura.

Violet is rather vague about her own reception from Aunt Emma at this point in their stay, but Ford was made welcome. He enlisted his aunt's support against Elsie by giving her his account of the money he had paid out for his children, which he continued to pay. He showed her the expensive presents he had bought for Katherine and Christina, and Aunt Emma thoroughly approved. But what proved Ford's strongest point was the fact that Elsie had gone so far as to be responsible for sending him to gaol. Not only did such behaviour violate all Aunt Emma's notions of wifely responsibilities she also felt mortified that a nephew of hers should have been subjected to such an indignity. She felt strongly that the honour of the family had been attacked.

In the meantime Violet was making a friend and ally of Ford's cousin Mimi. Mimi had read Violet's books and she was eager to have a first-hand account of the suffragettes. She had read many garbled stories of their activities in the German newspapers, and was surprised by the different version of events Violet had to tell her. Inevitably marriage and divorce were very much on Violet's mind, and these subjects were topics of conversation between the two women. In *The Flurried Years* Violet uses her recalling of these conversations as an occasion to spell out in detail her own views on these subjects.

However much like an easy chair Lita Brown might have been, she began to grow weary of Assmanshausen and Boppard and longed to return to her own circle of older ladies taking the waters at Nauheim. So Violet and Ford were obliged to accompany her back to the place of her cure. While inactive in Assmanshausen she had been thinking a great deal about the problems her two charges faced. She thought she could see a possible solution, and she suggested that Ford should consult a German lawyer.

Nauheim was a quiet place. The ladies stayed in one hotel and Ford in another. With strict regard to the proprieties, Ford was only introduced into the room of one lady if the other was present.

However, Ford and Violet had time together alone in the early mornings when all the invalids were still in bed and only service people were about. They received letters from England which, for once, were not the occasions of distress. Even one from Silvia, along with the usual complaints and accusations, hinted at the possibility of a better relationship in the future. Violet had high hopes that 'the receivership plan was going to placate everybody.'

In order to take up the receivership Violet would have to return to England. Before she left she wanted to see Marburg. But then, following up the hint from Lita Brown, Ford decided to go to Giessen for a day. Her plan which was taking root in *his* mind was to take up his German citizenship and then divorce Elsie under German law. He had learned that if a father gave up his German nationality that did not preclude his children from claiming it once more. To verify his notions Ford wanted to consult a lawyer in Giessen recommended by Lita Brown. After his visit to Giessen he returned to Nauheim, arriving back in time for dinner where he announced to the ladies, 'looking as portentous as might be with his mild blue eyes, that we *would* all go on Wednesday to Marburg as arranged and leave *him* there behind us. He was going to stay in Germany.'

Ford's decision was based on the fact that he had been advised that to become a German citizen he must take up residence in Germany and prove himself to be a worthy member of his community. It was a surprising step for Ford to take since until now he had made a point of being more English than the English, with his claims of exceptional ability at cricket and the fabrication of a school career at Westminster School. For many years he had modelled himself on Arthur Marwood, who came from a long line of Yorkshire squires.

Violet assessed the situation accurately:

He had taken one of those sudden resolutions, those sudden burgeonings of resolve, poison flowers that blow in a single day out of a concealed and tedious growth of dull misgivings, daily distastes, and nightmare apprehensions: the root of this flower was a sense of injustice and injury; Brixtons, hecklings, humblings and lowering of natural pride had manured it; secret tears had watered it and brought it to the birth.

The two of them made a visit to Boppard to tell Aunt Emma of the decision Ford had made. They were confident of her approval. But the stress of this change of plans triggered off Violet's illness. She was haemorrhaging profusely and as a result fainted. Aunt Emma sent for her doctor. His examination of Violet caused her a good deal of pain. His verdict was that she must have a minor operation in his hospital. There appears to have been no suspicion on his part that syphilis might be responsible for Violet's condition.

The imminence of her taking up the receivership made Violet declare this to be an impossible course to take. In order to effect at least a temporary cure she was ordered to her bed and put on a light diet. However, as there were delays in her being able to become her mother's receiver she was able to stay on in Germany with Ford for a little longer than she had anticipated. But as her health continued precarious, she and Ford were not able to attend such lively events as the Kermesse but had to stay quietly on level ground. It was not a very happy time although Ford was able to proceed with his writing, dictating to Violet when she was well enough to sit up.

It was on her forty-eighth birthday, in September 1910, that Violet received the anxiously awaited summons to return home and officially take up the receivership. And so, still ill and weak, she made her way back to England. She was accompanied as far as Cologne by Ford, but there they had to part company. Ford set off for his voluntary exile in Giessen.

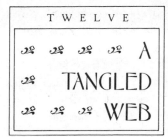

Ford's attempts to be received back into his fatherland did not begin auspiciously. He had arranged to take rooms at 29 Nordanlage in Giessen. From the outset his letters to Violet were full of complaints. He disliked his rooms intensely, he liked his landlady no better, and her cooking even less. He complained of loneliness, of boredom, of having insufficient to eat. To cap matters he had a recurrence of the problem that stress always brought on – severe writer's cramp.

Violet could do little to help or comfort him. She had sufficient troubles of her own.

She had assumed that since she was in South Lodge alone with her mother and the servants, Rosamond would be allowed to visit her once again. But a letter from her niece in response to one from her making such an invitation disabused her of such hopes. Rosamond's father had refused to allow her to see Violet and the young woman was sufficiently under his thumb that there was no question of her going against his wishes.

Violet's temperament was such that she was incapable of sitting back and admitting defeat in the face of her troubles. She cast about for some positive action she could take instead of simply waiting on Ford and events. Eventually she decided to consult an old friend of her father's, Sir John Westlake, an eminent international lawyer, now retired. Her account of his response to her enquiries about the feasibility of what she and Ford had planned is vague and elliptical: 'His answer, though hard and contradictious of certain ready and fallacious assumptions of mine, was kindly and reassured me completely as to the main point, telling me plainly what rested with *me* to do.'

Whatever the details of the reply, Violet was able to interpret them as suggesting that, in broad terms, Ford could regain his citizenship and could then divorce Elsie and be free to marry her. Westlake impressed on her that Ford's continued absence from England was vital if he wished to acquire German citizenship, and she in her turn tried to impress this on Ford.

She was encouraged in her belief that all would turn out for the best by the fact that Holman Hunt, a deeply religious and law-abiding man, had been unable to marry his deceased wife's sister because such a marriage was against the laws of consanguinity: but 'He had solved the problem by going to Holland where he was able to contract a legal marriage.' Violet's not altogether logical reasoning was that 'If Holman Hunt could marry his deceased wife's sister by going to Holland, surely there was a possibility that by going to Germany, and resuming the nationality of his ancestors, Ford might be able to secure a divorce, under German law, and thus be free to make Violet an honest woman.' This was Douglas Goldring's reconstruction of Violet's thinking on the matter.

As always, Violet failed to keep Ford's 'clever plan' to herself. She confided in her good friends Ethel Colburn Mayne and Dollie Radford.* They were alarmed on her behalf and consulted the lawyer R. Ellis Roberts for an expert opinion. His advice was that, although Ford's divorce and even his marriage might be considered valid in Germany, it would have no standing in English law and might even make him guilty of bigamy.

Violet would not or could not accept this reading of the situation, though a fear of Ford's being accused of bigamy was to surface later. To bolster up her belief in Ford's plan she set to work researching the life of Sir Herbert Herkomer, who had similarly resumed his German citizenship – though in his case, as in Holman Hunt's, he did so in order to marry his sister-in-law.

Ford himself was sufficiently confident of the course he had set out on to write to Elsie's lawyer informing him of his intention to seek a German divorce. Elsie was once again thrown into a panic by this news, despite reassurances from her lawyer, from Robert Garnett and from Hermann Hueffer that Ford's divorce would not be valid in English law.

The patching-up that Violet had had in Germany proved to be just that. She began to haemorrhage again, and the operation she had escaped in Germany became unavoidable. It was arranged that she should have the treatment in a private nursing home in Minden Terrace. Mary Martindale was her confidante and accompanied Violet to the clinic. She knew quite well that Violet had

---

*Dollie Radford and her husband Ernest were poets who were founding members of the New Reform Club to which Violet belonged. They were the parents of Lawrence's friend, Margaret Radford.

deliberately not told Ford about the operation. She also knew that he would be risking a great deal if he were to leave Germany and travel to England. However, she could not resist romance and drama and so, without telling Violet of her actions, she sent a telegram to Ford informing him of the situation.

Whether it was passionate concern for Violet or a similar desire for a romantically extravagant gesture coupled with utter boredom that motivated Ford, the result was that he travelled non-stop from Germany to be with Violet.

And so, the night before she was due for surgery Violet was summoned to the telephone:

> That evening, lonely, disconsolate, full of castor oil and little else, I sat on my bed like a frightened performer before the play, when I was suddenly summoned to the phone downstairs, and, lifting the receiver, listened again to a voice not heard since two months ago on Cologne platform.

The operation was performed in Violet's room at the nursing home by a woman surgeon, as Violet the suffragette was careful to point out. Once it was over Violet felt quite well and her time of convalescing proved to be very happy.

Again no mention was made of syphilis. Could it be that not even doctors expected to encounter the disease in a middle-class woman? It is quite evident that no one in the nursing home treated Violet with the disgust Dr Paget had displayed.

The matron of the nursing home had read and admired Violet's books, so she was prepared to allow Violet to have visitors. Violet was delighted that Ford had cared enough for her to rush to England. His daily visits, with the exception of a day on which he went to see his children in their convent school, gave Violet the kind of status in the clinic as a woman obviously loved by a man that she craved. After being the object of her sisters' disapproval and after taking responsibility for Ford and her mother for so long, it was a great pleasure to be looked after and to be the centre of attention.

The Irish nurses in the clinic were full of admiration for her decorative Parisian nightdresses and made excuses to visit her in order to examine them. She was in sufficiently good spirits to get on with her work, to write letters and to give an opinion on *The*

Widowing of Mrs Holroyd, the play which D.H. Lawrence had sent to her via Grace Crawford. She even received a letter of sympathy from Silvia. But it is a measure of how unhappy the year had been that Violet could say of her time in the nursing home 'Taken all in all, those ten days were the happiest of my life. I corrected my own new book, covered my bed with MS and papers, boxes and rolls, till the nurses squeaked with amusement every time they came in.'

After ten days Violet returned to South Lodge and Ford journeyed back to Germany. However, Violet decided that her need to convalesce entitled her to a holiday. As usual, money was a problem, so she wrote to Canon Greenwell, her god-father. He sent her the money for her trip on condition that she went to La Roche in the Ardennes and bought him a ham from a pig that had been fed on juniper. So that there should be no mistake, he sent Violet the label from a parcel that had once contained such a delicacy. Violet was later to use this incident to good effect in her novel *The House of Many Mirrors*.

Ford was sure that a few days at Spa in Belgium would not harm his case for naturalisation, so he arranged to meet Violet there. Of necessity they spent a quiet time for the most part. There were journeys to Liège, and Ford took the opportunity to indulge in the pastime he was passionately fond of – golf. He also began to give Violet German lessons in optimistic preparation for the day when they could marry and live in Germany. Evidently Violet's German, learnt when young from the peasant girl Milly, was nursery German, sufficient to make herself understood to a sympathetic listener, but not good enough to hold her own in a conversation of any sophistication.

The couple's expressed determination to live in Germany after their marriage suggests that even then they were not entirely confident how Ford's German divorce would hold up in England. By living in Germany they could avoid any problems about the legality of their relationship.

Violet's friend Thérèse Descours was in Spa with her husband. Violet and Ford spent New Year's Eve with them, and Ford made the punch for which he was famous. This party to mark the end of the year also marked the end of the brief period of happiness Ford and Violet enjoyed together.

On New Year's Day they went to the cathedral in Aix-la-

Chapelle to hear Mass. Perhaps because such occasions inevitably invite a looking back and a looking forward, Violet found herself taking stock of her situation and realising that she was not entirely happy with it. Her doubts about how serious Ford was in his efforts to divorce Elsie and marry her came to the surface, as well as doubts about how compatible the two of them were. Her description of the occasion was written with the benefit of hindsight and her conclusions are presented as harsher and more clear-cut than perhaps they were in fact. In *The Flurried Years* Violet writes that she suddenly felt that Ford was 'in a sense unsympathetic to me. A cold, patient man, without fire, lazy of habit: his heart, dull beating, was perhaps more faint about it all than he was willing to let it appear.' Violet saw her own personality as being in distinct contrast to that of Ford:

> I won't bear things unless I have to. I have to live always in the boiling middle of things or, to mix metaphors, in a world of thin ice and broken eggs that will never make an omelette ... I was always one that, refusing to notice when the signals were against me, made haste to a rendezvous that is to bring down misfortune on my head.

In quoting Violet's description of herself, Douglas Goldring confirms its accuracy and also that of her description of Ford. Certainly the difference in their temperaments and methods of doing things clouded Violet's judgement of Ford's good faith in what he had undertaken to achieve for her. The correspondence between Ford and his doctor, Dr Tebb, who was also Violet's doctor, makes it clear that Ford was ardent in pursuit of any evidence that would support his cause. And why else would he subject himself to the undoubted boredom of living in Giessen and the endless legal wranglings of the case if, at least initially, he did not intend to see it through to the end?

A combination of ill health and impatience undermined Violet's faith in the whole enterprise. But even at her most pessimistic she could not have foreseen what a miserable and humiliating year lay ahead of them.

Violet's fear that Ford was not being sufficiently active spurred her on to visit Paris to stay with the Farleys. Her main objective, however, was to visit those of the Hueffer family who had moved to Paris and, in particular, Ford's cousin Hermann. He had so far resolutely taken Elsie's side and urged her to resist a divorce. However, after an exchange of letters, he expressed willingness to meet Violet. As she had hoped, Violet personally made a favourable impression on Hermann Hueffer. But his liking for her in no way affected his principles, and she achieved nothing in that direction.

Arnold Bennett was in Paris at the time with his wife Marguerite, and Ford and Violet were invited to lunch at the Bennetts' home on the Rue de Grenelle, where they were treated to 'an English leg of mutton and potatoes and greens'. During this visit to Paris they went to the Bal Bullier and saw the dances currently fashionable, the tango, the fox-trot and the bunny hop.

Their gaiety did not last long. A letter from England announcing Rosamond's marriage threw Violet into despair: whatever hopes she had had of renewing an intimacy with her niece were now gone for ever. Rosamond had married a local clergyman. It was a marriage that met with her parents' full approval and one that Violet would not have chosen for her. Rosamond's husband disapproved of Violet as much as her father. Rosamond had simply exchanged the control of one male for that of another one equally determined to keep her away from the pernicious influence of the immoral Violet. It was a situation which Douglas Goldring's description of Rosamond suggests was inevitable.

By now it was time to leave Paris for Spa, from where Ford would return to Giessen and Violet to London. This time, they hoped, the parting would not be for too long as Ford had already, theoretically at least, spent a good part of the six months he had originally been told he must live in Giessen.

Violet's journey back to England was not a pleasant one. She met up with a Belgian who insisted on paying court to her. She felt that her rejection of his advances was strongly disapproved of by her travelling companions. The train was late arriving in Brussels and Violet missed her connection to Calais. Desperately trying to escape the insistent Belgian, who thought his opportunity had arrived, she ended up in a hotel which turned out to be little better than a brothel.

The next few months put a further strain on the relationship between Violet and Ford. Back in Giessen Ford found his living conditions more intolerable than ever. He wanted grander, more comfortable premises. He justified this desire by saying that he was more likely to be accepted as a solid citizen of Giessen if his outward circumstances had a more prosperous appearance. Violet was already feeling the strain of being Ford's financial support. Indeed she asked herself why she had 'taken the responsibility for keeping him alive'. She had already invested so much money and emotional energy in trying to achieve marriage to Ford that she found it difficult either to turn her back on the situation or utterly to discount Ford's claims that he needed better premises. After an argument between them, conducted by letters, Violet finally gave in with the words 'I honestly just want you to do what you can that will get the German citizenship.' Ford took her at her word and immediately moved into a comfortable apartment, complete with servants, at 15 Friedrichstrasse. Although he was happier in these new premises, he still felt that he needed a break from the monotony of his life in Giessen, so he returned to England for a brief holiday with Violet at Inchamery. Violet's account of their time suggests that it was not altogether happy. Ford spent much of his time playing cards with their hostess and a priest – an incident he later used in *Some Do Not*.

When Ford returned to Germany he took his mother with him. It was arranged that Violet should join them for Easter.

While Ford was away Violet continued to lead a life much like the one she had had before she met Ford. She worked on her books, and reviewed D.H. Lawrence's *The White Peacock* in the *Daily Chronicle* in February. She entertained her young friends at South Lodge and at her clubs, and kept up with her old friends. Despite the increasing friction between herself and Ford, when he was absent she missed him. She recorded that 'Giessen was worse than Brixton, where at least I could go and see him once a week.'*

Always one to take an interest in fashion, Violet acquired a harem skirt in March. Her account of this new style in her letter to Ford aroused much interest among his German acquaintances. When she left for Giessen the by now famous harem skirt went with her.

Violet's first impression of Ford's place of exile was a favourable

---

*'Once a week' was a characteristic exaggeration. Ford was in prison for exactly ten days.

one. She describes her initial reactions: 'Giessen is a junction, a very smart junction, decorated *art nouveau* like the rest of Germany. The roof is frescoed with wild flowers, and electric lights, in the form of campanulas, are hung in elegant festoons on long, thin, metal cords like organ pipes.' However, the gaiety and lightness of this welcoming scene proved to be deceptive.

In order to keep up appearances Violet did not stay in Ford's flat, for which she was paying, but in the Hotel Prinz Heinrich. Again for reasons of respectability, Ford's mother moved out of the flat and into the hotel so that she could better chaperone Violet. Indeed she proved to be rather too ardent in pursuing her task, and Violet complained that she had hardly a minute alone with Ford.

Much of Violet's visit was spent in exchanging formal calls and eating heavy food. Violet did not find Ford's new acquaintances to her taste. Her imperfect German excluded her from much of the conversation. But even if she had been able to participate fully the polite exchanges were far removed from the kind of lively conversations to which she was accustomed and at which she excelled.

She had hoped to create a sensation with her harem skirt, but she had not been prepared for the extremely prudish response she met with. Her principles as a suffragette were offended by this and by the demeanour of the wife of Ford's lawyer, whom she described tartly: 'She was an uncommonly clever woman, was Linchen, and against all women as a matter of course! Nothing of the suffragette about her!'

She also took a dislike to the lawyer himself, Herr Dr Rechtsanwalt Ludwig Leun, and became suspicious as to why the legal proceedings were being dragged out to such a length. Ford was made nervous by her attitude and urged her not to pry into matters:

> All this time I was being told, like Bluebeard's wife, not to go queering any pitches by the exhibition of unfeminine curiosity. I must on no account pump Herr John, or ask him how the naturalisation was going on. How could I have? 'Dumb Crambo' was all very well, but a legal term would have been utterly beyond my German.

After a month's visit Violet returned to London in late May. It had been arranged that Ford and the Leuns should visit London to see the coronation of George V on 22 June.

Back in London, Violet continued to quarrel with her sisters. Relations had deteriorated to such an extent that when Silvia and Venice visited their mother at South Lodge they went straight upstairs and had no contact with Violet. So when the Leuns and Ford arrived from Germany Violet decided that she could not have them all to stay at South Lodge. She was willing to stand up to her sisters for the right to have Ford to stay but she knew that they would regard the entertainment of his friends as a drain on their mother's finances. Her own dislike of the Leuns also played a part in her decision not to have them as her guests. The ever-willing Mary Martindale offered to have the Leuns to stay instead.

The novel Ford had begun writing at Fordingbridge after his release from Brixton, *Ladies Whose Bright Eyes*, was published this summer, after much wrangling with Constable. To mark this occasion, and to celebrate Ford's return to South Lodge, Violet threw one of her big parties.

That summer in England was an exceptionally hot one. By July there was a drought and the heat exacerbated the current political and social problems. London was especially hard hit. Violet describes the unswept streets, the lack of milk and the fear of a general food shortage. One piece of good news had come from Ford shortly after his return to Giessen. He had written to Violet to say that his lawyer seemed to think 'it is all right now about the naturalisation . . . Isn't it jolly?'

Violet was not satisfied with such a vague statement, especially since Leun was involved and Violet instinctively distrusted him. So she wrote to Ford asking him to write her a formal statement about the naturalisation. Ford complied with her request.

This pleasing news, however, was offset by other problems which had arisen during Ford's absence and were the cause of a temporary estrangement. For some reason Ford took it into his head that it was inappropriate for Violet to do any more journalism. As Violet had worked as a journalist since she was a young girl she bitterly resented this. Ford's timing of this demand was particularly unfortunate since Violet was once again desperately worried about money. She was also feeling ill and oppressed by the heat and dirt in London. She was, therefore, not disposed to look on with a kindly eye when Ford took time off from his writing to enjoy himself with

101

Ezra Pound, who was visiting Germany at the time. The last straw was when Ford wrote suggesting that they might buy a pony and trap for his children to enable them to enjoy their summer holiday to the full. Part of Violet knew that her jealousy of 'the children' was unreasonable, but this did not prevent her from responding to this request with a refusal to write to him at all.

Eventually Ford wrote to her in such a manner that she was completely won over.

> What ever you do or don't say or keep silent about, don't, don't Not Write. For there are cruelties and refinements of cruelties, but, however cruel you are in words, I would rather have it than silence. For you must remember, you must believe, that what ever you are or aren't, you are the only link I have with the visible world.

For some time Agnes Farley's dentist husband, whom Violet described as 'mad', had been urging Ford to have his teeth extracted and replaced by false ones. In late July 1911 Ford agreed to this and went to Paris where Farley had his practice to begin his treatment.

Violet was very anxious to join him there. She went through much heart-searching about the wisdom of leaving her mother when London was in such a disturbed state. However the threat of a railway strike proved a decisive factor, enabling her successfully to justify the need for her departure.

It was hardly a lovers' reunion when Ford met Violet at the station in Paris, as she recalled in *The Flurried Years*: 'At the Gare du Nord he met me, toothless, feckless, and attempted to see me through Customs. He had not a grinder in his head, and was still, perhaps for this reason, a little "limited in expression".' Violet was not only dismayed by Ford's appearance but also by the cost of all this dentistry: he told her that he was being charged eight pounds for each tooth.

After a short stay in Paris the two left via the Gare de L'Est for Rheims, and then on to Germany. By now Ford was aggressively pro-German and determined to have as little to do with England as possible. Violet was prepared to go along with him in this, but when she suggested a visit to Giessen to see Ford's naturalisation papers Ford opposed her, using as his excuse that he could not decently present himself before Leun in his toothless condition. Ezra Pound joined them for a while and as always his high spirits proved infectious. But then it was time to return to Paris, or at least to Bellevue, just outside Paris, from where they could go into Paris daily by boat for Ford to have more treatment. When the Farleys left Paris 'the teeth followed the dentist to Quend-sur-Mer'.

Violet left Ford in the hands of his dentist while she made a brief trip back to England. She had been invited to stay in her beloved North Riding at Hovingham Spa with Edith and George Stringer. Her friendship with this couple was a little odd, since they were Elsie's aunt and uncle. While she was away Ford was to attend to the final arrangements for his divorce.

By now, despite the fact that she had not been able to persuade Ford to let her see his naturalisation papers, Violet seems to have believed and trusted that Ford was doing as he had promised. She had written confidently to Ford's mother,

> I believe the German business is all right but the naturalisation did not come in time for the divorce to be pronounced before the courts rose for six weeks' holiday. So that would make it deferred until they 'set' again in October. Anyhow, no one will see me or Ford again till we are married.

When she rejoined Ford after her visit to Yorkshire they travelled via Luxembourg to Germany. Violet felt sufficiently close to being a married woman to be able to dispense with a chaperone: 'It was nice to be alone without the need for chaperonage: arranging it had been *my* task – Joseph Leopold* was so incurably Bohemian – and I had found it irksome.'

That year there was a bumper grape harvest in Germany. Violet and Ford put aside their troubles and threw themselves into the general bustle and merrymaking. Already, however, Violet's infatuation with all things German was diminishing and she greatly disliked the way the German army officers she encountered demanded to be treated with overweening respect by local civilians. She had already moved a long way from the feelings of admiration

---

*Throughout *The Flurried Years* Violet calls Ford 'Joseph Leopold'. These were the names he had been given when he became a Catholic convert before meeting Violet again.

and affinity she had expressed in her book about Germany, *The Desirable Alien*.

Her old illness flared up and in October she and Ford went to Spa once more where Violet had a minor operation, possibly a dilate and curettage. She was recovering from this when a reporter from the *Daily Mirror* arrived on the scene looking for an interview. Violet turned down his first request. She did not want publicity, even though both she and Ford had new books appearing – *The Doll* and *The New Humpty Dumpty*. But the reporter did not take no for an answer and, sensing that Violet was the stumbling-block, he sought out Ford that evening when he knew he would be unaccompanied by Violet, while playing billiards.

The interview provided by Ford was disastrous. On 22 October 1911 the following item appeared in the *Daily Mirror*:

Author Weds
Mr Ford Madox Hueffer Married Abroad
to Well-Known Lady Novelist.

The *Daily Mirror* is able to announce that Mr Ford Madox Hueffer, the famous novelist, has been married on the Continent to Miss Violet Hunt, the well-known authoress . . .

'I don't want to advertise myself,' he told the *Daily Mirror*, 'but it happens that both my wife and myself have books appearing today . . . I married her in Germany after divorcing my former wife on a technical ground, desertion, as I had a perfect right to do, being domiciled in Germany.'

Whatever happened subsequent to this interview there can be no doubt that there were absolutely no grounds for Ford's claim that he was at this time married to Violet. Brigit Patmore's comments perhaps illuminate the situation and its results most fully: 'Do habitual liars believe their lies? The lives of these two would probably have been arranged to the satisfaction of their social circle if Ford had not indulged in too much wishful thinking.'[1]

What happened next is not absolutely clear. As a result of various proceedings in court Violet never made a public statement about her 'marriage' to Ford and how it had come about. She simply insisted that it existed. The story can be pieced together.

Violet was appalled when she found out what Ford had done. She foresaw the repercussions in a way that he did not. For the sake of convenience she now accepted without question and without seeing any of the official documents that Ford was a naturalised German, and that he had obtained a German divorce from Elsie. It was difficult to go through a marriage ceremony in Germany after Ford's announcement that they had already been married there. At a later point in their relationship Violet wrote to Ford saying that she had been living with him as man and wife since 5 November 1911. She could have had no reason for using this particular date unless something significant had happened then of which both she and Ford were aware. She had, after all, actually been living with Ford for some time before that date. Further evidence for this comes from a letter from Ford to Violet quoted by Robert Secor in his monograph *The Return of the Good Soldier*, which states, 'I take it that these questions do not affect our marriage as that took place in France.'[2]

A letter from Ezra Pound to his mother adds to the confusion about dates but substantiates the fact that Ford and Violet had every intention of going through some kind of marriage ceremony in France. He writes: 'I had very little time to myself while with Hueffer. Not that there was much work done, but we disagree diametrically on art, religion, politics and all therein implied; and besides he's being married this afternoon or else this A.M. and going to the dentist's in the P.M.'[3]

The fact that some kind of ceremony was gone through as a result of Violet's justifiable panic over the *Daily Mirror* article is supported by Rebecca West's assurances to Robert Secor that Violet and Ford had a marriage ceremony in a hotel room in France, and by the foreword to *I Have This To Say*, the American edition of Violet's autobiography, in which she says, 'I never did become a legal wife. And leave it at that, and the whole truth at the bottom of the well at Selsey where it may lie until the Peninsula is all at sea.' Her clear implication is that subsequent events forced her to accept that she was not legally married, but that she had in her possession a document which proved that she and Ford had gone through a marriage ceremony. She had felt it necessary to get rid of this document when it was made clear to her what penalties Ford could be made to pay for committing bigamy.

Violet may have been naive and guilty of wishful thinking in believing that her marriage had any standing in law. But it seems unlikely, as some have suggested, that the whole affair was a deceitful stratagem concocted by Ford and Violet together when they found that they could not be legally married. After all, their relationship had already been totally accepted by their close friends and tacitly accepted by the larger society in which they moved. Only the kind of public scandal in which they became involved as a result of their insistence that they were married could have forced that society to reject them. The done thing was to refrain from drawing attention to an ambiguous situation.

It is true that when Elsie was shown the *Daily Mirror* piece by her gardener she threatened to sue the paper if a retraction was not forthcoming. But this was done with the minimum of publicity. Violet was already so entangled in legal problems concerning her mother and her sisters that she would surely not have willingly gone through all the publicity of the courts, and have brought René Byles, a loyal supporter, to ruin, if she had not felt she had some claim to call herself Ford's wife.

It would have taken a more cynical and arrogant woman than Violet was to reappear in England with Ford, to go for what amounted to a honeymoon at Littleston-on-Sea, and to have new stationery printed for herself and Ford, without the security of a marriage certificate. However, her confidence in her situation was given a frightening jolt when her publishers, Chatto & Windus, challenged her right to use the name Violet Hueffer on the title page of the novel *The Governess*. She insisted that she was entitled to do so.

Ford, who above all liked a quiet life without rows and scenes, went completely to pieces when he knew that Elsie had threatened legal action against the *Daily Mirror*. One morning at Littleston-on-Sea Violet got up to find that during the night Ford had so barricaded the house that it looked like a fortress. As she commented in *The Flurried Years*, 'It was the beginning of a fresh attack of neurasthenia that was to last three whole years and was responsible for many things, and much private and particular misery.'

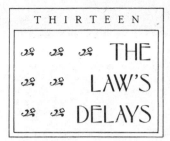

THIRTEEN

☙ ☙ ☙ THE
☙ ☙ LAW'S
☙ ☙ DELAYS

Meanwhile, unaware of all the trouble behind the scenes, friends of Violet and Ford accepted the marriage at face value. Lawrence had heard from Ford himself in October, long before any ceremony had taken place, and he wrote to give the news to all he thought might be interested. After a visit to Edward Garnett, who knew Elsie's side of the whole affair through his brother Robert, and who was not convinced that Ford had ever divorced Elsie, Lawrence realised the doubtful legal status of the marriage, but he does not appear to have been at all concerned. He wrote to his sister Ada: 'Did I tell you Ford Madox Hueffer had married Violet Hunt. I think it scarcely legal in England, as the divorce – so Garnett says – was never really accomplished. They were married in Germany.'[1]

By February 1912, when Lawrence met up with Ford and Violet in London, he appears to have accepted the marriage as accomplished even when writing to Edward Garnett. It is interesting to see from this letter how much Violet and Ford had been physically altered by all that they had recently gone through:

I found Hueffer getting very fat – 'be not puffed up' came into my mind. But he's rather nicer than he was. He seems to have had a crisis, when, dear Lord, he fizzed and bubbled all over the place. Now, don't you know, he seems quite considerate, even thoughtful for other folk. But he *is* fat. It's Violet's good influence. Do you know, I rather like her – she's such a neat assassin. I evoked the memory of various friends that were her friends twelve months ago. Behold she nicely showed me the effigies of these folk in her heart, each of their blemishes marked with a red asterisk like a dagger hole. I saluted her, she did the business so artistically: there was no loathsome gore spilt over murdered friends.

She looked old, yet she was gay – she was gay, she laughed, she bent and fluttered in the wind of joy. She coquetted and played beautifully with Hueffer: she loves him distractedly – she was charming, and I loved her. But my God, she looked old.

Perhaps because she wore – she was going to some afternoon affair of swell suffragettes – a gaudy witch-cap stitched with beads of scarlet and a delicate ravel of green and blue. It was a cap like a flat, square bag: the two points she pulled over her ears

– and she peeped coquettishly under the brim – but she looked damned old. It rather hurt me . . . I think Fordy liked it – but was rather scared. He feels, poor fish, the hooks are through his gills this time – and they *are*. Yet he's lucky to be so well caught – she'll handle him with marvellous skill.[2]

Ezra Pound too accepted the marriage, though he seems to have been a little sceptical about its legality. When his edition of Guido Cavalcanti came out in May he included a carefully-worded dedication which was sufficiently ambiguous to allow for the fact that Violet and Ford might not in fact be married. It reads: 'As much of this book as is mine I send to my friends Violet and Ford Madox Hueffer'.

When Dorothy Shakespear met Violet and Ford at a social occasion in June, Violet expressed her great pleasure at the book's dedication. Dorothy wrote to tell Pound about this: 'Mrs F.M.H. was evidently pleased at the dedication of the Guido. I lay low: and didn't say *I* had sent them the copy! "My name first, too," said V.H. I should hope it was put first.'[3]

Such pleasures were few and far between in this difficult year. They spent the spring at Selsey in an effort to help Ford through what was in effect a nervous breakdown. Violet tried to rouse Ford out of his depression by inviting lively company. René Byles was a frequent visitor. He had worked at the publishing house of Alston Rivers and had seen several of Ford's books through the press. By now he was the business manager of a not too secure review called *The Throne*. Ford and Violet were fortunate to have Byles for a friend, as Douglas Goldring makes clear in *South Lodge*:

> In a world in which, alas, 'most friendship is feigning', Byles was remarkable for his loyalty and unselfish devotion to those he cared for. He was a little man, thin and emaciated, of Huguenot extraction, and in appearance and temperament rather like the type of Frenchman of which Voltaire is the supreme example . . . his disinterested love of justice, and fiery honesty of purpose often led him and his associates into trouble . . . He was an uncompromising enemy and a tenacious, unselfish, long-suffering friend.[4]

It was a friendship that was to be severely tested in the coming months.

The Conrads were close by and could be persuaded to visit from time to time: 'The way to Conrad's heart just then was a motor-car, so we used to get one from Clayson's and go out to Orlestone to bring the Conrads and the little boy, Jacko, back to lunch.' It was unfortunate, however, that at this time of tension Violet should have made matters worse by quarrelling with Conrad about whether Marie Antoinette was a traitor to France.

After some coolness occasioned by Elsie's accusations that he had made improper advances to her, Arthur Marwood resumed his friendship with Ford and Violet. He not only visited them at this time, but he added his voice to those of the Conrads in advising his friends to leave England temporarily. He may have known of Elsie's threats of litigation or he might simply have been afraid of the consequences of Ford's assertion that he had married Violet after a German divorce. The case of Earl Russell, who had been tried by the House of Lords, fined five thousand pounds and put in gaol for three months for remarrying after a foreign divorce was well known.

Did Violet have sufficient confidence in her case to allow her to ignore these warnings? Was Ford's illness the result of his knowledge that there never had been a divorce?

For some time Violet had been fighting on two legal fronts – one to assert her marriage, the other to establish her integrity against her sisters' accusations. Now the two cases were to merge in a nightmarish way.

Violet claimed, and it seems an altogether reasonable claim, that her mother had given her permission to do as she liked with her unfinished and unpublished novel *The Governess*. A desperate need for money determined Violet and Ford to finish the book and write an introduction to it. The first response of the family, that of Aunt Jane, was promising, as Violet indicates in *The Flurried Years*:

'Just the kind of book your dear mother would write,' my Aunt Jane wrote from the North, which showed how cleverly I and Joseph Leopold had caught mother's style and 'joined' her flats. 'A nice quiet book,' my Aunt Jane continued, and was going to lend it to the vicar.

At this time Aunt Jane and Canon Greenwell believed in Violet's marriage. They rather liked Ford when they thought he was Violet's husband, and Aunt Jane in particular was impressed by Violet's titled acquaintances.

Violet's sisters, however, were not pleased by the imminent publication of the novel. They objected on several grounds: 'It was sought to gain an injunction on the ground that its publication was unauthorised . . . the book had *not* been given to me . . . it was not good. My mother, had she been sensible, would have deplored its publication.'

The old question as to whether Violet was acting responsibly towards her mother was raised once more. This time Violet had had enough of 'the petty policy of pin pricks that ends by bleeding one to death,' and in April she resigned her receivership of her mother's affairs. An injunction was not granted to Violet's sisters. A typical legal compromise was reached instead which satisfied no one. The book was to be published, but any earnings made by its publication were to be paid straight into the court until Mrs Hunt's financial affairs were finally sorted out.

Before she could legally resign the receivership Violet had to give an account of her management. Once again, in May, she had to appear before the Master of Lunacy, to whom all those acting as receivers for persons declared unfit to handle their own affairs had to justify their financial transactions. This particular Master of Lunacy had been an old friend of Margaret Hunt's, and this, coupled with his blindness, made Violet dread her interviews with him. Ford was present on some of these difficult occasions. Violet reports that 'a disconsolate author was at my side to support me. Sulky, top-hatted, loathing it – and almost me!' Like Margaret Hunt herself, the Master had a biting tongue and caused Violet great distress with his sarcasms and ironies.

As a mark of friendship René Byles tried to promote *The Governess* in *The Throne*. A promotional piece about the book was published in the issue of 3 April. Byles had seized upon the unusual situation of a novel co-authored by mother and daughter, and emphasised this by printing the portrait of Margaret Hunt and Violet side by side at the head of his article. This, of course, enraged Silvia and Venice. But the real damage was done in describing Violet as Mrs Hueffer, although in doing so Byles was merely recording how Violet's name appeared on the book, and that this was the name used by Ford in his introduction to *The Governess*.

Elsie's anger and her determination to make a public declaration that Violet was not married to Ford was fuelled by the article in *The Throne*. In the first instance she demanded a withdrawal of the article and a printed apology for calling Violet Mrs Hueffer instead of Miss Hunt. René Byles consulted Violet and Ford and was assured by them that Violet was fully entitled to use the name of Hueffer. As a result, the owner of *The Throne*, William C. Beaumont, refused to back down and print the apology Elsie had demanded. In June Elsie began proceedings against *The Throne* for the implications of their use of the name Hueffer for Violet.

But, as Violet herself remarked, 'The saddest thing about the law is the law's delays.' All through that nerve-racking year Violet watched the case climbing higher and higher in the list of those to be heard in court which was printed weekly in the *Daily Telegraph*, but it was not until February 1913 that it came before the courts.

The delay undermined Violet's confidence. She began to lose her nerve. She thought that, after all, confrontation was not worthwhile. She lunched with Beaumont and suggested to him that no real harm would be done to her by a printed apology as her 'friends would kindly ignore any apology he chose to insert and put the matter out of their minds.'

Beaumont, however, had the bit between his teeth. He was no longer primarily concerned about Violet but about the principles involved in the case. He felt that it was not the responsibility of a magazine to check up on the names people chose to use, especially when that name had already been printed elsewhere.

Elsie's determination to make life as difficult as possible for Ford and Violet can only have been strengthened by the appearance of Ford's new novel, *The New Humpty Dumpty*, a very thinly disguised account of the breakdown of her marriage to Ford and his subsequent love for Violet. No one who knew the story would have failed to recognise the portrait of Elsie.

She was not the only one to be angered by the book. H.G. Wells protested violently at the portrayal of himself, while more serious repercussions were to come from Marwood's recognition of himself in the book: credence was given to Elsie's claims that Marwood had tried to initiate an affair with her, and this caused him to break off his friendship with Ford and Violet once again.

One piece of good fortune resulted from the book's publication: the introduction of Rebecca West into the South Lodge circle. The beginning of the acquaintance was not propitious, for Rebecca gave *The New Humpty Dumpty* a devastatingly bad review. Violet decided that the only possible response was to meet the reviewer with the wicked pen and so she invited Rebecca West to tea at South Lodge.

Both Ford and Violet were more than a little surprised when the formidable reviewer appeared. They had expected to have to deal with someone quite other than the very young and very attractive woman who arrived at the door. Her appearance was totally at odds with her writing.

> She came. She had a pink dress on and a large, wide-brimmed, country-girlish straw hat that hid her splendid liquid eyes, which, however, no brim of any kind could hinder one from apprehending. She kept her feet planted very regularly and firmly together, and throughout the interview retained her handsome handbag (which was rather like a satchel) on her lap.

Thus began a friendship which, at least as far as the two women were concerned, was to prove strong and long-lasting.

Throughout the hot and airless summer of 1912, Violet was preoccupied with the legal battle with her sisters and worried about the outcome of *The Throne* trial. As a result, she was not as sympathetic as she might otherwise have been when Ford was threatened with bankruptcy. Upset by her seeming indifference and by her constant harping on legal matters, Ford threatened to end the relationship. Violet wrote of this time: 'Talk of poverty and the consequent flight of Love out of the window – it does not clear the room of all amatory stuff like a woman with a lawsuit on.'

Dr Tebb, who was already treating Ford for his breakdown, now began to prescribe a sedative for Violet as well. At least this had the desired effect of quietening her down, and Ford began to talk of escaping the distress and confusion by going to Germany. Violet was not enthusiastic, so Ford tried to make the prospect rosier with the promise of trips to San Sebastian, Montjoie and Le Touquet. In the event all they did was to retire to Selsey for much of the summer.

'The sweetest Violet in England'
– Portrait of Violet Hunt by a fellow art student.

Violet's father, the painter
Alfred William Hunt.

'A kind of wolf with bushy eyebrows'
– Photograph of John Ruskin in
Alfred Hunt's family album.

Alfred Hunt's painting 'Brignal Banks' which was given to Violet as a gift
and which she sold to finance her travels with Ford.

Violet's mother, the novelist Margaret Hunt.

'The flower of the flock'
– Violet's sister Venice, much envied by
Violet for being Ruskin's god-daughter.

'. . . kind and capricious, cunning and silly . . .'
Violet's youngest sister, Silvia.

'My favourite niece' – Rosamond Fogg Elliot,
Silvia's daughter.

1 Tor Villas, Violet's childhood home, leased by her father from Holman Hunt.

'A thin viperish-looking beauty with a long pointed chin. . .'
Violet drawn by Kathleen Shackleton.

South Lodge to which Violet and her mother moved after the death of Alfred Hunt.

'The wittiest woman in London'
– Margaret Hunt drawn by Violet.

'A fashionable and faintly vicious blue-stocking' – Violet at the time of her involvement with Ford Madox Ford.

84 Holland Park Avenue: office of *The English Review*, Ford's home, and the place where he and Violet first became lovers.

Ford and Violet at Selsey in the early days of their relationship.

'A walking temptation to women' – Ford in uniform with some of his other ladies:

His wife, Elsie

His mistress, Mary Martindale: Elsie's sister and Violet's friend

Stella Bowen for whom he left Violet

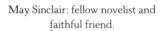

May Sinclair: fellow novelist and
faithful friend.

Henry James: fellow novelist and would-be
faithful friend whose patience was taxed
by Violet's indecorous behaviour.

Rebecca West: staunch friend and ally – 'A shining example of "the Newest Woman" ' –
seen here with her baby son Anthony, Violet and Ford.

In October Violet made one last attempt to be reconciled with her sister Silvia. She travelled with Ford to Northumberland and then Violet went alone to Bedburne to see her sister. But Silvia refused to speak directly to her or to see her. She merely instructed Rosamond to give her aunt tea and tell her that everything between them had to be handled by the lawyers.

When Violet and Ford returned to London it was apparent that Mrs Hunt was dying. She no longer recognised Violet and her appearance was shockingly changed: 'My mother had been a tall, large, wide-faced woman. As she lay there, breathing with difficulty, of a dull ferocious red like a smouldering coal, she seemed a small, brown, wizened changeling.' The doctor held out little hope, even if an operation which Violet could ill afford were to be undertaken.

Throughout the following difficult days Ford was a surprisingly strong support. He took his turn to watch over the dying woman at night so that the nurse could snatch some sleep.

Telegrams were sent to Venice and Silvia to warn them of the impending death. Yet even now they refused to be reconciled with Violet. Ford and his mother were more supportive and kind than Violet's own family.

Margaret Hunt died at the end of October 1912 and was dressed in the new white nightgown that she had kept specially for the occasion. She was to be buried with her husband at Woking. The night before the funeral the body was taken away in a carriage drawn by one black horse to spend the night in the station ready for the last train journey and the burial.

Immediately after the death of Margaret Hunt her lawyer announced that because Silvia and Venice had contested the will it was to be put into Chancery, so that none of them could touch the money until matters had been resolved. It took four years to achieve this.

In some ways the death of Mrs Hunt was a relief. It was far less painful for Violet to have the will contested than to have to pay frequent visits to the Master of Lunacy. And she no longer needed to fear that somehow word of the scandal about her marriage and about The Governess would reach her mother.

In an attempt to put all the misery and the anxiety about the coming trial of The Throne behind them for a while, Violet organised a Christmas house party at Farnham. Ezra Pound was one of those invited. He wrote to his mother to say that he was 'down here for a week with the Hueffers in a dingy old cottage that belonged to Milton. FMH and I being the only two people who couldn't be in the least impressed by the fact makes it a bit more ironical.'[5]

Ford, however, distressed at not being allowed to have his children with him at Christmas time, refused to celebrate Christmas Day. While Pound and Violet attempted to cook a sucking pig Ford locked himself into his bedroom and refused to speak to anyone. Faith Compton Mackenzie remembered that Christmas vividly:

> I once spent Christmas with the Hueffers at a cottage near Burnham Beeches. My contribution to the household was a Sudbury ham, which was fallen upon with greedy enthusiasm by the other guest, Ezra Pound, who talked without ceasing throughout the festival. On Christmas Day Ford could only be approached through the keyhole of his bedroom, in which he was firmly locked against all comers. The cause of this retirement was not made known, but it gave a spice to the party, since Violet was continually running upstairs to entreat him, speculating loudly as to why he was up there at all, and giving a touch of drama to the whole affair, so that the trumpery little cottage (which was only lent) achieved a sort of sublimity as the setting of a scene in history. Meanwhile Ezra's monologue went on without serious interruption.
>
> Ford, releasing himself from bondage on St Stephen's Day, descended upon us with his store of intellectual energy unimpaired by festive excess, full of benevolence, good cheer and lively conversation; in short he was himself again. And Violet, her great eyes blazing, carved the turkey and what remained of the ham with more than her usual dexterity, her cheeks flushed at the excitement of his restoration. It was a really notable Christmas, for I was, and have always been, devoted to Ford and Violet.[6]

Mary Martindale, who also spent Christmas with them, had recently returned from Germany. Her account of what was happening there was disquieting. Ford had felt it necessary to keep on his rooms in Giessen to maintain his claim to residency and thus to naturalisation. In his absence Mary and the lawyer Leun's wife had been looking after the rooms. Leun was showing signs of jealousy about the care his wife was taking over Ford. Further emotional stresses resulted from the fact that Mary had received a proposal of marriage from a friend of the Leuns. Frau Leun was piqued because she had considered this man one of her admirers, and Herr Leun was annoyed because Mary had rejected the proposal. The final complication was an unpaid legal bill which Leun was taking measures to make Ford pay. It was clear that Ford had to return to Giessen to sort matters out. A date had been set for *The Throne* trial, so it was arranged that once the trial was over Ford would meet Violet at Boulogne and from there they would both return to Giessen.

As usual their careful plans were of no avail. Ford played his part and dutifully arrived at the Hôtel Dervaux on the date agreed. But the case was postponed. It was too late for Violet to prevent his journey, so all she could do was to dash over to Boulogne to be with him until the case was called.

The hotel was in a miserable state because it was undergoing renovations. Ford had a cold and he was irritated by the delay as he was anxious to return to Giessen, where he had some social engagements.

While she was in Boulogne Violet struck up an acquaintance with another Englishwoman to whom she lent her newly-published novel *The Celebrity's Daughter*, which had also appeared under the name of Violet Hueffer.

A telegram arrived to announce that the trial would take place the next day, so Violet did a quick turnaround and made a thoroughly miserable journey back to England.

There was no question of Ford being called as a witness. His doctor had written to the court saying that in his opinion Ford Madox Heuffer, 'in consequence of certain symptoms of neurasthenia affecting the central circulation', was not fit to appear in court. Violet did not know whether she would be called, so she waited on tenterhooks by the telephone in the Soskices' house. A phone call from her solicitor came at eleven o'clock saying that in view of what was happening in court he advised having counsel watch the case for her.

That evening Violet read an account of the case in the newspapers. It made depressing reading. But there was more to come as the trial continued the following day. Once again Violet spent the day at the

115

Soskices', returning home in the evening. She did not know what the outcome of the trial was and she was afraid to find out. When she finally plucked up her courage to make enquiries she did not phone any of her close friends but spoke instead to her accountant. What she learned from him came as a great shock. *The Throne* had lost its case. Elsie Hueffer had been awarded three hundred pounds damages and the magazine had been ordered to pay costs, which amounted to a thousand pounds. This proved to be the ruin of *The Throne*, which was already in a precarious financial state.

The implications for Ford and Violet were equally serious. Things had been said in court which were damaging to the reputations of them both.

Elsie Hueffer had allowed the whole story of her marriage to and parting from Ford to be told in court. Her basic contention was that by publishing the article on *The Governess* which referred to Violet as 'Mrs Ford Madox Hueffer', *The Throne* had created a situation in which people would either think that she had never been married to Ford or that she was divorced. This, she maintained, exposed her to ridicule, hatred and contempt. *The Throne* responded by saying that the action should never have been brought. Why should they question what a woman chose to call herself when she was generally known by that name in society? Counsel for *The Throne* suggested that this was a fight between two women; the object of the bringing up of the case was to enable Mrs Hueffer to brand Miss Hunt an adultress.

One aspect of the case which did not show Elsie Hueffer in a favourable light at all was her allowing to stand the accusation that Ford had caused his wife and children great suffering by keeping them short of money. Elsie knew this was not at all true. She was only able to get away with it because neither Ford nor Violet was able to offer any defence under the terms of the trial. The notion of Ford's dereliction of his responsibilities cannot fail to have had an impact on the jury and its decision.

The repercussions of the verdict came quickly. Some old friends commiserated with Violet and said the verdict made no difference. But Violet's clubs asked her to resign, her sisters felt that their attitude towards her was completely vindicated, and Canon Greenwell cut her out of his will.

On top of everything else, Violet had the miserable task of

making the journey back to France to inform Ford of the judgement. A tearful and shocked Mary Martindale saw her off at the station. Throughout the proceedings she had remained loyal to Violet and Ford rather than to her sister. She was reduced to hysterics when she saw the portraits of Violet and Ford on newspaper placards and in all the newspapers. Violet sent Mary off to buy copies of all the papers, and for the rest of her journey had the experience of seeing fellow-passengers read about herself and Ford. Fortunately the portrait the newspapers had acquired was not a specially good one and no one appeared to realise that they were travelling with the person they were reading about.

Ford met Violet in the dark and rain at Boulogne. He was ill with worry and had lost his voice. Violet began to tell him about the trial but he would not listen and took to his bed. Violet put the newspapers away for a later occasion.

Her new position in society was brought home to her with full force the next morning. As she breakfasted alone the Englishwoman to whom she had lent *The Celebrity's Daughter* came up to her table, laid the novel on it and said loudly, 'There's your book, *Miss* Hunt!' And during the days the couple were forced to remain at the Hôtel Dervaux awaiting Ford's recovery, not one of the other guests spoke to them.

FOURTEEN

DEFYING CONVENTION

When Ford did recover it was not to Germany they went but, on the advice of their French doctor, to the South of France. Violet, who had never before been further south than Paris, was eager to see a part of the world about which both Ford and Conrad had expressed a good deal of enthusiasm. Ford's father had written about the troubadours of Provence in his book *The Troubadours: A History of Provençal Life and Literature in the Middle Ages*.

Conrad had urged them to visit Montpellier. He had written rapturously to Ford about 'the beauty of the land and the delicacy of the colours at sunset and sunrise,' which he keenly wished to share with 'the inheritor of the great Pre-Raphaelite tradition of colour'. He had described to Violet 'the villages perched on conical hills, standing out all around against "the great and sweeping lines of violet ranges as if in an enchanted country."'

Whether things had changed since Conrad was there, or whether Violet and Ford projected their own depression onto the place, it was far less than they had expected. Violet described it as 'a wash-out, ugly and ordinary'. Their dissatisfaction was not improved by the loss of their luggage. So they moved on to Carcassone, only to find that rabies was rampant there. They settled for a while at the Grand Hôtel de Provence in St Remy de Provence, braving the mistral, taking walks to Les Baux and, ironically, to the Château d'Amour. Ford worked most days, using a desk improvised from the lid of the bath. But they were both deeply disturbed and unhappy. Violet says that the best they could manage was to force 'a calmness that spoke less of emotion controlled than an utter atrophy of all the springs of feeling'.

They maintained contact with England through letters. Conrad wrote to say that his friendship towards them was unaffected by all the scandal and that he would take the earliest opportunity of making a formal visit on their return to London. Even while the scandal was brewing Henry James had had a change of heart and written kindly to Violet. He followed this up with another letter which seemed to express a resigned acceptance of her situation for he concluded with the words: 'Well, patch with purple if you must, so long as the piece holds. Yours, my dear Violet, ever, Henry James.'

Other correspondents took the scandal more seriously even while expressing their undiminished friendship and support. Violet did not reproduce these letters in either *The Flurried Years* or *I Have This To Say*, but they were found by Douglas Goldring after her death and reproduced in *South Lodge*.

Lilian, Lady Aberconway, wrote to Violet to offer what assistance she could to re-establish Violet's position in society and to express her sympathy for all the distress the couple had endured. It was typical of Violet that she could not simply accept this expression of friendship but had to justify herself, and it was equally typical of Ford that he wanted to let matters rest. The difference in their two attitudes is revealed by two letters which show a basic difference in temperament. This difference was to become more pronounced and was, at least in part, the reason for their growing incompatibility. Ford's letter reads:

> I hold very strongly the view that friends are people before whom one does not need to justify oneself and, personally, I am absolutely determined to speak to no-one about those matters. The fact is that I prefer not to know people who think that I am capable of, let us say, basely deserting an unwilling woman, leaving my children insufficiently provided for, or any of the other things alleged against me at the trial to which your letter to Violet refers. I am, you see, not English and the whole process of washing dirty linen in public, so essential to the English point of view, appears to me to be repulsive . . . I wish Violet took that view; but she considers – and no doubt very rightly from her standpoint – that she owes it to her friends to justify herself.

It was not just Violet but her friends also who urged justification. Violet had written from Provence to Mrs W.K. Clifford, a close friend and someone who had moved in the same circles as her parents. She had announced her intention of returning home shortly to South Lodge, but Mrs Clifford had replied by urging Violet not to return to London and face the scandal but to stay abroad until the whole affair had been forgotten. She recommended an absence of three years. In her opinion Violet would not be well received in respectable circles and her attempts to be so would bring embarrassment and distress to those who cared for her and wished her well.

Indignantly Violet replied that she expected her friends to accept the legality of her marriage despite the mud flung in court: 'I should expect all my real friends to accept my version of the affair naturally and easily – and if other friends walked out, let them.'

Mrs Clifford was not content to let matters rest there. She wrote to Violet giving her what she believed to be sound advice. First of all she told her what conclusion the majority of society had reached: 'They say that it is impossible to believe that Ford had definite reason for divorcing his wife or that he did divorce her, or that he thought he had divorced her, that you went through no marriage ceremony, and that you have no reason for believing yourself legally married to Ford.'

As she saw it, the simplest solution to the tangle was for Violet to instruct her solicitor to issue a statement that would put an end to the gossip. She outlined what should be included in the statement:

(1)   That Ford divorced his wife on the – of the – . Give dates. That the citation was served on her on such a date at such a place – *give time, places above all things.*

(2)   That the divorce decree was procured at such a court or before such a Judge – *give dates and places.*

(3)   That the decree became absolute on such a date.

(4)   That on *such a date* you two went through the ceremony of marriage *at such a place*, believing it, as you now do, to be legal.

She concludes her letter with a P.S. in which she says 'For goodness sake, dear woman, set forth in plain, clear words the facts, and say you do so not for your own sake but for the sake of friends who do believe in you.'

If Violet could only have complied with Mrs Clifford's request what pleasure it would have given her. But now, if she had ever believed in the legality of her marriage, she had to accept that she had been gullible in not insisting on asking the very questions Mrs Clifford had posed and in not insisting on seeing all the relevant legal documents. This realisation did not improve the already strained relationship between the two exiles.

The greatest blow was a letter from May Sinclair written on 10 May 1913. Violet could be in no doubt about the fact that May Sinclair would stick to her through all her troubles, but she too urged the wisdom of staying abroad for a while:

My dear Violet,
            I was at the women writers' Committee on Saturday – and I may say at once that there was hardly anyone there who was not entirely friendly – in fact, none who was hostile, but the majority decided to accept your offer to resign from the Committee, with the utmost appreciation of your kindness

in offering. The idea seemed to be that some foolish persons might object if you remained on the Committee and that they might make a fuss which would cause injury to the dinner – the sacred dinner!

We also decided, as far as this Committee-meeting is concerned that you should be asked to come to it – the dinner – if you still cared to.

The only thing is that, considering the absurdly strong feeling this case has roused, most of us – Marie and Mrs Clifford and Evelyn and I – *just because we care for you* and can't bear your being hurt more than you have been, think that it would be wiser if you waited till all this has blown over and been forgotten before coming back to England. You know we don't share in the least in that feeling. Personally, I don't care two straws whether your marriage holds good in this country or not, (and should *not* care if it had never taken place). I'm only thinking of what will be the best for you both in the long run. People have short memories, and in another six months nobody will remember that they ever made a fuss and you can be sure of taking your place as if nobody had ever minded. It's much better, ten times more dignified – than trying to fight them at the present moment.

I hate to have to suggest it, but I do believe it's 'wisdom'.

Never forget that we love you and are on your side whatever happens. And do forgive me if I've proposed a course that is distasteful to you. With love to you and kindest regards to Mr Hueffer – always affectionately, May Sinclair.

From Provence the unhappy couple went to Corsica, where Violet's mother had discovered the two sisters so many years before. Ford disliked Corsica and his dislike of the place was intensified by a letter from Marwood demanding the repayment of a loan. Although, on the surface, to make such a demand at such a moment seemed gratuitously malicious, Violet and Ford learned later that Marwood knew he was dying and he was anxious to ensure that he left his estate in good order.

Tired of their exile, Violet and Ford decided to ignore all the advice they had been given to the contrary and returned to South Lodge. With characteristic bravado Violet immediately began to issue invitations to a garden party on 1 July. To her distress she found that members of the family and the older friends she knew through her parents were inclined to behave exactly in the way predicted by Mrs Clifford. There were those who straightforwardly refused because of the distaste they felt for what they saw as Violet's immorality, and those who apologised for not having the courage to defy society and associate themselves with her.

In *The Flurried Years* Violet does not admit this setback. She claimed that 'my yearly garden-party [was] never so well attended. Cabinet Ministers, by Jove.' But in effect those who attended were Ford's family and old friends.

The nature of South Lodge and its salon began to change. If the old and the self-consciously respectable gave it a wide berth, the young and 'charming artist rabble who were on the top of the vogue' were happy to attend parties there. Ford dispelled his neurasthenia to some extent by taking to drinking whisky. By the end of Christmas 1913 the parties at South Lodge were as brilliant as ever, though the guest list had changed.

To some extent Ezra Pound symbolised the kind of change that took place. Until now Violet had insisted on maintaining the same decorum of dress and behaviour in her drawing-room as her mother had done. But now Ezra Pound was able to appear looking the very essence of young bohemia with his luxuriant auburn hair and beard, his pince-nez, a turquoise in his ear and big blue glass buttons on his coat. Wyndham Lewis, the writer and painter, and Henri Gaudier-Brzeska, the sculptor, were among the regular visitors. The latter was very much Pound's protégé. Violet describes the young Frenchman as 'quiet, ill-looking, almost toothless, wearing his blue workman's shirt, clean, on all occasions'. He would certainly not have gained admittance to one of Mrs Hunt's 'at homes' in such an outfit. The young sculptor was desperately short of money even for the marble he needed for his work. Pound acquired an unusually large piece for him as a gift, which Gaudier-Brzeska used to carve a hieratic head of the poet.

The problem of where to put the huge sculpture when it was finished was solved when Violet offered to have it in her garden. There it stood, a public declaration of Violet's and Ford's support for the new art of the time, looking 'ghastly and terrible' when the moon shone on it and the source of much speculation amongst the neighbours.

They introduced the new art inside the house as well. Since Margaret Hunt had died a number of alterations had been made to the house. In the dining-room at the back of the house on the ground floor a service lift for hauling dishes up from the basement kitchen had been constructed to Ford's design. On the first floor the front room had been turned into a study for Ford, and what had been the dressing-room adjoining this room was now lined with bookshelves.

Over the fireplace in the study was a large and disturbing abstract painting which Ford and Violet had commissioned from Wyndham Lewis. In this room the new art work determined the rest of the decor. There was no longer the familiar William Morris curtaining but brick-red tapestry curtains, the colour of which was picked up in the newly painted red woodwork. Mrs Hunt would not have recognised the room as belonging to her house.

Much of that very hot summer was spent at Knapp Cottage, with Brigit Patmore as a guest. Despite Violet's great and persistent affection for her younger guest – Brigit was thirty-one at the time – she was more than a little irritated when she realised that Ford was in love with her.

During this summer Ford began to write one of his best novels, *The Good Soldier*, and, provoked by Violet, he produced for her what many critics regard as one of his finest poems, 'To V.H. Who Asked for a Working Heaven.' In a bad mood as a result of her many worries, the hot summer and Ford's attraction towards Brigit Patmore, Violet had told him that 'You say you believe in heaven; I wish you'd write one for me. I want no beauty; I want no damned optimism; I want just a plain, workaday heaven that I can go to some day and enjoy it when I'm there.'

The poem did not please Violet. She saw in it a clear indication of how differently she and Ford defined love, and she found his definition limited and unsatisfactory.

All through the summer Violet had seethed with resentment against Leun, Ford's German lawyer. After all the misery she had gone through she wanted to get to the bottom of exactly what had happened, to confront Leun and to find out how he could justify the large fees he had charged in return for what seemed to be nothing at all.

She had enough sense to know that she would achieve nothing by saying straight out what her objectives were. Ford wanted no more scandal or probing into murky legal matters. So what she proposed

was a trip down the Rhine with their good friends the Mastermans.*
She set out quite deliberately to paint a glowing picture of what
the voyage would be like, and she managed to convince Ford and
the Mastermans of the desirability of such a holiday. Ezra Pound,
watching events from his nearby rooms, expressed his scepticism
about the journey in a letter to Dorothy Shakespear in September
1913: 'That pillar of your government together with their respec-
tive wives or concubines are now enjoying (or otherwise, probably
otherwise in the case of V.) the Rhine.'[1]

His perception was an accurate one. For although Violet enjoyed
the early part of the holiday, once they drew close to Assmanshausen
memories of the events that had taken place since her last visit,
when she had been so full of hope, made her bitter. Her attitude
to Germany now was in complete contrast to that expressed in
The Desirable Alien, which she had written when she had believed
and hoped that she and Ford could have a life together as solid,
respectable, German citizens. Now nothing pleased her – not the
hotel, nor the food, nor the landscape, nor the Germans themselves.

A hotel was found at Rudesheim. With some difficulty the party
arranged to pay a visit to the battlefields of Sedan, of Gavelotte
and Mars-la-Tour. It was Masterman's particular desire to see these
sights. But the excursion was not a great success. Whether justifiably
or not, Ford became very alarmed by the attitude of the coachman
they had hired. This fear was intensified when he discovered that
the books that he and Violet had taken to read on the train part
of the journey had disappeared. Ironically, among them was *The
Desirable Alien*. Ford later came to the conclusion that they had
been treated with such suspicion and watched so closely because

---

*Charles Frederick Gurney Masterman (1874–1927) was a Liberal Christian Socialist. In
1911 he had been the first chairman of the National Insurance commission. He worked
closely with Winston Churchill and in 1912 was financial secretary to the Treasury. In
his capacity as Director of Wellington House, in charge of the literary department of
the Ministry of Information, he was to prove a good friend to Ford. He
refuted charges of Ford's being in contact with an enemy alien and gave
him propaganda assignments.

He and his wife Lucy, whom he had married in 1908, were not at all perturbed by
Violet and Ford's irregular relationship. They were accustomed to mixing with the upper
classes and the nobility, where extra-marital relationships were commonplace.

Ford had a great respect for Masterman and did his best to enlist his support
against Violet when he had made his mind up to end the relationship.

Masterman had been mistaken for Churchill. In her biography of her husband, Lucy Masterman dismisses this idea. But this scare, together with a feeling of war in the air, made Ford aware of the difficulty of his position if Germany was to go to war. He dissuaded Violet from protracting their time in Germany with a visit to his cousin Mimi at Boppard. He responded to Violet's request that they should go to Giessen, the main objective of the whole enterprise as far as Violet was concerned, with the following melodramatic speech: 'Do you want me to be shot or forced to fight against France? If you're prepared to risk that, dear, we'll go.' Violet had to return to England with none of her questions answered.

1914 was very much the year of the Vorticists, who had begun to make an impact as a group in 1913. Violet had been persuaded by her young friends to dress in Vorticist style, which involved wearing brightly coloured angular clothes. It had been pointed out to her that such clothes looked much better in the context of Vorticist art exhibitions than the French pastel-coloured dresses she was accustomed to wearing. Violet was never very happy about dressing in the new style despite Wyndham Lewis's assurances that she looked 'better than a dying stag or a virgin in a Greek dress picking daisies'. Nor was she entirely pleased by the mural decorations at the Rebel Art Centre, which she described as evocative of a butcher's shop full of prime cuts.

Violet and Ford were much older than most of the young people who comprised the Vorticist group, of which Pound and Lewis were the most emphatic members. The group's common aims had crystalised after Wyndham Lewis had pronounced unsatisfactory the Futurist Manifesto as set out by Marinetti. He described the Vorticist Movement to Violet in the following terms, which she recorded in *I Have This To Say*: 'You think at once of a whirlpool. At the heart of the whirlpool is a great silent place where all the energy is concentrated. And there, at the point of concentration is The Vorticist.'

South Lodge was not the only meeting place for the group. Another was the Rebel Arts Centre in one of the old houses in Great Ormond Street, with its membership fee of one guinea. Violet was intrigued by the fact that this meeting place was so close to the Queen's Square house where the Pre-Raphaelites had met. Another favourite meeting place was the Golden Calf Club, run by Madame

Strindberg in a basement in Heddon Street. Edgar Jepson, who was a regular attender, describes it in *Memories of An Edwardian*:

> It was indeed an uncommon night-club: the food and wine were good and served in a civilised fashion, and not only could you dance there those obsolete Vorticist dances, the turkey trot and the bunny hug, but between the dances you could observe violent, Vorticist assaults on the drama. An expensive club, it was frequented by the intelligent, wealthy, interested in letters and the arts. Before or since there has been no club like it.[2]

Ford makes the club one of the settings of his novel *The Marsden Case*, and a detailed description of it as The Silver Cow appears in Violet's novel *The House of Many Mirrors*.

Although Violet and Ford threw themselves into the activities of their younger friends, Violet at least was beginning to feel how much older she was than the rest of the group. Perhaps the attitude she attributed to one of her characters in *The House of Many Mirrors* was also true of herself at this time: 'She had the modern woman's half real, half feigned appreciation of and interest in the development of the arts.' Her comment on this hectic time also suggests this to have been the case:

> We were poised on the point of a needle, trembling in space, and all this remue-menage, this nervous gaiety, this singing of German Lieder and performing of amateur plays at the Cabaret Club under the walls covered with Wyndham Lewis's raw meat designs, this crackling of thorns under the social pot was all very well, but it wasn't life, either of the heart or the mind.

The Vorticists felt the need for an 'organ' which would promote their particular view of the arts. In June 1914 there were several occasions organised to launch *Blast*. One was held in the Rebel Art Centre, and began in true Vorticist style with a row between W.H. Nevinson and Wyndham Lewis; while a dinner at the Dieudonne restaurant was marked by a falling-out between Ford and the formidable American poet, Amy Lowell. At a tea party in Lewis's studio the by now famous lists of Blasts and Blessings were proclaimed. Violet took on the job of selling copies of *Blast* at her parties, and she found that many copies sold simply because the purchasers were anxious to see if their names appeared and, if so, on which list.

During this very active social year there were also quieter, regular dinner meetings arranged by Pound in Belloti's, a Soho restaurant. The Vorticist group formed the core of regular diners, but Edgar Jepson appeared from time to time, as did T.S. Eliot. It was to one of these dinners that Pound invited Stella Bowen, a young Australian painter, and he introduced her to his other friends including Ford and Violet.

It was during this year also that Pound became engaged to and married Dorothy Shakespear. When the engagement was announced Ford promised the couple a set of six High Wycombe chairs. This was a somewhat ironic gift, as Ford clearly felt that the Pound household would need such sturdy wooden chairs. He had seen the way Pound treated chairs and had been present when Pound had accidentally destroyed one of Violet's fragile antique chairs. The letter in which Pound tells Dorothy of this promised gift also reveals the fact that the growing tension between Violet and Ford was apparent to their friends: 'Fat Ford is going to give six High Wycombe chairs. He says V. has got to give us something else and she says they are both going to give us something together. Unanimission again!'3

It was through Wyndham Lewis that Violet and Ford became acquainted with Mary Borden. Lewis had begun by painting the portrait of the Chicago millionairess, who was already established as a novelist. She had, inevitably, become his mistress. In the July of 1914 Lewis was staying with Mary Borden and her husband of that time at their rented summer house in Berwick-on-Tweed. Violet and Ford were also invited. Ford recalls reading parts of *The Good Soldier*, which had been published in *Blast*. Mary Borden was reading a serialisation of *A Portrait of The Artist* by James Joyce in *The Egoist*. Pound was responsible for its inclusion, and since it was Violet who had suggested that Pound be given a position on *The Egoist* (at that time, in 1913, it was still called *The New Freewoman*) she was indirectly responsible for this publication of Joyce's work.

But the real concern of everyone during that July was whether or not England would go to war. Ford and Violet had been sufficiently anxious about leaving London at such a time that they had arranged for Richard Aldington* to send them telegrams keeping them in touch with developments.

In his autobiography *Blasting and Bombardiering* Lewis recalls the conversation which took place outside in the sunlight on the lawn. Mary Borden was emphatic that there would not be a war. She is reported as saying 'There won't be any war, Ford. Not here – England won't go into a war.' Ford disagreed with his hostess.

> Ford thrust his mouth out, fish-fashion, as if about to gasp for breath. He juggled his eyes and waggled one eyelid about. He just moved his lips a little and we heard him say, in a breathless sotto voce –
> 'England will.'
> 'England will! But Ford,' said Mrs Turner, 'England has a Liberal government. A Liberal government cannot declare war . . .'
> 'I don't agree,' Ford answered in his faintest voice, with consummate indifference, 'because it has always been the Liberals who have gone to war. It is *because* it is a Liberal Government that it *will* declare war.'[4]

There was sufficient unease among the group about the possibility of war being declared that Wyndham Lewis left earlier than he intended, closely followed by Ford and Violet. The evening of their return Violet heard shouts from the street.

War had been declared.

It was a war which was to change much in English society, and alter the course of Violet's life irrevocably.

---

*Richard Aldington was a young writer who was a friend of Ezra Pound. Through Pound he met and then married the American poet Hilda Doolittle (H.D.). At this time he was living in Church Walk, Kensington.

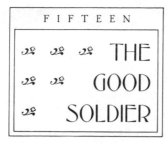

FIFTEEN

∂º ∂º ∂º THE
∂º ∂º GOOD
∂º SOLDIER

Violet responded to this crisis as she had responded to so many, by fleeing to Selsey and Knapp Cottage. Although the cottage had a reputation for being haunted and although many of their friends were not easy with its atmosphere, for Ford and Violet it had so far been a satisfactory retreat and a place where they both could work well. It was close enough to London for them to be able to keep in contact with their social life there if they so wished. Violet describes the cottage with some affection in *I Have This To Say:*

> Our little lonely tree-embosomed cottage by the sea was easily the uneasiest place in an uneasy village, a long narrow but important carriage drive led by a concealed turning to the furtive little abode where Joseph Leopold and I retired to write. Two tall trees grew at one side of the cottage, their lower boughs caressing its roof, making the parlour dark at noonday, while at night they painstakingly ground away at the chimney stack like cows or cats rubbing at a post.

This time, however, they were not to find the peace and tranquillity to which they were accustomed. It was not the reputed ghosts that disturbed them, but the consequences of their own earlier actions.

For a while they lived pleasantly enough, planting a vegetable garden as a part of the war effort. Ford was always happiest in the role of smallholder, as later events emphasised.

Edward Heron Allen, who had once nursed an unrequited passion for Violet, was also living in Selsey. He was, in fact, Violet's landlord. Ford had always appeared to find him congenial even though Heron Allen had always been cool towards him personally and actively hostile to his relationship with Violet. The wartime situation brought the latent hostility between the two men to the surface. Heron Allen was obsessed with the war and convinced that the Germans had targeted that particular part of the coast for submarine landings. His talk of an invasion spread uneasiness amongst the villagers, and Ford remonstrated with him

129

about this. But it appears to have been malice rather than a genuine desire to redress the balance of opinion that motivated Ford to write his story 'The Scaremonger', which was published in *The Bystander* in November 1914. There was no doubt in anyone's mind about who was portrayed in the story. Even close friends of Ford and Violet were shocked by the story, as Brigit Patmore's comment in a letter of 30 December 1914 indicates: 'The attack on Ned is flagrant, & all the more astounding as Ford pretended to like Ned. Why did he do it?'

Heron Allen was naturally outraged. He felt that his friendship and hospitality had been grossly abused. Ford's evidently insincere apology did nothing to abate his anger. In the circumstances it was hardly tactful of Ford to then publish an article on the gallant enemy in *The Outlook*. Anti-German feelings were running very high in England. Suddenly Ford and Violet's German adventure took on a different complexion. Ford's German surname 'Hueffer' made him an obvious target for suspicion. His claim to have taken up his German citizenship in order to get a German divorce and to marry Violet now proved an embarrassment. If he proved that he was not in fact a German citizen he would also be conceding that everything he had said about his divorce and his marriage was a fiction.

In January 1915 the ambiguity of their position was brought home forcefully and unpleasantly to Ford and Violet when the Chief Constable of West Sussex ordered Ford, as a German and therefore an enemy alien, to leave the area. He was suspected of being in communication with the enemy and of giving information about possible landing sites along the coast. It was Edward Heron Allen's revenge for Ford's story.

He was not, however, successful in having Ford removed from the area. Ford was quickly in contact with his friend Masterman, whose intervention caused the order to be withdrawn. But in other respects Heron Allen succeeded in creating the mischief he had intended. Ford knew very clearly who was behind the investigation by the Sussex police. He blamed Violet for her friendship with Heron Allen and for her refusal to drop him. More importantly, he blamed her for the whole German fiasco, suggesting that had it not been for her urgent desire for marriage and respectability there would never have been any question of his renewing his German citizenship.

And, of course, there was in print for anyone who cared to read, Violet's book *The Desirable Alien*, which presents Ford as a solid worthy German citizen and herself as aspiring to follow suit.

The publication of *The Good Soldier* in March 1915 did not ease the increasing strain in the household at Selsey. Although Ford suppressed many passages which made the link between Violet and Florence absolutely clear, few of their acquaintance could have failed to mistake the portrait.

In addition there are passages in the novel which could be read as direct addresses from Ford to Violet, explaining his position with regard to their relationship. The words quoted here are those of the narrator Dowell:

> For, whatever may be said of the relation of the sexes, there is no man who loves a woman that does not desire to come to her for the renewal of his courage, for the cutting asunder of his difficulties. And that will be the mainspring of his desire for her. We are all so afraid, we are all so alone, we all so need from outside the assurance of our own worthiness to exist.

This is a remarkably accurate description of how Ford and Violet first became involved over the bottle marked 'poison'. But Dowell goes on to describe what happens to such promising love affairs. Once again the description is accurate about the stage Ford and Violet had reached: 'But these things pass away; inevitably they pass away as the shadows pass across sundials. It is sad, but it is so. The pages of the book will become familiar; the beautiful corner of the road will have been turned too many times. Well, this is the saddest story.'

It is to Violet's credit that she never did other than praise the novel, whatever pain it must have caused her in its public revelation of Ford's changed attitude towards her.

Increasingly Ford found his situation uncomfortable. His German connections continued to make him an object of suspicion, Violet was ever more irritable and bad-tempered. It may have been as a result of consulting Violet's doctor about her tantrums that Ford first discovered that Violet had syphilis, which was by then in its tertiary stage. The disease was no longer transmittable and he had never been in any danger from it himself. He tried to be kind and sympathetic towards her, but she herself felt that from then on he was somewhat repelled by her. So his decision to seek a commission in the Army appeared to her what in many ways it was, a rejection of their relationship.

Violet would, of course, have opposed Ford's taking such a step. There was no legal need for him to enlist because at forty-two he was above the age limit. He avoided confrontation for as long as possible, but one day in July 1915 he disappeared to London, apparently on business to do with his writing. When he returned to Selsey later that day, having obtained his commission, Violet knew at once that things had changed irrevocably:

> A man I hardly seemed to know though I knew his coat, with a *serviette* full of papers under his arm, got in beside me and said dryly, in incisive, biting tones that were strange to me, as his secretary got in after him and covered his speech a little:
> 'I have got my commission.'

Violet felt the irony of the situation bitterly: 'We rolled along the twisted road from Chi' to Selsey, to the village that was trying to get rid of him because he was a German, and he was carrying the King's commission in his pocket.' She made as big a scene and fuss as Ford had feared, spending hours crying in her room. But she could not change the course of events, and by 13 August Ford was in uniform.

Even with his uniform as a visible expression of his patriotism, Ford was touchy about his German connections. It was, therefore, a difficult situation that he found himself in when he and Violet visited the Lawrences in the cottage in Sussex which had been lent to them by the Meynells. Frieda Lawrence, as a German by birth, expected some fellow-feeling from Ford. This he adamantly refused to give. Frieda and Violet, both very strong-willed women prone to be quarrelsome, fell into an argument which was still raging when Ford and Violet left. It was as a result of this occasion that Violet nicknamed Frieda 'the Valkyrie'. The quarrel marked the end of any intimacy between Lawrence and Ford and Violet – though Violet and Frieda did correspond at a later date, and Violet's description of Frieda Lawrence in *I Have This To Say* expresses her admiration for the younger woman's beauty and forceful personality.

Before Ford's departure to join his regiment Violet threw a party at South Lodge for close friends to say their goodbyes. It was a 'whisky and sandwich' party. But after the party the tensions between the host and hostess, exacerbated by whisky, came to a head and after a violent row Ford left South Lodge and spent his last night in London elsewhere. Their parting on this occasion was to establish the pattern for their relationship over the next few years.

Ford's absence did not put an end to Violet's social life. All her women friends were still in London. She resumed her friendship with Marguerite Radclyffe Hall. There was the continuing presence of Ezra Pound, who organised the activities of his friends both young and old round a series of lively dinner parties in Soho and continued to visit South Lodge with his usual frequency. He was often Violet's confidant, and did his best to give her good advice. Violet busied herself helping Wyndham Lewis to get a commission. She kept in close contact with those of her friends who were not in the forces – among them H.G. Wells and Joseph Conrad. The latter had agreed to be her fellow-literary executor for Ford.

In the early part of the war, when Ford was on leave, some of the old gaiety would surface. Grace Lovat Fraser recalls an occasion when she and her husband threw a party in his studio and Ford turned up with Violet, who was wearing his tin helmet tied on with pink ribbons.

But life in London was not just a frantic social whirl as young men came and went. The war made itself felt in the shortages of food, the impossibility of buying new clothes and, of course, in the air raids.

In response to the strange life everyone was forced to lead Violet and Ford wrote *Zeppelin Nights*. Loosely modelled on the form of Boccacio's *Decameron*, it consisted of a series of stories, each of which dealt with a critical moment in history. It also advocated a greater degree of humanity, especially towards enemies whose values were not understood and appreciated. It should have helped to establish Ford as being on the right side in the war as there is a strong patriotic element, but its effect was the opposite to what Violet and Ford had hoped. One reviewer went so far as to call Ford 'a foreigner and a coward' and to say of the book that 'There are flashes of Miss Hunt's genius dispersed throughout the volume, and one is sensible that she had made a heroic attempt to leaven the mass of Mr Hueffer's dull offensiveness.'[1] Such a review could only serve to drive a further wedge between the two authors, especially since Ford was in fact responsible for the greater part of the book.

The German connection continued to plague both Violet and Ford. An unsympathetic commanding officer confronted Ford with the article in the *Daily Mirror* which had already caused them so many problems. Ford was asked to explain how he could simultaneously claim to be a German citizen and a German landowner and serve as an officer in the British Army. Once again Ford had to confess that there was no truth in the *Daily Mirror*'s report. But even at this late stage he could not confront facts clearly and without muddle. He felt quite able to write to Violet after this incident, 'I take it that these questions do not affect our marriage as that took place in France.'

Meanwhile Violet was also experiencing the disadvantages of claiming to be Mrs Hueffer. After a particularly bad air raid, during which a bomb had been dropped on Campden Hill Road, she went out with the rest of the neighbourhood to inspect the damage. She was greeted with open hostility and roundly abused for being a German.

Throughout these troubled years with Ford, Violet continued to write novels and short stories. But the work of this period is not her best. Was she too busy bolstering up Ford to give her full energy to her own work? Was she so concerned to sell her work because she needed the income that she could not afford to take risks and write innovatively?

After such novels as *Sooner or Later* and *White Rose of Weary Leaf, The Celebrity's Daughter* represents a return to a kind of fiction that was more calculated to please. The Austenian conclusion to the novel, in which marriage is presented as the most desirable happy ending, is clearly a reflection of her hopes for herself at this time; but it sits uneasily with the rest of the novel, which is mostly about divorce and votes for women.

Perhaps Violet felt that she was risking enough in introducing these previously taboo topics into her fiction. She uses the Elsie–Ford situation as the basis for her plot, but wisely distances the experience by an element of comedy. Like Elsie, the heroine's mother Lucy has set in motion divorce proceedings against her husband. But, again like Elsie, she has only gone as far as to bring an action for restitution. Like Ford, the heroine's father, George, is left in a strange limbo, unable to act himself and unable to marry his mistress. When the court orders George to pay seven pounds a week, the wife ends up paying him; but later, when she is annoyed with her husband, she has him put into Brixton Gaol for arrears of alimony. Through the novel Violet is able to mock Elsie for taking the same action against Ford: 'It seems such an outrageous thing to do, to put your own husband in gaol, however bad his conduct is.'

There are similar snippets of autobiographical experience in *The House of Many Mirrors*. These include visits to the Cave of the Golden Calf, the request from a relative of a particular kind of ham, the gift of a tortoise, and illness in a spa town. But the novels are not autobiographical, and these elements drawn from Violet's own life often sit oddly with the main plot. In *The Celebrity's Daughter* we once again have a situation which is resolved by marriage. The heroine may not end up with a love match, but she does have plenty of money of her own and a famous, sophisticated and titled husband. The plot of *The House of Many Mirrors* is quite simply maudlin and melodramatic. It may well have been a response to *The Good Soldier* and Ford's tendency to wax romantic about younger women.

However, there is in *The House of Many Mirrors* a refusal to gloss over unpleasantness in behaviour and character which again had been unusual in the work of earlier women writers. This aspect of Violet's work is most pronounced in the collections of short stories.

Tales of the Uneasy was published in 1911. Its title emphasises the kind of subject Violet was interested in. In the preface to *More Tales of the Uneasy*, published in 1925, Violet recounts how Henry James had provided her with the word 'uneasy' for her titles. He understood exactly the element which binds the stories together:

> The little thing and how much it is! The irrelevant incident, or the speech that won't somehow and wonderfully fit in with the preconceived hypothesis of the ingenuous *raconteur* who is so distressed because there is a detail that won't tally . . . the unexplained increment . . . that constant factor of the uneasy.

In 1898 Henry James had published *The Turn of the Screw*. Violet realised that the power of this story lay not only in the shocking incidents it related, but in the sheer nastiness of its implications. She felt that James himself was not completely aware of this aspect of his story. When she came to write her stories in a similar vein she was in no doubt about their power to disturb, for she had deliberately set out to achieve this. The stories in *Tales of the Uneasy* all have as their titles the names of objects. This is appropriate, in that they are characterised by a lack of warmth and humanity – not because the writer lacks warmth or humanity, but because she sees how many relationships lack these qualities. Wildean wit is employed, but this time in order to show the emotional inadequacy of those who use it. In 'The Telegram', for example, the central character makes a flippant and heartless remark which she later regrets, when she says of her husband's first wife, 'Greater love hath no woman than she lay down her marriage lines for her husband.' Similarly Lady Greenwell's assertion in 'The Memoir' that she 'was neither young nor beautiful: it behoved her to be clever,' leads her to behave in a way that is certainly 'clever' but is in the end also cynically cruel.

Many of the stories could be classed as ghost stories. But their emphasis is not on making our spines chill with the horror of ghosts but with horror at the coldness and cynicism they bring to light in those whom they haunt.

Henry James was very much on Violet's mind at this time. He had taken a house in Chelsea, and once again Violet was able to visit him regularly. He had become a British subject after all his years of living in England because he wanted to make clear his support for the war effort. But he wanted to do more than make such a gesture; he wanted to make a contribution through his writing. He knew only too well his reputation for obscurity. So he invited Violet to his home to be an audience for his new kind of writing designed to be easily understood by a wider audience than he was accustomed to reaching.

Violet was half amused by his earnestness, as her comments in *The Flurried Years* reveal: 'Greater love hath no man than he lay down his *style* for his friend. He was so willing to help that he was eager to be comprehended by the people.' He admonished Violet not to forget 'that in this article I am addressing not a Woman, but a Nation!'

136

The description of the frail Henry James reading aloud shows how moved Violet was by the occasion. It was a reminder to her that a world she had known was coming to an end. This meeting did, in fact, prove to be their last. In February 1916 Henry James died.

Family affairs continued to distress Violet. She had hoped that once Rosamond was married she would once again be free to come to London and be with her aunt. But Rosamond never visited; her husband was just as hostile to Violet as Walton Fogg Elliot had been. She encountered more disapproval when she visited her god-father, Canon Greenwell. Despite his great age, he was angry enough with her to denounce her and say, 'I wish to have nothing to do with you! You are not his wife.'[2]

Although Ford and Violet had parted with a bitter quarrel, the break between them was not final. They corresponded, even if their letters were not always friendly. Ford continued to spend his leaves at South Lodge or Selsey. Violet sent him the proofs of *Their Lives* to correct. He wrote a preface for it and in letters to friends spoke of it as being really very good. He sent her his work to place as best she could. But there was always an undercurrent of tension and suspicion. True to her nature, Violet did not keep her troubles with Ford to herself but discussed them with friends. At her prompting, H.G. Wells wrote to Ford in an attempt to achieve a reconciliation between him and Violet. Ford also acted in characteristic fashion in writing a letter to Wells denying that any problem existed. But the cutting tone in which he refers to Violet belies his assertions:

> My dear H.G.
>
> I am much touched by your letter – tho' I do not really know what to make of it. I hadn't the least idea that there was any difference between Violet and myself – or at least anything to make her face the necessity of talking about it. I, at any rate, haven't any grievance against her and want nothing better than to live with her the life of a peaceable regimental officer with a peaceable wife. Of course that is not very exciting for her and her enjoyment of life depends so much on excitement. But one's preoccupations can't, now, be what they were in the 90's – or even three or two years ago ... At any rate, if you see V., do impress on her with the fact that, short of absence without leave

or cutting parades, I shall always be and am at her disposal. I have the greatest possible affection and esteem for her; there isn't anyone else (but I don't know what she has got into her always romantic head) and I am frightfully sorry that these bad years are such bad years for her.[3]

Ford was being ingenuous when he said that he did not know what Violet had got into her always romantic head. He knew full well that she had heard rumours of his frequenting prostitutes while he was stationed in Rouen, and even uses this incident in *No More Parades*. He was also aware that she knew of his affair with a girl in Wales. And he was quite open about his feelings for Brigit Patmore.

Many of Violet's friends saw clearly that it was simply a question of time before Ford left her for someone else, and they urged her to take the initiative and make the break. Others, including Ezra Pound, felt that the problem was simply that Violet expected too much of Ford. Violet herself began to feel that all Ford looked to her for was money. In July 1916 she instructed her solicitor, Dollymore, to inform Ford that she was withdrawing her financial guarantee. The estrangement that this caused persisted until Ford's next leave in March. She ignored his message that he was going to be in London at the Y.M.C.A., despite Lucy Masterman's advice to the contrary. But she was incapable of leaving the matter alone. She went to a party, got drunk and then phoned Ford. The result was that Ford moved back into South Lodge for the remainder of his leave and their relationship moved into a strange, ambiguous phase.

Violet found that she could not bear to have Ford in the same house with her on the basis of friendship rather than as her lover, despite her intention to do so. During this week and during subsequent periods when they were together she insisted on sharing Ford's bed with the resulting frustration and anger on both sides. There were occasions when Violet's anger took the form of physical violence. One night when she was staying with Ford in Redcar she scratched his face so badly that he had to go on sick leave rather than face the regiment.

Violet was not proud of her rages. In part the development of syphilis was responsible, but Ford's behaviour was such that it would have enraged any woman. When he was away from Violet he would write declaring his undying love for her; but when they were together he was impotent with her, and his explanations and suggestions for improving the situation were deeply hurtful and humiliating to Violet.

On one occasion he told Violet that it was the changes in her that were responsible for their difficulties: if she wanted to attract him, she must be attractive. 'It's the lot of all women!' he declared. Violet brooded over what she must do to make herself attractive to Ford. Her forthright friend Eleanor Jackson told her 'When he told you to make yourself attractive if you wanted to attract him: he didn't mean dye your hair or paint or make love – he doesn't care if you look a hundred, so long as you give him money and make South Lodge pleasant!'[4]

These words must have come to mind at Selsey in October when Ford claimed that 'he couldn't love or think of making love till he was no longer worried to death about money. He is overdrawn.' When Violet suggested that she was prepared to be his financial guarantor once more, Ford was prepared to be kind and loving.

Another line Ford pursued was that he needed more than one woman. He said to Violet, 'If I could have another woman I might desire *you*. I was nice to you in the Brigit time.'

Mutual friends were beginning to say that what Ford needed was a young healthy woman who would give him a baby. Events were to prove how accurate this judgement was.

A new friend whom Violet had made in Ford's absence was Stella Bowen. As we have seen, this young Australian painter, who was sharing a studio with Phillis Reid, had been introduced into the group by Ezra Pound. Ironically enough, Violet's initial feelings towards Stella were of jealousy, but not on account of Ford. Several young men had been attracted to Violet at the very time that she felt that Ford was ready to cast her off for a younger woman. One of these was Arthur Watts, an artist and caricaturist now in uniform, who was twenty years younger than her. In June 1917 he had declared his love for her. Violet's response was ambivalent. On the one hand she considered him far too young, with 'the face of a gnome'; on the other hand she felt in need of all the love she could get. So although she refused to take his attentions seriously at first, she was hurt when she thought Watts was paying court to Stella:

> I felt as if AW and I were married and had got to *that* stage
> of indifference and kind feeling. He is very young and danced
> well. A girl called Stella Bowen came in with Ezra and I was,
> I suppose, a little jealous of her. Yet I could have him. Why
> I would if I liked him physically as well as F – whom I hate
> rather.

That evening she refused to go along with the rest of the
group to Stella's studio, preferring to return home alone.

The affair with Watts fizzled out. Like many young men at
the time he was in a hurry to marry before going off to fight, and
within months he had found a wife. His friendship with Violet was
not affected, and they corresponded once he had left England.

After her initial hostility towards Stella, Violet changed her
mind and sought the younger woman's society. Stella and Phillis
were invited to dinner at South Lodge. Violet took Stella out on
her own to dinner, and even co-hosted a party with the two young
women in their studio. So when Ford clamoured for the society of
young people on his next leave, in October 1917, it seemed natural
for Violet to invite Stella and Phillis to Selsey to provide Ford with
the kind of company he desired. In the event only Stella went.

In his novel *Some Do Not* Ford depicts the end of his relationship with Violet and the beginning of that with Stella. When
Valentine (the Stella figure) meets Sylvia (Violet) for the first time
she forms a favourable impression of the older woman: 'Beautiful!
The most beautiful woman she had ever seen! And good! Kind!
. . . she, Valentine, ought to be ready to lay down her life for
Sylvia Tietjens.'

Stella's view of Violet, which she had formed by seeing her
apart from Ford, changed when she saw the two of them together
at Selsey. She witnessed their terrible rows and their incompatibility. Like Valentine, she had a change of heart, and from then on
her feelings were for Ford rather than Violet:

> The nature of Tietjens' wife occupied her mind. Before she
> had hardly thought about her. She had seemed so unreal; so
> mysterious as to be a myth. Radiant and high stepping like a
> great stag. But she must be cruel! She must be vindictively cruel
> to Tietjens himself, or she could not have revealed his private
> affairs.

In an ominous note in Violet's diary she records that Ford had got an extension of his leave, 'but will spend 24 hrs in London – S. Bowen will stop till Thursday and go with him.'

This last leave that Ford spent at Selsey had proved a complete disaster. Violet had restored good relations with Heron Allen, only to fall out again with him almost immediately over a dispute about burst pipes in the cottage. She had rowed violently with Ford and, despite his subsequent letter saying that the rows had not in 'the least affected his permanent feeling' for Violet, the relationship was at an end. The poem Ford sent to Violet in December, a lyric to Stella, was the final proof that he no longer cared for her.

In her preface to Stella Bowen's autobiography her daughter records her mother's favourite Spanish proverb, one which Ford also appreciated: 'Take what you want, said God, take it, and pay for it.' This is exactly what the two of them proceeded to do.

Violet suffered another severe blow during this difficult time. She had serious nose bleeds while at Selsey, which continued back in London. In November she had an 'electric' examination which revealed that the inside of her nose was disintegrating – another long-term effect of the syphilis. She now knew that Crawfurd had been responsible, and she knew also that she would get worse not better.

Throughout this stressful year René Byles was Violet's constant support. He took her side against Ford and repeatedly urged her to make a clean break with him. When the opportunity came to sell the lease on South Lodge he encouraged Violet to do so, knowing full well that this would speed up the parting. Violet's inability to sell was based on more than her relationship with Ford, as her story 'The Night of No Weather' in More Tales of the Uneasy makes clear. She had so many emotional attachments to her home that she could not imagine herself living anywhere else. It seems likely that it was René Byles with whom Violet was first unfaithful to Ford.

Although fully aware that a break was the only possible outcome, she was incapable of acting on her knowledge. She admitted that by now she neither loved nor respected Ford, but that she had a 'passion' for him. At times she felt that she could accept Ford's living with her at South Lodge without his being her lover, so great was her fear of the alternative – 'loneliness and neglect'. And she acknowledged that she made excessive demands on him: 'But I must come to see that I have not been so very good to Ford that he must be eternally grateful. He paid as he went along in caresses.' She felt herself to be 'a queer side-bone' of Ford, utterly dominated by him.

Regrettable as was Violet's sexual dependence on Ford, she was not the only intelligent woman to be so reduced. Some years later, when Ford had left England and was living in Paris with Stella Bowen, he established a similar relationship with the young impoverished writer, Jean Rhys. He went so far as to have her live in the house along with his wife and daughter. In *Quartet* Jean Rhys depicts through her central characters the sexual obsession and subsequent misery that she, like Violet, experienced in her relationship with Ford. She describes her central character's state of mind when her lover leaves her, in terms which could be applied without change to Violet: 'For perhaps thirty seconds she was able to keep her mind a blank; then her obsession gripped her, arid, torturing, gigantic, possessing her as utterly as the longing for water possesses someone who is dying of thirst.

In December 1917 Violet sent Ford birthday presents but when he invited her to attend the regiment's New Year ball in Redcar she refused. She did not join him for Christmas either, although she spent time with his sister and brother-in-law. On New Year's Eve she went to a party, dancing with friends.

Ford wrote in January, saying 'I suppose then our relations are at an end. I am very sorry, but I suppose it had to be.' Violet answered by agreeing with him.

She put the final seal on the break when Ford had some leave at the end of the month. Although she allowed him to stay at South Lodge, she herself went off and stayed with Ford's mother while he was in town. In her diary of the time she wrote 'F never forgave me for going to Mrs H's while he was on leave. That did it finally.' But looking back on this entry with the benefit of hindsight she saw that it was not her actions which had brought about the break. After the above words she added later, 'Did it? It was Stella – the new passion.'

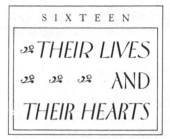

ᴐᵉ THEIR LIVES

ᴐᵉ ᴐᵉ ᴐᵉ AND

THEIR HEARTS

Miserable as Violet was at the break-up of her relationship with Ford, she turned the time when she was separated from him to good account and wrote her first frankly autobiographical novel, *Their Lives*. Just as her misery at the end of her affair with Crawfurd had stimulated her into writing her best novels to date, so too her unhappiness at this time was creative so far as her work was concerned.

Although *Their Hearts* was not published until some time later, in 1921, the two novels are so closely related that it makes good sense to consider them together. Taken together, they form a fictional account of Violet's own life. But they are not simply autobiographical novels; they are primarily carefully crafted fictions and their value as such is not diminished if the reader has no knowledge whatsoever of Violet Hunt's life.

In the interest of achieving particular emphases the events of the novels are put into a different time frame from the events in Violet's life. It would be impossible to date anything in the life with accuracy from the novels.

In her review of *Their Lives*, Rebecca West noted the relationship between Violet's work and that of Jane Austen. That relationship is especially important in these two novels. Violet focuses closely on the everyday lives of three sisters. There is very little mention of or reference to larger social and political events unless they directly affect that everyday life; and, like Jane Austen, Violet focuses on marriage and its central position in a woman's life. But, as noted earlier, Violet Hunt's perspective is of necessity quite different from that of Jane Austen. She is fully aware that conventions and attitudes are being applied to a society which they will no longer fit. Again Rebecca West pinpoints the crucial distinction when she says of Mrs Radmall that 'She was characteristic of an age when people neither lived according to the wisdom of strong instincts, nor elaborated a system of beautiful manners to compensate for the weakness of their instincts.'[1]

The women in these novels occupy a no-man's-land between the world of Jane Austen and the world Rebecca West herself lived in. It is significant that when Violet published these novels

143

she was looking back on the time of her youth from wartime and later. The war had made the lives of younger women very different from her own. One of the objectives of the novels is to dramatise the plight of the women of Violet's generation and to explain and perhaps justify the manner in which her own life had developed.

The three sisters of the novels are three very different personalities, but marriage is a central preoccupation in all three lives. The fact that such different women should all share this preoccupation shows how impossible it was for a woman of that generation to avoid the common obsession.

Their Lives is written largely from the point of view of Christina, the oldest of the sisters and the Violet figure. Because she is precociously intelligent and desirous of excitement and even of independence, the restrictions imposed on her as a female are hard to bear. Rebecca West accurately summarised the difficulties facing a girl such as Christina:

> There was no escape from this inadequate society into intellectual activities, for the pre-Raphaelite and the aesthetic movements described here with such gentle malice had nothing more to do with a woman than to put her on a brocade settee with a sunflower. So all a girl could do was to sit in the 'Trust' position till a husband was given one, and one could drop into the happy relaxation of 'Paid For'.[2]

Even as very young children Christina and Virgilia begin their rivalry for a husband when they both propose to the Professor, the fictionalised version of John Ruskin.

Christina then embarks upon a series of relationships. She is first wooed by Philip Wynyard. She likes his mind and he likes hers. In the world of Jane Austen there would have been the basis for a marriage in their mutual respect. But Philip Wynyard is not a hero from Jane Austen. He is not rich enough to marry unless he can find a wife with enough money for them both. When he does meet a rich girl he ceases to pay attention to Christina – so in her very first relationship with a man she learns that marriage is as much as anything else a commercial transaction. In this way she is taught to make a distinction between love and marriage, and for a while she seeks only the excitement of love in affairs with men whom she could not possibly marry, either because they are too young or too old or already married. She causes her family great distress by turning down a most eligible suitor without consulting her parents. Even one of her lovers becomes worried that their relationship is almost certainly diminishing her value in the marriage market.

Only when Virgilia becomes engaged is Christina pulled up short and realises that she is not altogether attracted to the prospect of life as a single woman. So, against her true instincts, 'henceforth she relentlessly, clumsily, inefficiently pursued the unmarried.'

Her efforts to free herself from the patterns imposed upon women by writing for the press are only marginally successful, as Mrs Radmall is quick to point out:

> She revenged herself for her odiously sheltered position by writing every week about 'Revolting Daughters' and 'The New and the Newer Woman'. She insisted that she herself was a New Woman. Mrs Radmall mockingly said that Editors knew better, and that she would not have had more or less everything she wrote accepted, if she had really been that undesirable product of disaffected womanhood.

Mrs Radmall knows only too well what men expect of women. She is prepared to play the role assigned to her, but she maintains the view that 'Men, the best of them, were dangerous animals, and a little of them went a long way.'

This cynical view of the relationships between men and women underlies all that Virgilia does. Her principal objective is to marry well. She is clear that her virginity has a market value and she is, therefore, prepared to present herself as the Ice Maiden to potential husbands. In her relationships with other men, such as John Dempster Blenkinsop, whom she has no intention of marrying, she is far more physically available than her apparently fast sister Christina. Virgilia is never afraid of hypocrisy if it helps her to get what she wants.

The issues raised in *Their Lives* are explored in greater depth in *Their Hearts*. The earlier novel deals with the upbringing of the three girls; *Their Hearts* shows how this shapes their subsequent lives.

Virgilia finds it easy to meet the demands of society and to obey the rules of the sexual game without in any way violating her nature. She has complete control over herself, and knows exactly when to give and when to hold back. She knows what she wants and how to get it. She is never upset by double standards, even when confronted by them. When she declares categorically that she would never entertain a man who lived with a woman who was not his wife, her friend brings up Ser Giove, a fashionable painter who is well known for his affairs. Virgilia has decided that he is sufficiently important to her socially for her to ignore his irregular affairs, and she directs her anger not against him but against the girl, who was not prepared to leave the truth unsaid.

She applies a double standard to her own behaviour. She flirts with John Blenkinsop and is not unwilling to be alone with him at night in a house in which all the other adults are asleep. But once her engagement to Marmaduke Hall has been announced she insists on being chaperoned by Christina to all her meetings with him.

Appropriately enough, *Their Hearts* begins with a wedding – Virgilia's. Everything that the girls have ever been taught has been in preparation for achieving this goal. There is some uneasiness about whether the educational process has been entirely successful, for, if all had gone according to plan, the first wedding should have been that of the oldest daughter, Christina, a fact of which she is made painfully aware.

Christina, however, cannot so easily adapt to the role assigned to her as a woman in that society. She is confused by the conflict between her need to conform and her need to use her intelligence to acquire independence, not a husband. If she is to follow the journalistic career on which she has already embarked, she cannot always be chaperoned in the way that a girl seeking marriage should be. Once she earns some money she acquires a freedom of movement denied to her sisters. She is the only one of the three sisters who demands and gets the key to the door of the parental home.

The independence she has achieved so far is, however, limited. She is still dependent on her parents for a roof over her head: she is unable to maintain even a modest establishment of her own. Her independent life does not fit well with life at home with her parents. Christina has to resort to all kinds of stratagems and deceits to maintain a balance between the two. When Orinthia deplores her lies she justifies herself by blaming her basic lack of freedom. She retorts 'It's what Ulysses did. It's only being an opportunist.' Interestingly, Christina has to use a male for her role model; in her society there are no satisfactory females upon whom she can model herself.

Yet for all her bravado, Christina is not altogether sure she has taken the right path. Her upbringing has sufficiently affected her to make her feel that she too would like to have a husband, to come first with someone, to have a home of her own – even though she has come to believe that the love she passionately desires is not to be found in the kind of marriage she observes and can expect to make. She accepts, half mockingly, what Virgilia has to say on the subject:

> 'No passion without a proposal, eh?' jibed Christina.
> 'My dear child, I suppose when one talks of love, one usually means the kind that leads to marriage. And marriage is generally introduced by a proposal, or ought to be, in our class. You don't seem to realise that, with a man, making love and proposing are a different pair of shoes. You will go confounding them and get neither!'

For a while she tests Virgilia's wisdom and falls in with Virgilia's match-making schemes. But all the while she is as much an observer as a participant:

> It was a plot to make her leave Bohemia for society, Christina knew, and considered the scheme on its merits. Two quite different lives were open to her, she had a foot in both worlds . . . The 'roses and raptures' of the Bohemian restaurant gave zest to the 'lilies and languors' of parties like Virgilia's.

Orinthia, the youngest sister, is the most devastating comment on a Victorian upbringing. She does not have Virgilia's single-minded strength of character and ability to zero in on what she wants. Nor does she have Christina's good looks, intelligence, talent and confidence. She has been the least loved of the daughters and the least educated. She is the sister who is made most vulnerable and who is most damaged by the Radmall family.

She has learnt from her mother that the man of the house is the most important member of the household, and that the lives of his womenfolk must be sacrificed if necessary to his comfort and well-being. Although she is slightly annoyed during her first pregnancy that her mother still puts Papa first, when her father is dying she abandons her own child and her husband and, despite the imminence of a second pregnancy, insists on being with her parents. The lesson of putting father first is so well learnt that Orinthia has great difficulty in transferring her allegiance to her husband from her father. There is a suggestion of incestuous feelings as Orinthia travels home from her honeymoon: 'She was now assured that Papa was the kind of man she could have just tolerated as a lover . . . Did fathers ever fall in love with daughters?' This suggestion is reinforced in the depiction of Orinthia's pleasure in sleeping in her mother's bed in the room next to her dead father.

Orinthia knows that she can never be the most important person in her father's life. She sees Virgilia with Dukie and Christina involved in passionate if unconventional love affairs. Even the strangely sexed Marjorie, John Dempster's sister, has a fiancé. So she obeys the instinct nurtured by her mother's training and seeks a man on whom to bestow the affection no one else appears to want. In this way she begins a relationship with John Dempster:

> She sighed for the merging of her scant thought with that of another, not necessarily a lover . . . Yet only a lover attends to what you say, and even then only at the height of his passion . . . She chose the nearest thing to Prince Charming that came her way . . . the eldest son of the house.

As a child and even as a young woman Orinthia is totally and humiliatingly financially dependent. It is only at Christina's prompting that Mrs Radmall buys Orinthia new clothes – there is no question of her being given money to buy them herself. The situation does not change when Orinthia is married. She has no money of her own at all. When her doctor presents a bill while her husband is away she makes a childish muddle of trying to pay him with a cheque drawn on her husband's account.

All her life Orinthia is impressed by the fact that looks are very important in gaining a suitor and keeping him. She is also made to understand as a child that she does not meet Mrs Radmall's expectations in terms of her looks. So once she is a woman and is suddenly attractive she becomes vain and careful of her looks, even to the point of insisting on tightly-laced stays to disguise what she considers to be the ugly bulk of her pregnancy. The warnings of her doctor and Christina go unheeded.

Ignorance is partly to blame for Orinthia's foolish attitude. She has only the vaguest of notions about what to expect on her wedding night, for example: 'She had mixed Grace Colvin's hints with Middleton Rowe's lectures and was puzzled to death by it all. She wasn't so much afraid of pain as of suggested inroads in her personal delicacies and fastidiousness.' She thinks she can avoid having a child simply by will-power, and it takes the unmarried Christina to perceive that she is pregnant. The confirmatory examination by a doctor is a deep humiliation for her.

When her labour begins she is totally unprepared. She has learnt by now that her mother cannot or will not help her, so she sends for her cook, a young woman who has recently had an illegitimate child: 'Mamma's experience was too long back, and besides, no one ever asked her things. Carrie's disaster was fairly recent. Perhaps Carrie could tell her how to avoid the pain, how to do without having the baby at all.'

Violet Hunt's exploration of the effects on girls of keeping them in ignorance about sexual matters is frank, and this frankness is a new departure in fiction written by women. Most of the novel is written from Orinthia's point of view. Because her mother has refused to educate her, and because she has always implied some disgust about the physical relations between men and women, Orinthia is obsessed with sex. This morbid obsession finds expression in two ways. First of all the incident with the man on the beach*

---

*Orinthia had been left temporarily in the care of two maiden aunts who had left her very much to her own devices. Bored and lonely she had struck up an acquaintance with an elderly man who made much of her; bought her ice-creams and called her his 'little girl'. Orinthia was charmed by his attentions but told no one about him.

One day he took her onto the beach and it was there while he was exposing himself to her that the pair were found by a shocked and frightened housemaid who rushed Orinthia home and reported the incident to her employers. There was so much fuss but so little of substance was actually said that for a long time Orinthia feared that the mere sight of a man's penis could have been enough to make her pregnant.

is kept constantly before us by references to the aunt with whom she had been staying at the time. Even Virgilia's wedding is linked to the episode, because the death of Great-Aunt Eliza threatens a postponement of the wedding. A balancing motif is provided by the repeated appearances of Middleton Rowe, the young man who had seen it as his responsibility to lecture the Radmall girls on basic female physiology.

But the most striking feature of the novel is the way in which Orinthia's obsession means that she sees everything she experiences in terms of sexuality. Virgilia's wedding inevitably leads her into a meditation on love and marriage. But, though basically ignorant, she is not romantic. The image which pervades her mind is that of the young woman whose husband left her the morning after the wedding and refused to acknowledge as his the daughter who is born later. Orinthia knows that something dreadful and nasty lies behind this story, but she cannot fathom out what. A series of young women who have 'got into trouble' interest her. Once again she observes the disgrace but is not sure of its basis. She looks for enlightenment from her married sister but Virgilia too wishes to keep the dark and apparently dirty secret from her. She knows that Christina has fathomed the mystery and she attributes this to all the reading, especially of French novels, that she has done. She determines 'to let her daughters, if she had any, read what they liked. With her sons she would be far more particular.'

It is a worthy notion, but we see how unlikely it is to be carried out. For one of the most devastating conclusions that the novel leads us to is that Orinthia will not learn from her own miserable experience and treat her own daughter differently. Once she is a mother she begins to behave in the same way that her own mother had behaved towards her. She does not breast-feed her baby. She looks upon it coldly, with no physical affection, and is content to leave others to look after the child even when it is sick, because she regards it as more important to be with her father.

Their Hearts is not an optimistic novel. It may begin with a wedding, but it ends with a funeral. The one sister who has stood out for independence feels her solitary and unmarried state most painfully. The biblical implications of the final passage do not give the conclusion of the novel a hopeful note: 'For, frankly weeping, tottering a little, leaning on the arms of love that was not disallowed, her two sisters had suffered their husbands to lead them away into the wilderness.'

The best summary of the effectiveness and achievement of Violet Hunt's fictions was provided by her closest friend, May Sinclair:

> If you care for nothing but beauty, beauty of subject, beauty of form and pattern, beauty of technique, you will not care for the novels of Violet Hunt. But to the lover of austere truth telling, who would rather see things as they sometimes are than as they are not and cannot be, who prefer a natural ugliness to artificial and sentimental beauty, they will appeal by their sincerity, their unhesitating courage, their incorruptible reality.[3]

SEVENTEEN

ALONE

Had Violet known about the relationship Ford had established with Stella Bowen, she might have acted differently. But she did not know that he was already writing love letters to the younger woman, that she was visiting him in Redcar, and the two had planned to set up in a country cottage once Ford had left the Army.

For a while Ford and Stella were careful to keep their secret. Not only did Ford, with justification, fear the violence of Violet's reaction to his new relationship, but Stella was also afraid that her brother Tom, then on leave in London, would find out about the affair and have the family summon her back to Australia. Tom regarded himself as the head of the family and responsible for Stella's well being. He would not have looked favourably upon her liaison with an older and impoverished man.

As a result, when Ford left the army in 1919 he did not immediately join Stella but took a single room in London. His choice of location at 20A Campden Hill Gardens, close to South Lodge, was surely provocative – as too was his appearance. He dressed in old rags and looked little better than a tramp. He was clearly signalling to the world that Violet had abandoned him

151

and left him in a poverty-stricken state, and was trying to ensure that their friends' sympathy would be directed towards him as the wronged party.

The arrangements for setting up with Stella were made with as much secrecy as Ford's trip to France with Violet had been. There were some people, such as his agent, Pinker, to whom he had to give his new address, but he swore them all to secrecy. He told Violet nothing of what he was planning, but made arrangements for her close friend Ethel Colburn Mayne to present her with a *fait accompli* once he had left London. As a final gesture towards the new life he proposed to lead he changed his name from Ford Hermann Hueffer to Ford Madox Ford. His German phase was thus at an end, and Violet's claims to be Mrs Hueffer would be of no further consequence to him.

In June 1919 Ford left London for Red Ford Cottage in Pulborough, Sussex. It was characteristic of him that he should write to such close friends as the Mastermans announcing his new name and his new address at the same time as putting the blame for the break upon Violet and failing to mention that his new love was already established at his new address. He wrote to Masterman as follows:

> I don't want to bother you with my reasons for doing this, further than by saying that, at the beginning of the year, I gave Violet the choice between my leaving South Lodge or her giving up the acquaintanceship of certain people whom I regarded as my enemies . . . Violet's course seemed to me to be so radical a disloyalty to any form of joint life that I saw no other way open than to retire the scene.[1]

Violet was devastated by the news of Ford's defection. Although she had just ended her relationship with him, she had done so several times before and then resumed it. She could have better accepted a final break had there not been another woman involved. But the fact that Ford had set up house with Stella made it clear to her how irrevocable the break was this time.

It was a great humiliation to be left for a younger woman, although she had feared this possibility for some years. And what now was the status of the marriage they had together proclaimed to the world? How could she face her social life as an abandoned woman? She had done very well without Ford throughout the war, but everyone had known that he was there in the background.

Her first desperate response was to insist that he should not abandon her altogether. She claimed that he owed her some of his time, and that he should continue to visit her regularly and to host parties with her at South Lodge. It is a measure of how bad a conscience Ford had about his behaviour that he initially agreed to Violet's demands. He explained his position in a letter to Masterman: 'In order to spare Violet the mortification of the appearance of an official abandonment, I shall figure at her larger parties from time to time – as, for instance, on Monday next. I don't like doing it, but I take it to be a duty.'[2]

The result of this agreement was a very strange party. Alec Waugh was present and he gave the following account of the occasion to Douglas Goldring, who reproduced his letter in *South Lodge*:

> Has anyone told you about a curious party Violet gave in July 1919? I only realised later the dramatic undertones. (I had dined with them at South Lodge in January '19 where I met W.L. George for the first time, and knew nothing about their having parted.) I heard later that by July 1919 they were apart but that Violet wanted there to be a public occasion when they could appear together. It was one of the biggest parties I have ever been to – champagne, white ties, etc. I got there a little early and Violet kept saying 'I wonder what's keeping Ford. I wish he'd hurry.' When eventually he did arrive it was to moon around looking very lost. He did not seem to know if he was a guest or host. He appeared surprised when I went to say 'goodbye' and 'thank you'. I suppose it was their last public bow. It certainly was a party.

This occasion, however, did not reconcile Violet to her loss. For a while she was almost insane with desperation and frustration. She drafted numerous letters to Ford berating him for his betrayal of her and insisting on her rights. Fortunately she usually showed these letters to close friends, of whom Edgar Jepson was one, and was dissuaded from sending them. Perhaps the satisfaction of putting her side of the matter before friends was enough. She visited Juliet

Soskice and Ford's mother, and poured out her grievances to them. Most strangely, she visited Elsie Hueffer, as if at last she understood what Elsie had suffered at Ford's hands.

When, in 1920, Ford moved to Bedham in Sussex – where he and Stella stayed for a while at Scamell's Farm until their new home was ready – Violet got wind of his address. Together with May Sinclair, she turned up in the village and watched him as he went about his work, much to the distress of both Ford and Stella. Ford wrote to Pound describing the situation from his point of view on the 30th of August:

> I am getting along with the *Dial* article – with interruptions from Violet who has planted herself in the neighbourhood and runs about interrupting my workmen and generally making things lively. I fancy she had you followed by a detective when you came down and so got the address. But I may be wrong about that.[3]

Violet did not stop at visiting Ford. When she returned to London she persuaded the wife of the carpenter who was working for Ford to send her regular reports on her 'husband' in return for a small payment. It was in this way she learned that on 29 November Stella had given birth to a daughter.

Gradually Violet settled into life as a single woman once again. She was now fifty-seven. After the failure of all her other affairs she had quickly flung herself into a new one. But the pattern was not repeated this time. She was sadly aware that she was losing her looks as a result of ageing, syphilis and her earlier use of arsenic for her complexion. The hair of which she was so proud was thinning – one of the side effects of syphilis – and she had to have scalp massages. But the main reason why she did not embark on a new affair was that she was still emotionally involved with Ford. She had spoken only too truly when she had written in her diary for 1917, 'I have . . . an unholy passion that will last till I die.'

She made several efforts through her friends to persuade Ford to visit her but he was firm in his refusal to do so. Then, in 1922, he and Stella with their baby daughter set off for Paris. He was never to live permanently in England again. Violet kept track of his movements and, as the epilogue to *I Have This To Say* makes plain, she was never completely reconciled to losing him. She always retained a hope that he would see the error of his ways and return to her at last.

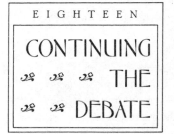

EIGHTEEN

CONTINUING
    THE
   DEBATE

Although by 1920 Violet's 'flurried years', with all their pains and pleasures, were over, their effects eddied on. Violet and Ford did not meet again once he had left for Paris, but the dialogue and the disputes between the two of them were to continue in their published works.

In 1924 Ford published *Some Do Not*, the first of his four novels which were to be collected under the title 'Parade's End'. When Violet first read this work she must have experienced both dismay and pleasure. She would have been pleased that Sylvia Tietjens, who is largely modelled on her, is the wife of the hero Christopher Tietjens: it was better to be a fictional wife than no wife at all. The description of her beauty and her power over men would also have been flattering to her ego. What would have dismayed her was to find so many incidents of the last years presented in a way that put her in a very bad light.

Mercilessly Ford describes Violet's affair with Crawfurd from his perspective, and with no element of the sentimentality with which Violet was prone to regard it: 'She had certainly been taken advantage of, after champagne, by a married man called Drake. A bit of a brute she acknowledged him now to be. But after the event passion had developed; intense on her side and quite intense enough on his.'

He takes his revenge for all those scenes of physical violence to which Violet had subjected him, especially when he was stationed in the Army at Redcar, by reproducing one in his novel:

> Being near Tietjens she lifted her plate, which contained two cold cutlets in aspic and several leaves of salad; she wavered a little to one side and, with a circular motion of her hand, let the whole contents fly at Tietjens' head. She placed the plate on the table and drifted slowly towards the enormous mirror over the fireplace.

155

'I'm bored,' she said. 'Bored! Bored!'

And Ford's resentment at Violet's friendship with the wealthy Monds comes out in Tietjens' relief that he need spend 'no more weekends with Sylvia in the mansions of the Chosen People'.

What must have distressed Violet most was Ford's accurate depiction of her mental attitude towards him in the last few years of their relationship:

> 'You want to know why I hate my husband. I'll tell you; it's because of his simple, sheer immorality. I don't mean his actions; his views. Every speech he utters about everything makes me – I swear it makes me – in spite of myself, want to stick a knife into him, and I can't prove he's wrong, not ever, about the simplest thing. But I can pain him. And I will . . .'

The year after Ford published *Some Do Not*, Violet published *More Tales of the Uneasy*. It is not as closely related to the first volume of short stories as the title might suggest. Significantly, it is altogether more autobiographical and it has an uncharacteristically long preface, in which Violet describes writing techniques in a way that is new for her. In discussing the work of the modernist writers of the younger generation in relation to her own, she is challenging Ford at his own game. He was the acknowledged expert on the style of their young friends.

Most of the stories in this collection are longer than their predecessors. She has consciously chosen a new form, even though she realises that 'it is ever so difficult today for the modern author to write up to this specification, confronted with the terrible expansion of the modern mind and its wide and stormy outlook, its millions or so more facets to consider and moods to chronicle.'

She takes as her model Rodin's head of Balzac, and sets out to achieve stories in which 'the motif is chiselled with every care and refinement so that a certain looseness and indefiniteness can be allowed to prevail round the central knot of interest.'

She achieves all she had aimed at in the last story in the collection, 'The Corsican Sisters', which is keenly observed and keeps the reader in a state of uneasiness from start to finish. Her description of a particular quality of the Pre-Raphaelite paintings with which both she and Ford were so familiar can be applied with relevance to this story which leads us

> to realise the mysteries of romance in terms of every day, subconsciously aware of the psychological fact that the merest irrelevant detail lingers in the mind and takes root there when the state of exaltation in which some form of spiritual vision has been granted departs, and fixes it there for a sign.

The story is based on the lives of Marguerite and Reine Dausoignes, the two girls who had been taken to England from Corsica by Margaret Hunt, and it deals with the discoveries which Violet made when she and Ford went to Vivario during their exile in 1913. Ford was very unhappy at the time: he did not like Corsica, and made his dislike felt. All this appears in the story. Is it a measure of Violet's frustration with Ford at this time that the character based on him meets a violent end?

In this same year, 1925, Ford continued his attack with the publication of *No More Parades*, the second volume in the Tietjens quartet. Violet can have found little to please her in this novel beyond a recognition of what had made her relationship with Ford go wrong. Tietjens says 'Our differences were caused by ... differences of temperament. She, as you say, is a beautiful and reckless woman. Reckless in an admirable way.'

For the rest, her fictional counterpart Sylvia is described by her husband as 'without mitigation a whore', a woman who is capable of 'hating ... slowly and coldly'. Tietjens' description of his married life is surely how Ford had come to view his last troubled years with Violet: 'She had lived for years beside him, apparently on terms of hatred and miscomprehension ... Then, during the tenuous, lugubrious small hours, before his coming out there again to France, she had given evidence of a madly vindictive passion for his person. A physical passion at any rate.' How well Ford knew Violet!

He even turns Violet's pride in her Pre-Raphaelite appearance against her: 'There's a picture that my mother's got, by Burne-Jones ... A cruel-looking woman with a distant smile ... some vampire ... *La belle Dame sans Merci*. That's what you're like.' Ford's choice of this painting to make his point is particularly telling, since it is the same one that Christina broods upon in *Their Lives* – the last work of Violet's with which Ford had any close contact.

It was in the context of these exchanges in print that Violet published not a fictional account of her years with Ford, but her autobiography.

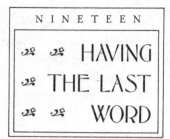

NINETEEN

◦ ◦ HAVING

◦ THE LAST

◦ ◦ WORD

It was in 1926 that Violet published *The Flurried Years* in London with Hurst and Blackett. By the time she came to publish *I Have This to Say: The Story of My Flurried Years* with Boni and Liveright later that same year in New York she had had a chance to reflect on reactions to the English publication. The American edition differs in several major ways from the English one and, because it includes so much more, this chapter will concentrate upon it.

Inevitably, the book raised a great deal of dust. Violet had known and still knew too many established figures about whom she is not always respectful or discreet. Her friends and acquaintances were divided between those who admired her courage and those who deplored the laying bare of old wounds. It was, above all, a great embarrassment to Ford. He was in the States when it was published there, and for a while he would not deal with Boni and Liveright because of their involvement with Violet. His anger at Rebecca West's outspoken defence of Violet's book effectively ended what remained of his friendship with her.

Then there were those who questioned the 'facts' revealed in the book and who accused Violet of deliberate and gross inaccuracies. Douglas Goldring, for example, shows some embarrassment when he comes to discuss it in *South Lodge*. Goldring remained a loyal friend to Violet to the end of her days, and his reaction is indicative of a general misreading of the book which has persisted until today. Goldring values the book as 'a fascinating human document which sheds light on a social system in the last stages of decay'. He admires the 'full length portraits of men and women who achieved fame and are not likely to be forgotten . . . the thumbnail sketches of a crowd of minor characters in whom the author contrives to waken our interest.' His conclusion about its importance is that 'Its most valuable quality, however, apart from its importance to literary historians of the future, is the reflection it gives us of the enormous power exercised by the Victorian conventions up till August 1914.'

In other words, like most other writers and critics, he treats the book as a document of social history rather than as an example of the very different genre of autobiography. In fact, he criticises it for something which is, and is intended to be, its very essence. He says 'she told – *naturally from her own standpoint* [my emphasis] – as much of the story of her affaire with Ford and the resulting matrimonial imbroglio as the laws of libel would permit.'

The Flurried Years and *I Have This To Say* are not social history, literary criticism or art criticism, although they contain elements of all these. They are rather two versions of an autobiography, and as such are only of value in as far as they are written 'from her own standpoint'. The very title of the American edition, with its emphasis on the words 'I' and 'my', asserts that the book is to be read as an autobiography, with all that the genre implies.

It is perhaps because the books succeed so well in depicting the years 1908–1915 and those people who impinged on Violet's life during those years that they have been read in terms of a form they do not pretend to be – and this despite the fact that Violet makes clear how well aware she is of the limitations of her books as purely historical documents:

> Yes, I know they are puzzling, my great white silences, and that there are the absurdest lacunas in my narration of the things that impressed me, the things that depressed me as they fell in the course of the flurried years 1908–1914. I am aware that there *are* the most distracting contradictions .here and there and that 'in many places the text, as it stands, *is* confusing.' I am aware that 'the lawsuits are *not* lucidly explained' and that 'conditions that led to certain legal situations are *not* clear without such explanations.'

Those same critics who point to flaws in Violet's historical accuracy are nevertheless eager to make use of those parts of the book which bring alive situations and people. Even so, a

159

careful reading shows the autobiographies to be quite different from Goldring's description of books in which Violet 'released her pent-up emotions and distraught nerves in a long, intensely personal, rather incoherent but eminently 'human' book, called *The Flurried Years*'.

I Have This To Say and *The Flurried Years* are, in fact, very carefully structured works of art which show a clear awareness in both form and content of the nature of autobiography. Violet was quite capable of writing autobiographical novels, as *Sooner or Later*, *Their Lives* and *Their Hearts*, made clear but she did not write of the years 1908–1915 in novel form for particular reasons connected with the very nature of autobiography.

Roy Pascal describes autobiography as

> not so much a remembrance of the past as poetic re-enactment and creation, that is, a new creative experience of the author, whereby he grasps himself in a new way, shapes and re-shapes himself anew. The reader does not merely take in historical facts, but participates in an integrated succession of experiences.[1]

This description of the nature of autobiography is a good starting point for an examination of Violet Hunt's experiments in that form.

By the time *The Flurried Years* was published it was ten years since Ford had left Violet. By then a good deal of the raw pain and hysteria were over. Ford no longer lived in England, and his relationship with Stella Bowen had been long since established. So what this account of their time together represents is not Violet's attempt to take her revenge on Ford for his abandonment of her, but rather her attempt to recreate those days so that others might understand the reasons for her actions. More importantly, she is trying to understand herself and what had happened to her. It is towards this end that the autobiographies are patterned and focused in the way they are.

Although the books are about a crucial eight years in Violet's life and in society at large, they do not consist of a ragbag of everything that happened to Violet during those years, nor do they exclude events and people from earlier stages of her life. There is a readily observable pattern in the selection of material for inclusion: everything that is included throws light on Violet's relationship with Ford and on the nature of a society which had neither truly abandoned Victorian values nor fully accepted the new moral standards that were to prevail during and after the war. Both Violet and her society were in the process of undergoing important changes.

The many references to Violet's childhood, for example, are carefully selected. Some are to do with the Pre-Raphaelite background she shared with Ford. Others point out a relationship to the German language and to Germany itself which reached back to her early years. For example, she tells of her parents' visit to Germany to see an eye specialist before they were married, refers to *Grimms' Fairy Tales*, which her mother translated and which were her childhood reading, and mentions her German nursery maid, Milly from Paderborn, who made her into a 'good little German'.

The effect of these carefully chosen recollections of childhood is to build up the suggestion that everything in her life was leading her towards an inevitable relationship with Ford and subsequently with Germany. In the light of inevitability she can better understand why she became so involved with Ford, and why she readily accepted the idea of becoming a German citizen.

This is not the only way in which she tries to understand her relationship to Ford and why she took on the burden she eventually found herself bearing. Ford is just one of many writers and artists to be mentioned in the autobiographies. There are writers of an older generation, such as W.H. Hudson, Henry James, Thomas Hardy, John Galsworthy; some contemporaries of Ford, such as H.G. Wells, Conrad, Bennett; and younger writers, such as Lawrence and Pound. Violet seeks to establish through this context of great men with whom Ford was intimate that Ford too was a great writer, indeed a genius. For if she can establish this for herself and for her reader, then her succumbing to Ford, the unhappily married man, becomes a matter not simply of seeking to achieve her own end of the excitement of a love affair followed by respectability and marriage: it becomes a matter of saving a genius for posterity. This objective also explains her detailed account of some of Ford's writing and her generous assessment of a novel for which she provided the model and which shows her in a far from kindly light. She is, in her autobiographies, consciously putting art first and excusing a good deal in its interests. To avoid any sense

161

of special pleading on Ford's behalf, she shows how both she and Ford put aside their middle-aged scruples and comfort and whole-heartedly supported the younger artists such as Wyndham Lewis, Jacob Epstein and Gaudier-Brzeska, despite not fully understanding their work.

Because she sacrificed so much for Ford, she is intent not only on seeing it as an important gesture towards the preservation of an artist but also as the prime relationship of her life. As we know from her other writings, Violet had no reservations about speaking and writing of her many love affairs. But mention of these is curiously absent from the two autobiographies. It is true that she mentions the fact that Oscar Wilde had proposed to her, but the effect of this is to suggest that she was saving herself for a greater genius. She mentions several times that a former lover – Crawfurd – had died recently, but again she uses this to illuminate her susceptibility to Ford. She is suggesting that, since her capacity for passion expired with the man who had first inspired it, in this new relationship she is able to be a generous support, the one who gives, rather than a woman needing desperately to be loved. The particular and highly selective way in which she refers to this earlier important love affair is shown clearly by her never mentioning that the woman she selected as her chaperone in Germany, the Countess, or Lita Brown, had in fact ousted her in Crawfurd's affections and become his wife. If this autobiography were the only evidence available, it would be possible to suppose that Crawfurd was still involved with Violet when he died. Her affair with Boughton is equally carefully handled. Boughton is mentioned several times as a renowned art-ist, and his cynical attitude to marriage is quoted. But there is no suggestion that Violet knew him other than socially. The desire to focus on her relationship with Ford is further emphasised by the mention of other lovers as being just good friends – such as Somerset Maugham and H.G. Wells.

These omissions should not be regarded as dishonesty but as a necessary feature of the autobiographical form. Pascal says that 'those autobiographers who have taken their task seriously have recognised that for their purpose *they have to be reticent about whole aspects of their life in the interest of their task*'[2] (the emphasis is mine).

By carefully focusing on her relationship with Ford, Violet

achieves an emotional truth rather than a series of historically accurate facts. For there can be no question but that she came to see her time with Ford as the focal point of her life. And not only did Violet see these eight years with Ford as being special for her but as of great importance in the social and artistic life of London, and an entity with particular and unique characteristics. This sense of a time irrevocably lost is common to most autobiographies since the nineteenth century.

There are several ways in which Violet shows how she has come to see the eight years as being clearly marked off from what went before and what came afterwards. At the very beginning of both autobiographies the mention of Ford as a soldier reveals that the writer is looking back to a lost time, and to that war which was to make an end of the 'flurried years'. What marks the beginning of this special time is the launching of *The English Review*. Because this coincided with the beginning of Violet's relationship with Ford, the interconnection between what was happening in the larger world and what was happening to Violet personally is firmly established.

The publication of *The English Review* symbolised a coming together of artists and the creation of an artistic community in Kensington during the period 1908–14. Not only was Violet carried along by the burst of artistic energy, but so was everyone else she knew in that Kensington group – which is why the autobiographies pay such close attention to the artists and the artistic movements which were taking place round them. One of the remarkable aspects of this flowering was that it bridged generations and social classes in a new way – just as, at South Lodge, Violet entertained the eighteen-year-old firebrand Rebecca West along with established older writers such as W.H. Hudson and Henry James. Standing between two generations, she and Ford could appreciate both Thomas Hardy and Wyndham Lewis. It is no accident that Violet pays special attention to Vorticism and all it represented, for she clearly feels that the kind of fever pitch to which this movement brought all the artists she knew was reflected in her own life. She says, quoting Wyndham Lewis's summary of Vorticism, '"And there, at the point of concentration is The Vorticist" – in the boiling middle of things, as I used to say.' She makes the connection even more specific when she writes 'Well, Vorticism is a meet name for the flicker of a *genre* that flourished just before the appearance in the world of the Maelstrom of woe that sucked us all down in its vortex. It coincided with my own smash, with Joseph Leopold's.' What amounted to the real end of her affair with Ford in August 1914 is marked in the autobiographies by an account of Wyndham Lewis hastening away from Scotland to take his part in the war.

It was not only in the artistic community that changes were taking place that made a distinct gap between the Victorians and the Edwardians. Within society at large there was the burning Woman Question. The vote was not the only issue. Should and could women play a more decisive role in society? Should women be judged by different moral standards than those used to judge men? Were women as capable of independent adult behaviour as men? These are all questions in which Violet shows a great interest because they affect her personally. She sees herself as caught between two worlds. She is the 'New Woman that people wrote about in the nineties', whereas Rebecca West is a shining example of the 'Newest Woman'.

One of the differences between *The Flurried Years* and *I Have This To Say* is that in the latter Violet writes at much greater length about Rebecca West. She writes with great admiration, respect and affection. She emphasises her friend's ability to take on the world and her skill as a writer in supporting herself by her own pen, and she sees her attitude towards men as the only one possible for the New Woman: 'She is in the boat with all women. Men, she sensibly enough, does not hate, for, as the American girl said to Matthew Arnold, "It's all there is."' She quoted with some relish West's comment, 'Most men have so much to repent that they *must* be amusing to justify their existence.'

A striking feature of the autobiographies is the number of deaths they record. Each of them again represents not only the end of something in Violet's life but also in English society. There is first the death of her mother. For Violet this involves a change in status and function and material well-being. She no longer has the care of her mother as a *raison d'être*, nor does she have the benefit of her mother's care in terms of financial help. It becomes, therefore, doubly important to establish herself in the new role of Ford's wife and his support. There is also a larger significance to Margaret Hunt's death which Violet underlines by her detailed account of the publication of *The Governess*, Margaret Hunt's last novel which was finished and polished up by Violet and Ford. The death of Margaret Hunt marks the end of the possibility of a particular kind of novel-writing by women for women. Violet cannot write out of the same certainties as had her mother, nor can those other women writers she is close to such as May Sinclair, Ethel Colburn Mayne and Rebecca West. In a similar way, the deaths of Henry James and W.H. Hudson represent the end of a particular era of writing, while news of the death of the sculptor Gaudier-Brzeska foreshadows the breaking up of the artistic community of the younger generation by the war.

Goldring accuses Violet of indiscretion. But, as in the case of Rebecca West, Violet can be discretion itself. Rebecca West had a sexual and moral courage which Violet did not see in herself. But she does not mention West's protracted affair with H.G. Wells, nor does she mention that Rebecca West achieved all she did despite bearing and bringing up her son by Wells. But she surely had her and her ability to overcome scandal in mind when she says ruefully, 'Does post-war woman realise the differentiation of the standard of manners that has obtained since 1918?'

She further underlines her sense of being excluded from new attitudes towards and the possibilities open to women when she mentions with some envy that all her young friends, such as Rebecca West and Stella Bowen, are actively involved in war work, for which she feels too old.

The most obvious way in which Violet places these years as a time apart is in her use of a framing foreword and envoi in *I Have This To Say*. Both these pieces display a different kind of writing. Within the body of the text we have the sense of the writer recreating and reliving the experience of those times. In fact at times she becomes so thoroughly involved in the present of the autobiography that she forgets that the outcome has already been determined. The following passage, in which she describes Selsey, is a particularly striking example: 'The church and the churchyard . . . where I intend to lay my bones and those of Joseph Leopold when the time comes.'

In the foreword and envoi, however, she establishes a distance in time from the body of the text when she writes:

And I sit by the fire in England, under the fearsome masterpiece of Wyndham Lewis that becomes me so, with Mary finer, stouter, and Maleine,* a worker, with small, precise, red-tipped mouth no longer torture and generous; her hair not any more toppling but bobbed, of course, and with a great, grown-up son to protect her . . . And Joseph Leopold wanders, wanders, among the fleur de luce of the Castle of Beaucaire with another, hardier, sturdier Egeria.

She establishes a difference in perspective in the foreword when she writes using the language of law about what had been seized on as flaws in her autobiography. Her inclusion of reports from *The Times* covering the crucial legal battles also serves to provide a perspective on the account of these matters in the body of the text and to establish firmly the difference between autobiographical writing and the factual recording of evidence.

Violet's strong awareness of forming a precarious balance between two generations is suggested by the very structure of her books. She begins by referring to John Ruskin, who was such an important influence on her life and very much a figure of her mother's generation. She recounts an incident in which Ruskin had advised her to 'find someone you can love and trust and then count no sacrifice too great to make in that one's service.' She then establishes how difficult it had proved in her own life to follow Ruskin's advice: '*And trust!* Yes, leave it at that and life is very simple.'

Because her own experience is so different she cannot write the kind of autobiography which Ruskin had urged in *Praeterita*, one which dwells 'at length on things that give men joy, passing in total silence things which I have no pleasure in reviewing, and which the reader would find no help in the account of'. On the contrary, she asserts in her first paragraph that her autobiography will be about pain and error: 'And there comes, sooner or later, according to the sets and the entries and exits of the other actors, one's own supreme moment. One is on. And that entry, being but human, one may so easily muff. That moment, some will say, I did muff.'

She decisively rejects at the outset Ford's reservations about the usefulness and truthfulness of autobiography based on his notion

---

*Maleine was Violet's code name for Brigit Patmore.

that 'not . . . till a person comes to lie on his deathbed . . . does a person know which is *the* affair of all.' She firmly claims that 'Life is a succession of affairs, but there is always one affair for which the years, from birth, are a preparation, a hardening, a tempering.'

She does, however, retain an almost ironic connection with Victorian notions of autobiography in her use of prefatory material for each chapter. The headings which appear to sum up the contents of each chapter prove to be deceptive. They suggest a firmness and a chronological clarity which is noticeably absent from the body of the text.

Violet is doing in her writing what her young friend Ezra Pound did in his early poetry: looking back to Robert Browning's poetry for a form suitable for her needs. Browning's *Men and Women* and *The Ring and the Book* represent that searching for a truth by individuals who are painfully aware of how limiting the individual perspective is. Like Browning's fictional characters, she puts her case in her own particular voice and leaves the reader to judge its strengths and weaknesses.

We are back once again to Goldring's assertion that the events of the autobiography are told from 'her own standpoint'.

The real test of how successful *The Flurried Years* and *I Have This To Say* are as autobiographies is not so much what they tell us about the events of Violet's life as how much they reveal about the personality of the writer. There is no question but that a fully rounded portrait of Violet Hunt emerges from her pages. Her novelistic skills are apparent in her ability to recreate vividly people and places. She has an ear for the pertinent anecdote which gives us a sudden flash of insight into a personality. A particularly good example of this, and one which shows also that witty tongue that she inherited from her mother, has to do with Henry James. She describes how he encourages her and others to relate interesting gossip to him. The moment he has seized what is to him, as a novelist, the useful kernel of the story he loses further interest. She sums up her observation as follows: 'The role of the priest in the confessional, armed with plenary powers, would just have suited him. For, the moment he was bored, all he would have to do would be to say, "Go, my daughter, go in peace and sin some more."'

She also shows herself to be her father's daughter in the way in which she regularly considers people and occasions in painterly terms. For example, she compares her sister to a Giovanni Bellini portrait and her niece to Romney's portrait of Lady Hamilton and describes Ford's proposal as 'Pre-Raphaelite'. Elsewhere she remarks on the fact that Conrad does not have a painterly eye, and that he lacks a precise sense of colour.

The very fact that Violet chose to focus on the 'flurried years' of her life is indicative of her character. She was a woman who insisted on making her position clear and justifying it where necessary, as we see in her letters relating to the scandal over her 'marriage' to Ford. It would have been quite out of character for her to have remained silent rather than making a public statement.

The books also do justice to the complexity and contradictions of her personality. She presents to us on the one hand the notion of herself as the North Country woman with all that that suggests. It is to this side of her nature that she attributes a certain unromantic commonsense quality. It is the side of her that sees Ford's irresponsibility and fecklessness, which drives her to sort out his domestic tangles and financial problems, to try to prevent him from spending extravagantly on his children when he is going short himself. It is as a North Country woman that she tries to make her sisters deal fairly with her in the matter of her mother's affairs. If Aunt Jane keeps account of what Violet spends on South Lodge, Violet is equally ready to point out that there are expenses involved in having to look after her mother. She finds nothing strange in declaring that her mother is her tenant and as such should pay something towards the upkeep of the house and the food bills. When she has a sudden fancy to travel she carefully cost accounts the journey and then devises ways of acquiring the necessary money. She has no hesitation about telling her reader what sums of money were exchanged when, to finance her journeys, she sold some of her father's paintings.

Yet this shrewd businesswoman can also present herself repeatedly as the little sparrow constantly threatened by the horses' hooves. And she shows just how unbusinesslike she can be when she chooses to be deceived. She knows that she is 'credulous', a 'non-sifter of evidence'. Her failure to insist on seeing documentary evidence of Ford's naturalisation and divorce is indicative of this side of her. Although she sees the physical Ford with an unblinkered vision, presenting him at times as shabby and toothless, she has a romantic vision of him as the genius entitled to behave with gross selfishness. This tolerance goes against her otherwise clear-sighted perceptions. In her attitude towards her sisters, particularly Silvia, she reveals the same kind of contradictions. On the one hand she can hardly condemn them enough for what she sees as their avaricious spitefulness – the very names she chooses for them, Goneril and Regan, suggests wickedness and brutality. For much of the autobiographies she uses Shakespeare's *King Lear* as an image for her own family. She sees herself as the misunderstood Cordelia and her mother as a Lear-figure about to be put into an asylum by unfeeling daughters who all the while protest their loving concern to protect her from the wicked Violet. Despite the harsh judgement she implies by this image and these names, she can still say of her youngest sister 'Dear Little Goneril, how I loved her! Shrewd and weak, kind and capricious, cunning and silly, and very lovely, like a Gian Bellini, with deep-blue, sombre eyes . . .' This kind of contradictory attitude marks all her comments on Silvia. On the one hand Silvia's actions are condemned as heartless, and on the other she is always making excuses for her sister's harsh behaviour and gleaning every hope she can that at bottom her sister really cares for her. The hard-bitten Violet is also a woman who desperately needs to be loved.

In the matter of women's suffrage, once again contradictions and ambivalences emerge of which she is fully aware. On the one hand she wholeheartedly supports the fight for the vote. She is publicly proud of her acquaintance with Christabel Pankhurst. She is prepared to write in support of suffrage and she collects money and holds meetings at South Lodge. But a part of her is very much afraid. She gives her responsibility for caring for her mother as a reason for not being in the front line in the fight and for not going to prison for the cause. But she is not convincing in her excuses. When Ford returns from Brixton Gaol she experiments with the idea of her possibly serving a sentence as well. But once again she is not convincing when she says 'I treasured up these details because if, some day I was sent to prison as a suffragette, this was what I should have to eat.'

Even in her attitude towards women's suffrage she is hampered by the ingrained habits of her Victorian upbringing. She bewails the fact that as a woman she does not know enough about the law at the same time as she continues to put her faith in male lawyers. She feels that she has as great a right to opportunities as any man, but she sacrifices herself to Ford's need to work and even, for a time, gives up journalism because that is what Ford wants.

If we look at her attitude towards sexual freedom we see the same pattern. While she is prepared to have an affair with Ford she also wants to maintain the appearance of respectability. Her whole desperate emphasis on chaperones is the result. When she thinks that at last she is about to be Mrs Hueffer, a respectable married woman with no need for a chaperone, she reveals, perhaps unwittingly in this case, a sense of the ridiculousness of her position: 'It was so nice to be done with the need for chaperonage: arranging for it had been *my* task – Joseph Leopold was so incurably Bohemian – and I had found it irksome.'

While she is prepared to condemn marriage as 'a tyranny tempered by divorce', as long as Ford still acknowledges that he is married to Elsie, she is anxious to assume the yoke of that tyranny herself.

Paradoxically, these revelations of ambiguity and weakness in Violet's character do not lessen our respect for her. The sheer honesty of her presentation of herself with all her flaws gains our admiration. The fact that she was very conscious of herself as a woman writing with a frankness unusual for a woman of her background commands our respect. This is further enhanced when we see how Goldring unself-consciously takes cognizance only of male responses to Violet's autobiographies. He quotes a friend of his who, although he had not actually read *The Flurried Years* at the time, commented that 'From what I hear of it I imagine V.H. has cleaned up her mind once and for all of *that* topic: but, Lord, what a cat she is. (Most women are, really).'[3] Goldring himself describes *The Flurried Years* as 'heavily biased and written in tones of bitterness and self-pity which the author makes heroic efforts to conceal or overcome'. In my view his emphasis is completely wrong. Violet Hunt has the courage to present herself honestly, and it is this honesty at that time which is heroic.

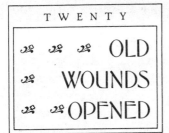

TWENTY

OLD
WOUNDS
OPENED

Once Ford had left England Violet settled into old routines, including literary luncheons. At one of these in 1922 she met up again with her old friend Somerset Maugham. The attention bestowed on her by that now famous author was a great salve to her damaged pride.

Her women friends continued to be important to her. She was grateful for the support given to her by May Sinclair, Ethel Colburn Mayne and Rebecca West. She remained on terms of intimacy with Mary Martindale, and with Ford out of the picture she could once more enjoy the company of Brigit Patmore without reservations. Indeed the two women became closer when Brigit too had the experience of being abandoned by her lover, Richard Aldington.

After the death of Marcel Proust in Paris in 1922, C.K. Scott Moncrieff decided to publish an English tribute to the great French writer. Violet was an obvious person to ask for a contribution to such a volume as she was well acquainted not only with the work of Proust but other French writers, many of whom she had met on her frequent visits to Paris. Several of her friends were also asked to contribute, including Joseph Conrad, Arnold Bennett, Compton Mackenzie, Alec Waugh and Ethel Colburn Mayne.

In her contribution Violet describes how she had first encountered the work of Proust in the form of a London Library book on the table of a Kensington society hostess, and how the reading of it had had a permanent effect on her: 'But I – I had become acquainted with Proust and had gained a world – one of the worlds in which, through a book, we can go to live awhile whenever we choose.'[1]

It pleased her greatly to find there was a link between the French writer and her old mentor John Ruskin, for Proust had translated Ruskin's *Bible of Amiens*. Douglas Goldring recalls that Violet even named one of her cats 'Proust'.

1922 was also the year in which W.H. Hudson died. His death affected Violet more than might have been expected. It was one more link with the past severed. She wrote extensively about his last days in *The Flurried Years* and made a point of being present at his funeral.

The comparative calm of these years was disturbed once more in 1924, not only by the publication of Ford's novel *Some Do Not* but also by a renewal of hostilities with Elsie Hueffer.

The meeting of the two women three years earlier had done little to effect a reconciliation between them. Violet was responsible for the fresh outbreak of antagonism.

On 12 January a letter from Violet was published in the weekly *Westminster Review*. She had taken it upon herself to correct a mistake in an earlier issue by writing as follows:

> Sir,
>
> May I point out to you an error in your list of Prize Poems, and the names of the volumes from which they are culled. My husband never published a book called *From Ireland and Other Poems* with Messrs Duckworth. It ought to run *From Inland, and Other Poems*. The book is now out of print.
>
> Violet Hunt Hueffer.

Elsie once more rose to defend her name. She took out an interim injunction to prevent Violet from calling herself Mrs Hueffer. The case came to court and was reported in *The Times* on the 12th of February. All the arguments over whether Violet and Ford had ever been married were revived. *The Times* reported the defence put forward on Violet's behalf:

> Mr Storry Deans said that, in justice to his client, it must be said that she had not formed a perfectly lawless association with the plaintiff's husband. Mr Hueffer who had now adopted another name and lived in another country, had represented that he was a German, and had obtained a divorce in Germany. Miss Hunt now knew that she was not lawfully married to Mr Hueffer. She had never intended to suggest, nor did she suggest, that Mrs Hueffer was other than a virtuous woman in every sense.

Justice Branson made a perpetual injunction restraining Violet from describing herself as the wife of Mr Hueffer or suggesting that Mrs Hueffer was not his wife. Violet was required to pay Elsie's costs for the case.

Why did Violet create a situation in which she could only suffer further humiliation? It can only be, as Ford himself suggests in *The*

Last Post, the final novel in the sequence 'No More Parades', which he published in 1928, that Violet could not stand to be ignored. Even a public humiliation, as long as it linked her name with Ford's and established that she had some claim on him, was preferable to anonymity and silence.

The third of Ford's novel sequence, *A Man Could Stand Up*, had been published in 1926, and 'Sylvia' had figured very little in it. But *The Last Post* contained the most devastating portrait of all. Had the publication of *The Flurried Years* and *I Have This To Say* opened up all the old resentments once more? The Sylvia of this novel is based to a very large extent on what Ford felt about Violet immediately after he had left her and gone to live with Stella. Some of the incidents from this period of his life appear in the novel, most notably the occasion on which Violet had spied on him and Stella and had, he believed, gone back to London to tell her friends all that he was doing:

> Normally she would not – the members of her circle would not – have made confidantes of her ex-husband's domestics. But she had to chance whether the details of Christopher's *ménage* as revealed by the wife of his carpenter would prove to her friends sufficiently amusing to make them forget the social trespass she committed in consorting with her husband's dependants and she had to chance whether the carpenter's wife would see that, by proclaiming her wrongs over the fact that her husband had left her, she was proclaiming her own unattractiveness.

In the novel, Sylvia's behaviour is attributed to two motives: 'But every other action of hers from that date had been inexcusable – except regarded as actions perpetrated under the impulsion of sex-viciousness.' And 'To be cruel is to draw attention to yourself; you cannot expect to be courted by a man whom you allow to forget you.'

In these passages Ford is commenting on Violet's frantic attempts to make him return to her. With chillingly accurate perception he describes what was the driving force in Violet's life in the first year after he had left her: 'For it is to be remembered that one of the chief torments of the woman who has been abandoned by a man is the sheer thirst of curiosity for material details as to how that man subsequently lives.'

What must have been the most distressing aspect of the novel, however, is the way in which Ford conflates aspects of Violet and his wife Elsie. It was Elsie who had taken Ford to court for restitution of conjugal rights and who had subsequently refused to divorce him. There is little doubt that Violet would have acted in the same way had she been in a position to do so; in the novel all these actions are attributed to Sylvia, who in other respects represents Violet.

There is a good deal of truth in Ford's portrait of Violet in the *Parade's End* sequence of novels. But the portrait is partial. He depicts Violet only at her worst and when she was tormented by his ceasing to care for her. Because he had rejected her he cannot afford to acknowledge those good aspects of her character which had attracted him to her in the first place. To Violet's credit she recognised the literary merits of the novels and judged them solely on that basis.

One consolation she could derive from them is that however disagreeable a character Sylvia is, she is a very forceful presence. She is described with an intensity of feeling which is absent from the depiction of the Stella character, Valentine, who remains shadowy and unconvincing. Violet can have had no doubt that she had made as lasting an impression on Ford's life as he had on hers.

During the years that followed Violet concentrated her energies on researching a biography of Elizabeth Siddal. In 1931 she was invited to contribute to an exhibition of author-artists at Foyle's Art Gallery and her work, some of which dated back to her days at Kensington Art School, was praised. Otherwise her contacts with the larger world were increasingly few. She missed her close relationship with May Sinclair who had begun to suffer from Parkinson's disease and who, in 1932, left London and moved to a house in Buckinghamshire.

The scandal surrounding Violet's relationship with Ford and her insistence on calling herself Mrs Hueffer had died away. Even in literary circles the story was no longer well understood. Nor did Violet herself still have the power to make people fear her biting tongue. Both points are amply illustrated by a letter written by Virginia Woolf to her sister Vanessa Bell on 23 May 1931, after she had met Violet to discuss the possibility of publishing *The Wife of Rossetti* at the Hogarth Press:

Then we had Violet Hunt-Hueffer (it appears she's a married woman in certain streets in Berlin, where she signed a document; but not otherwise) and had a lewd and lascivious talk about her statements as to Ruskin's private parts and so on. It is all based upon things she heard gentlemen saying to her mother as she was going up to bed at the age of 8. These she has since reflected upon and drawn her own conclusions – erratic slightly, and I ought to be going through the revised version at this moment, instead of scribbling to you.[2]

TWENTY-ONE

THE WIFE OF ROSSETTI

It was not the Hogarth Press, however, but John Lane who published Violet Hunt's last major literary work in 1932.

Even at this late stage in her career, she chose to experiment with a form new to her – biography. But why, having chosen this form, did she, who knew and had known so many major artists and literary and political figures, choose as her subject the wife of Dante Gabriel Rossetti, Elizabeth Siddal?

She was, after all, better acquainted with the lives and the work of Rossetti himself, Burne-Jones, Morris and Millais, to mention just a few of the most famous of the Pre-Raphaelites. Her mother had set an example by using Rossetti for the model for her hero in *Thornicroft's Model*. The Pre-Raphaelites are a constant presence in Margaret Hunt's works and in Violet's, and in her autobiographies Violet is at pains to establish Ford as a Pre-Raphaelite.

As a child she had accepted the Pre-Raphaelites' claim to her admiration wholeheartedly. It was a great joy to her to dress like a Burne-Jones figure and to monopolise the great man's time if only for a few minutes. Her home was always decorated with the products of William Morris's workshop.

By this stage of her life, however, she had a different perspective on the man who had founded the Brotherhood. She also knew with some bitterness what it meant to dedicate one's life to the bolstering up of genius.

Like her mother, she still recognised what the Pre-Raphaelites had achieved. In *The Leaden Casket* Margaret Hunt had celebrated the Brotherhood as bringers of fresh air, defiers of the stuffiness of Victorian society even to the extent of encouraging the women associated with them to abandon the fashionable crinoline in favour of looser, more flowing, less cumbersome and more picturesque garments. If Violet herself was a little sceptical about her mother's view of the Brotherhood, she was prepared to acknowledge that, led by Rossetti, they had fought against 'the Sanhedrin of old, mild but evil men who had sat down heavily in the High Places of British Art and persistently stifled all efforts to see things truly and well.'

From the perspective of 1932 she could see that the revolt against Victorian values was limited. The freedom the men strove for was for themselves as artists only. Their women in no way benefited from their revolt. She began to show her awareness of this in *The Flurried Years*, when she mentions how as a child she was taken by her nurse to the home of Edward Burne-Jones. Her mother wanted him to sign a petition for women's suffrage. The great man refused point-blank to be involved with any such disturbing enterprise.

In many ways the lives of the Brotherhood epitomised all that was wrong in the society in which they lived. The life of Elizabeth Siddal, therefore, the forgotten wife of Dante Gabriel Rossetti, provided an excellent basis for the kind of biography Violet wanted to write.

There has been a good deal of criticism by scholars about the inaccuracy of this biography. These criticisms come from those who would like to mine the book for factual information. To find fault with it on these grounds is to misunderstand the nature of the work Violet set out to achieve. In the preface to the book she states the limitations and the strengths of her enterprise. Her emphasis is on the personal nature of her biography. She indicates clearly that the starting point of her work is her own life and her own experience of the Pre-Raphaelites:

> My sources for this life are chiefly oral, from the circumstances of my childhood and early girlhood, spent much in the company of the actors in the scenes I am attempting to describe, wandering o' mornings in and out of their houses with messages, and, older,

with a good book in my hand which I did not read, hearkening as a servant waiting at table might, to words that I only half understood.

As a child she had been aware of a glamour and a mystery surrounding Rossetti himself. Her fascination with the Rossetti legend had been fostered because of what she sensed was kept hidden and left unsaid. Her curiosity was stimulated by Robert Browning's loud utterance, 'I never can forgive Rossetti,' by the painter Holman Hunt's sad comment, 'No, I never see Gabriel now . . . his life is so bad,' and by her own father's serious and solemn refusal to speak to her of Rossetti. She was aware of the visits of her parents to breakfast with Rossetti and her mother's attitude towards him as a man with a 'soft Italian voice and the wonderful eyes with the bar of Michelangelo across the brows . . . so that one could refuse him nothing.' She tells us how the mystery was further intensified for her by her own direct experience of the man on the day she saw his painting 'Dante's Dream' in the shed of the painter William Bell Scott and then saw through the window the strange figure with his *pardessus* "hugged up", as these North Country people said, over his face so that he looked like a monk. "Gabriel!" Mrs Scott exclaimed.' Violet began to realise that it was not Rossetti's relationship with his somewhat shadowy wife which troubled her parents' generation but his subsequent love for Jane Morris and his addiction to drugs.

She knew her mother's view of Elizabeth Siddal – 'Mr Rossetti's trying wife, peevish, uncertain-tempered and staring-eyed and to whom he was unfaithful'.

This dismissive comment on Elizabeth Siddal, coupled with the fact that not one of her parents' generation did other than to take Dante Gabriel Rossetti's side in the whole matter of the troubled relationship between man and wife, made Violet aware that 'The truth about Rossetti has been told, more or less: the truth about the woman he married, never.'

The biography of Elizabeth Siddal is the record of Violet's attempts to learn about and understand her subject. The fact that we are witnessing a process of exploration is emphasised towards the end of the biography, when, after the suicide of Elizabeth Siddal, Violet recreates the occasion in the coroner's court. As she

177

describes the testimony of Mrs Birrell, the caretaker of the building in which the Rossettis lived, her close identification with the dead woman becomes explicit: 'Mrs Birrell had known Mrs Rossetti for nine years, officially for two, when she began living there as his wife. That got out. Too late to matter, but she would have disliked it.'

This close identification with Elizabeth Siddal gives the biography its special quality. For as Violet learns more and more about Rossetti's wife and thinks about her life she realises how closely the events of the dead woman's life relate to her own. The biography, therefore, becomes as much an exploration of what has gone wrong in her own life as in Elizabeth Siddal's. Because Elizabeth Siddal's life is over it is possible for Violet to see the patterns and the inevitabilities in the other woman's life which she cannot see completely in her own.

One way in which Violet establishes a link between herself and her subject is in the use of bird imagery. In the autobiographies she represents herself as the sparrow forever being threatened by the horses' hooves. In the biography she makes a close association between Elizabeth Siddal and the dove. When Elizabeth Siddal dies her pet dove dies also and is buried in her coffin. It is the image which Rossetti used for his wife and which appears in his painting of her as 'Beata Beatrix'.

So what were the points of comparison Violet Hunt discovered between her own life and that of Elizabeth Siddal, a young woman from a very different background from her own, whose personality and talents were in many ways unlike Violet's?

The most obvious link between the two women is their close association with the Pre-Raphaelites. But as Violet grew older she began to perceive more clearly the malign influence this association had had on her life. Her research into Elizabeth Siddal's life confirmed her more mature perspective.

When she came to write her biography Violet was no longer so impressed by the Brotherhood. She was more aware of its implications and she resented them. She records how when they first came together they had proclaimed that they would 'force their women to dress like ladies in the pictures of the Primitives', and how at a later phase in the Brotherhood Edward Burne-Jones, imitating the notions of his leader, Rossetti, was prompted to declare that

'Domesticity is nice . . . but, in his opinion, a man who had any special work to do in the world was better without a mate.' Once William Morris and Burne-Jones and Rossetti found themselves married men together, they contained the damage of domesticity by 'the convention of the three friends that their wives, more or less, sufficed each other for company'. She makes it very clear that these men always subordinated women to the demands of their art. She attributes to Barbara Leigh-Smith, an earlier feminist, a perception of the Pre-Raphaelites which is surely her own:

> Barbara Leigh-Smith liked Gabriel; but not this Pre-Raphaelitism which, on the face of it, reminded her, a would-be-reformer, of the status of her sex, of the mental starvation undergone by Woman in mediaeval days, her disgustingly inferior position except during those few fleeting years when she is man's delight and may command him. Look, she said, at the faces of the young women in the pictures these young men admired – the tight waists, the overloaded heads that must have ached so frequently, the lined foreheads, the pinched mouths, the sly slanting eyes . . . Chattels, these ladies, inured to death and horror, with iron nerves, if they possessed them at all.

This description of the ladies in Pre-Raphaelite paintings is remarkably close to the description Violet gives of the kind of women Ford habitually made the heroines of his novels. And, of course, there were those, notably Douglas Goldring, who called the grandson of Ford Madox Brown the last Pre-Raphaelite. Because Ford Madox Brown is such a prominent figure in the biography of Elizabeth Siddal we cannot but be aware of how close to the forefront of Violet's mind Ford was when she was writing.

Many of Elizabeth Siddal's miseries arise, like those of Violet, because she is trapped within a role defined for her by her class and by her sex. Her retreat from the world of the over-worked, poorly-paid millinery business into the more lucrative enterprise of being an artist's model leads her into a strange and unfamiliar twilight world. In the same way, when Violet seeks independence through her writing, particularly journalism, she becomes part of a Bohemian world whose values do not fit easily with her middle-class, professional background. Elizabeth Siddal's position is much worse and much more ambiguous than that of Violet since the model, as a person, did not exist in polite society. 'It would have been in the nature of an insult for the artist to introduce his paid model to his lady friends.' But though her position is extreme it is representative of a problem facing all women who cannot or will not rely on men to support them. The man for whom Elizabeth Siddal models initially is aware of the limited possibilities available to her. He

> disapproved of the step she proposed to take, but what alter-
> native could he suggest? Her talent for stringing verses would
> not keep her and she would be no use on the stage, though
> she had a good figure, because of her voice – slightly sibilant,
> turning into the faintest little hiss whenever she got tired with
> talking too long . . . There really seemed nothing Walter could
> do for her but marry her, and he had not enough to marry on.

In Elizabeth Siddal's life, as in Violet's, marriage became a major problem. Neither woman lacked suitors but neither found it easy to achieve a marriage with the man to whom they chose to dedicate the greater part of their lives. Like Violet, Elizabeth Siddal was extremely aware of being regarded as immoral for living with the man she loved. But she too had the courage to flout convention:

> The other tenants, meeting her on the stairs, thought of her
> as Mr Rossetti's mistress. Mrs Birrell, though perfectly civil,
> probably thought so too – for gentlemen, even the most hard-
> working, do not care as a rule to live without female society of
> a kind. Lizzy was probably the first woman to live by herself in
> a bachelor's flat. Stiff, haughty and fearless, looking not in the
> least professional model or mistress – she just took her clothes,
> her baby easel and her big workbox to Gabriel's rooms and stayed
> there, living for days without speaking to a single creature except
> the caretaker and her daughter.

Violet expresses an admiration for Elizabeth Siddal's courage such as she would have liked to receive for her own defiance of convention. Despite their courage, both women felt the pressure on them to get married. Barbara Leigh-Smith, an independently wealthy woman, is a lone voice when she says, 'She knew of no particular reason why Gabriel should marry Lizzy unless he wanted to; if he did why not? Did he actually owe her marriage?'

Throughout the biography Barbara Leigh-Smith is presented as the antithesis of the Pre-Raphaelite woman Elizabeth Siddal is. She is the kind of woman Violet herself would have liked to be. Her life is devoted to improving the status of women in the most basic ways. She is involved in schemes to educate young girls. She works to provide proper medical care for sick women. She sees her sex as, for the most part, 'stultified' in the 'culpable resignation to circumstances'. She wants proper health education for women. Her position is almost diametrically opposed to that represented by Mrs Radmall in Violet's novels, for she says that 'girls should be taught the rules of health' even though 'it was actually contended – by men probably, with their queer fetish of female delicacy – that women should know as little as possible about that exceedingly delicate subject.'

There are many other points at which the lives of writer and subject touch. Both women were at one time the objects of John Ruskin's concern and encouragement, and he acted as something of a mentor to them both. Both women were scrupulously honest and businesslike, unlike the men with whom they were involved: Violet always kept Ford's accounts, while Elizabeth Siddal insisted on completing paintings and drawings for which Ruskin had paid in advance when her husband was inclined to default.

Each had a talent which was overshadowed by that of the man she loved, and each gave the most important part of her life to a relationship which ended in distress and recriminations. What Violet says of Elizabeth Siddal and Dante Gabriel Rossetti could be rephrased to describe her own relationship with Ford: 'Her history is that of the eleven years during which her orbit coincided with that of Gabriel Rossetti and the Pre-Raphaelites.'

When Violet describes the distress experienced by Elizabeth Siddal when faced with Rossetti's numerous and frequent infidelities, she writes from her own experience of seeing Ford falling in love with other women. She too felt that one day she might not be able to cope any longer and carried a poison ring.* She is,

---

*This was a ring she had had made for herself when she was writing *Unkist, Unkind*, and was described in her novel. Violet often showed the ring to her friends but, although she had access to arsenic, she does not appear to have actually carried poison in it.

therefore, completely sympathetic to Elizabeth Siddal's decision to take her own life. She presents suicide not as a cowardly escape from life but as Elizabeth Siddal's positive decision to put an end to what had become unbearable. She records the message the young woman wrote out and pinned to her nightdress before taking a fatal overdose of laudanum: 'My life is so miserable I wish for no more of it.'

The Wife of Rossetti has all the qualities of Violet Hunt's finest novels. She has a good ear for dialogue, an ability to recreate scenes from the past and a painterly, indeed Pre-Raphaelite, eye for the significant detail. The biography also breaks new ground in that it is one of the first declaredly feminist biographies in which the writer does not choose to focus on a hero or heroine whom the reader should strive to emulate. Her subject is an obscure woman whose struggles to contend with the restrictions imposed upon her by class, society and her sex ended in tragedy, but whose life nevertheless exhibits determination, strength of character and courage. Violet was no doubt aware that she too was, in late middle age, regarded by many of her acquaintance as a tiresome and difficult woman. Her attempt to make us understand and sympathise with what lay behind Elizabeth Siddal's difficult exterior is also a plea for tolerance of her own misunderstood life.

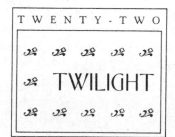

TWENTY-TWO

TWILIGHT

After the publication of *The Wife of Rossetti* there was little left for Violet to do. During the years she had been collecting material for the book and writing it she had been able to live in the past, evoking her vivid memories, and she had to some extent been able to ignore the fact that she no longer understood the world around her and that her short-term memory was failing.

She attempted to repeat the experience she had enjoyed when writing Elizabeth Siddal's biography by starting a life of Charles

August Howell.* But this did not have the same immediate relevance to her own life and her energy and enthusiasm for the project petered out.

If she ever reread her accounts of her own mother at an advanced age she must have recognised with horror how much history was repeating itself. But in Violet's case the decline of her mental powers was exacerbated by the long-term effects of the syphilis contracted all those years ago from the long-dead Oswald Crawfurd.

And her mother had been luckier than Violet in other ways also. To the end of her life the house in which she lived was filled with people and comings and goings and excitement. She could look back on her marriage and know that it had been an unusually happy one. She had had three daughters who, although she felt they had betrayed her when her independence was taken from her, continued to attend to her until her death. In her last days she was looked after by her daughter Violet. She had the satisfaction of knowing that her career as a writer had been successful. And, although the young men and women who frequented South Lodge in the heyday of the *English Review* were not of the same social class as she was accustomed to, at least they were poets, novelists and painters who felt that they were valued by society.

How different it was for Violet. The marriage she had worked so hard for and wanted so much had never materialised. She had no children to comfort her and look after her in her old age. And the world in which she had grown up and come to maturity was irrevocably lost. It was not simply that her friends were scattered

---

*Charles August Howell is described by Timothy Hilton in *The Pre-Raphaelites* as a 'thieving trickster'. Although he was of little importance in his own right, Violet would have been interested in him because his life touched on those of some major figures in the art world with whom she was acquainted. He had, for example, been Ruskin's secretary from 1865–70. He was closely associated with Dante Gabriel Rossetti because he acted as unofficial agent for the sale of his pictures and was always ready to carry out tasks for him. One of these was to go, in the company of two men from the Blackfriars Company, to Highgate Cemetery. There, by firelight, the three men dug up the coffin of Elizabeth Siddal, raised the lid, and removed from among her hair Rossetti's notebook of poems which in his guilty anguish at his wife's death he had placed there as a gesture of love and sacrifice. Howell took the notebook to a Kensington doctor who disinfected it before Howell restored it to its owner. His intimacy with Rossetti provided him with the opportunity for forging and selling Rossetti drawings.

or dead, but that the values they had held dear were no longer of importance in the larger world. She had lived through one world war and now another was imminent.

During the Twenties Violet's social life continued to be quite active. But there was a difference. Now she was invited to parties as something of a curiosity, a character, rather than as a celebrated writer and arbiter of taste. With the publication of *The Wife of Rossetti* she once again received some of the attention she craved. By now, however, her failing memory was making her an increasing social embarrassment both to herself and to her hosts. In *South Lodge*, Douglas Goldring recalls an incident which was typical of many such:

> I met Violet at a crowded cocktail party given by Alec Waugh, at which Michael Arlen was present. She waved to him and Arlen came across the room and greeted her. Afterwards, including both Arlen and myself in the conversation, she went on: 'You know I used to see quite a lot of Michael Arlen, at one time, but he never comes to visit me now. He's really quite a nice young man – and extremely clever. I wonder why it is that his books are so *awful*.'

She continued to think about Ford and their life together. Indeed how could she do otherwise, surrounded as she was by portraits of Ford and by Ford's possessions? In 1932, when she found out that Ford was in London, she complained bitterly because he did not visit her. She still did not understand how he hated the kind of emotional intensity she was capable of engendering and she seemed not to realise how the publication of *The Flurried Years* had so embarrassed and distressed Ford that further meetings between them were unthinkable as far as he was concerned.

A welcome visitor from the past came in 1936. Ezra Pound had been summoned to London because his mother-in-law, Olivia Shakespear, was dying. By the time he arrived she had died, and he was faced with the task of settling her affairs and selling her possessions. Olivia's home at 34 Abingdon Court was close to South Lodge, so Ezra visited his old friend and enlisted her help in tracing some of his friends from his bachelor days in London.

Ford died in France in 1939. He and Stella had parted long

ago, and Janice Biala, the painter, was with him at the time of his death.

When Ezra Pound heard of Ford's death he wanted to see Ford's papers collected together as a kind of memorial to the man he had so admired. With this in mind he wrote to Violet in October 1939, urging her to send all the papers she had in her possession to the library at Olivet College in the States where Ford had been teaching: 'They think no end of FMH out there. It is the one place where any papers, or a set of Fordie's books would be really preserved and used and done honour to.'[1] But the papers and the possessions were all that Violet had left of her grand passion. She did not feel able to give them up and clung to them till she died.

They were still there when Douglas Goldring made his last visit to South Lodge in July 1939. He has left an account of this occasion in *South Lodge*: 'Violet stood at the dark green door of South Lodge, a frail, witchlike figure, dressed in tattered chiffons, the assembled remains, no doubt, of some of her "fluffiest" frocks of bygone times.'

Despite Violet's dishevelled appearance it was one of those nights when her mind was clear and she was eager to talk about literature and the past. Her thoughts were on Ford:

> All passion spent, all bitterness forgotten, she talked of Ford objectively, but with a generous appreciation of his achievement. As she spoke, I looked up at the bearded face of Dr Francis Hueffer, Ford's father, whose eyes gravely regarded me from the shadows above a dark cabinet in a corner of the room. Behind my chair, on one side, was a portrait of Ford's grandfather sitting in a garden, with his palette and easel and, on the other, Madox Brown's picture of Ford as William Tell's son, holding in his hand the two halves of the apple split by his father's marksmanship . . . in a queer unaccountable way, he still dominated the house.

It had been just before the First World War that Gaudier-Brzeska's hieratic head of Ezra Pound had been put in the garden at South Lodge. Violet had seen its presence as a charm to ward off the destruction of the First World War. She must, therefore, have had some sad thoughts when the head was finally removed in the 1930s and transported to Rapallo, where Ezra was then living. It had been in her garden for twenty years, and its removal was a visible sign of the disintegration of the South Lodge salon.

Douglas Goldring was there when it was hauled away. He gives the following description of the occasion in *South Lodge*:

> It was enormously heavy and when I last saw it, after having weathered many drenching rainstorms, it had sunk into the grass and looked lopsided and slightly tipsy. During the period of Ezra's grandeur in the early 1930s, when he was organising concerts on the Italian Riviera and was being courted by the Fascists, the bust was sent for by his admirers. Strong men arrived one day, in green baize aprons, yanked it on to a lorry and despatched it to Rapallo.

It was, therefore, without the symbolic protection of the sculpture that Violet faced the bombing of the Second World War. She had been afraid of bombs in the First World War, but she was terrified this time. She lived to see her former house in Tor Villas demolished by bombs, and South Lodge itself had its front windows blown out. Violet, along with her cook and a young Welsh parlourmaid, slept in the basement. During the Blitz Violet's mind finally gave way. She no longer knew that she was in London under bombardment, but she believed that she was in the Welsh mountains with her father braving a terrific thunderstorm.

By a strange irony, after such a very untidy life, Violet's death in January 1942 was neatly timed: the lease she had bought on South Lodge was about to expire, and the fate she had most dreaded, to be consigned to a home, would otherwise surely have come about.

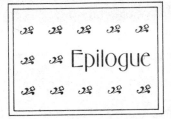

Epilogue

It was Violet Hunt's dearest wish to achieve some kind of immortality, and the careful preservation of her papers and family records and photographs was to that end. She was concerned that the truth of her life should finally be known, and to facilitate this she had stuffed 'significant' letters into various books, confident that they would thus come to the attention of her literary executors, in particular Douglas Goldring and Ethel Colburn Mayne.

She had even determinedly set the record straight about the edition of *The Memoirs of Jacques Casanova de Seingalt* which she had translated with Agnes Farley. She put the following statement in her copy of the book where, as she had hoped, it was found by Goldring, who published it in *South Lodge*: 'I should like to get Messrs Chapman and Hall to place it on record that I, Violet Hunt, am responsible for the translation, and now that I am seventy-four the impropriety of it would hardly "lie" as they say of winter snow.'

In other respects things did not work out quite as Violet had hoped. Ethel Colburn Mayne predeceased Violet and so could not act as her executor. The papers, books and paintings which she had regarded as treasures were, by the time she died, something of an embarrassment to those who had to clear her house. Eventually her papers were bought for Cornell University Library, where they are still kept – ironically, as part of the Ford Madox Ford Archive. For many years scholars have used her papers for the light they throw on her contemporaries. Violet herself has largely been ignored.

Douglas Goldring feared that Violet would sink into oblivion. When he last saw South Lodge it was covered in dust and in general disrepair, and he was told that the house would be pulled down. He knew from earlier occasions when he had tried to help Violet to sell some of her Pre-Raphaelite possessions and paintings, including Ford Madox Brown's portrait of Ford as William Tell's son, that the Brotherhood was out of fashion and that no one was interested in their work.

But things have changed since then. Not only is South Lodge still standing, but it carries a plaque recording the fact that Ford lived there, even if it does not mention Violet. The Pre-Raphaelites are no longer out of favour. Ford himself is at last beginning to get some of the recognition he deserves.

It is an appropriate time to look again at Violet Hunt. Both her life and her work have an importance and a relevance that is only now becoming apparent.

NOTES

Chapter 1: THE LOVE MATCH
1. John Ruskin, *Modern Painters*, edited and abridged by David Barrie (London, André Deutsch, 1987), p. xii.
2. Quoted by Timothy Hilton, *The Pre-Raphaelites* (London, Thames and Hudson, 1983), p. 38.
3. Penelope Fitzgerald, *Edward Burne-Jones: A Biography* (London, Michael Joseph, 1975), p. 33.

Chapter 2: GROWING UP PRE-RAPHAELITE
1. Violet Hunt, 'Alfred William Hunt, R.W.S. 1830–1896', *Old Water Colour Society Club 1924–25*, p. 37.
2. Quoted by Robert and Marie Secor in 'Lives and Hearts in Pre-Raphaelite England: The Autobiographical Novels of Violet Hunt', *The Pre-Raphaelite Review*, May 1979, pp. 59–70.
3. Patricia Hutchins, *Ezra Pound's Kensington* (London, Faber and Faber, 1965), p. 69.
4. Quoted by Douglas Goldring, *South Lodge: Reminiscences of Violet Hunt, Ford Madox Ford and the English Review Circle* (London, Constable, 1943), p. 3. Goldring describes how when he went through Violet Hunt's papers he found a number of press cuttings which Margaret Hunt had preserved about Alfred Hunt's work. The piece by W. Newall is one of them.
5. Violet Hunt, 'Alfred William Hunt', p. 31.
6. Philip Henderson, *William Morris, His Life, Work and Friends* (London, Thames and Hudson, 1967), p. 224.
7. Robert Secor, *John Ruskin and Alfred Hunt. New letters and the Record of a Friendship* (Victoria, the University of Victoria Press, 1982), p. 63.

Chapter 3: RUSKIN AS A GUIDE TO YOUTH
1. Quoted by Patricia Hutchins, *op. cit.*
2. All letters quoted in this chapter are from Robert Secor's edition of the letters of John Ruskin and Alfred Hunt.

Chapter 4: THE SWEETEST VIOLET
1. Robert Secor, 'Aesthetes and Pre-Raphaelites: Oscar Wilde and the Sweetest Violet in England', *Texas Studies in Literature and Language*, Vol. 21, 1979, pp. 396–412.

Chapter 5: IN AND OUT OF LOVE
1. The extracts from Violet Hunt's diaries quoted in this chapter are from Arthur Mizener, *The Saddest Story: A Biography of Ford Madox Ford* (New York, World Publishing Co., 1971).
2. Secor, Hunt–Ruskin Letters, p. 115.
3. *The Young Rebecca. Writings of Rebecca West 1911–1917*, selected and introduced by Jane Marcus (London, Macmillan and Virago, 1982), p. 206.

Chapter 6: THE FIRST FRUITS OF EXPERIENCE
1. Humphrey Carpenter, *A Serious Character: The Life of Ezra Pound* (London, Faber and Faber, 1988), p. 130. It is evident that this critic has not actually read the novels he dismisses.

Chapter 7: SOUTH LODGE
1. Quoted by Ted Morgan, *Maugham: A Biography* (New York, Simon and Schuster, 1980), p. 76.
2. *ibid.*
3. Violet Hunt, 'Arnold Bennett in Paris', *The Bookman*, August 1932, Vol. 75, pp. 345–8.
4. *ibid.*

Chapter 8: ANOTHER PRE-RAPHAELITE
1. Quoted by Mizener from Ford's biography of his grandfather Ford Madox Brown, p. 246.

Chapter 9: LOVE AND LITERATURE
1. Victoria Glendinning, *Rebecca West* (London, Weidenfeld and Nicolson, 1987), p. 36.
2. David Garnett, *The Golden Echo* (London, Chatto and Windus, 1957), p. 129.
3. *The Letters of D.H. Lawrence, Volume I September 1901–May 1913*, edited by James Boulton (Cambridge, Cambridge University Press, 1979), p. 138.
4. *ibid.*
5. *South Lodge*, p. 15.
6. Stella Bowen, *Drawn From Life* (London, Virago, 1984), p. 62.
7. Douglas Goldring, *Trained For Genius: The Life and Writings of Ford Madox Ford* (New York, Dutton, 1949), p. 155.
8. *ibid.*, p. 156.
9. I am indebted to Professor Joseph Kestner of the University of Tulsa for a stimulating lecture he gave on this topic at the

University of British Columbia in 1988.
10. May Sinclair, 'The Novels of Violet Hunt', *English Review*, February 1922, p. 110.
11. *South Lodge*, p. 42.
12. *The Golden Echo*, p. 128.
13. *Lawrence Letters Vol I*, p. 107.
14. Brigit Patmore, *My Friends When Young: The Memoirs of Brigit Patmore*, edited by Derek Patmore (London, Heinemann, 1968), p. 9.
15. *ibid.*, p. 50.
16. Douglas Goldring, *Life Interests* (London, Macdonald, 1948), p. 51.
17. *My Friends When Young*, p. 53.
18. *Lawrence Letters Vol. I*, p. 167.
19. *South Lodge*, p. 113.

Chapter 10: A CHAPTER OF ACCIDENTS
1. *The Letters of Ford Madox Ford*, edited by Richard M. Ludwig (Princeton, Princeton University Press, 1965), p. 39.
2. Grace Lovat Fraser *In The Days of My Youth* (London, Cassell, 1970), pp. 129–130.
3. *ibid.*, p. 128.
4. *ibid.*, p. 141.
5. *My Friends When Young*, p. 55.

Chapter 12: A TANGLED WEB
1. *My Friends When Young*, p. 56.
2. Robert and Marie Secor, *The Return of the Good Soldier: Ford Madox Ford and Violet Hunt's 1917 Diary* (Victoria, University of Victoria Press, 1983), p. 21.
3. *Pound/Ford. The Story of a Literary Friendship*, edited by Brita Lindberg-Seyersted (New York, New Directions, 1982), p. 8.

Chapter 13: THE LAW'S DELAYS
1. *Lawrence Letters, Vol. I*, p. 315.
2. *ibid.*, pp. 363–4.
3. *Ezra Pound and Dorothy Shakespear: Their Letters 1909–1914*, edited by Omar Pound and A. Walton Litz (New York, New Directions, 1984), p. 123.
4. *South Lodge*, p. 59.
5. *Ezra Pound and Dorothy Shakespear*, p. 171.
6. Faith Compton Mackenzie, *As Much As I Dare* (London, Collins, 1938), pp. 271–2.

Chapter 14: DEFYING CONVENTION
1. *Ezra Pound and Dorothy Shakespear*, p. 260.
2. Edgar Jepson, *Memories of an Edwardian and Neo-Georgian* (London, Martin Secker, 1937), p. 154.
3. *Ezra Pound and Dorothy Shakespear*, p. 322.
4. P. Wyndham Lewis, *Blasting and Bombardiering* (London, Calder, 1982), p. 48.

Chapter 15: THE GOOD SOLDIER
1. Quoted in *The Return of The Good Soldier* p. 24.
2. *ibid.*, p. 74.
3. *The Letters of Ford Madox Ford*, p. 63.
4. *The Return of The Good Soldier*. All future references to Violet Hunt's diary for 1917 are taken from this edition.

Chapter 16: *THEIR LIVES AND THEIR HEARTS*
1. *The Young Rebecca*, p. 336.
2. *ibid.*
3. May Sinclair, p. 118.

Chapter 17: ALONE
1. *The Letters of Ford Madox Ford*, p. 95.
2. *ibid.*, p. 96.
3. *Pound/Ford*, p. 39.

Chapter 19: HAVING THE LAST WORD
1. Roy Pascal, *Design and Truth in Autobiography* (London, Routledge and Kegan Paul, 1960), p. 23.
2. *ibid.*, p. 96.
3. *South Lodge*, p. 76.

Chapter 20: OLD WOUNDS OPENED
1. Violet Hunt, 'Proust's Way', in *Marcel Proust: An English Tribute*, collected by C.K. Scott Moncrieff (London, Chatto and Windus, 1923), p. 112.
2. Virginia Woolf, *A Reflection of the Other Person: The letters of Virginia Woolf Vol. IV 1929–1931*, edited by Nigel Nicolson (London, Hogarth Press, 1978), p. 335.

Chapter 22: TWILIGHT
1. *Pound/Ford Letters*, p. 171.

The Maiden's Progress: A Novel In Dialogue, Osgoode, McIlvaine &
  Co., 1894.
A Hard Woman, Chapman & Hall, 1895.
The Way Of Marriage, Chapman & Hall, 1896.
Unkist, Unkind!, Chapman & Hall, 1897.
The Human Interest, Methuen, 1899.
Affairs Of The Heart, Freemantle, 1900.
The Memoirs of Jacques Casanova De Seingalt, Chapman & Hall, 1902.
The Heart Of Ruby by Berthe Tosti (translation), Chapman & Hall, 1903.
The Celebrity At Home, Chapman & Hall, 1904.
Sooner Or Later, Chapman & Hall, 1904.
The Cat. Animal Autobiographies, A. & C. Black, 1905.
The Workaday Woman, T. Werner Laurie, 1906.
White Rose Of Weary Leaf, Heinemann, 1908.
The Wife of Altamont, Heinemann, 1910.
Tales Of The Uneasy, Heinemann, 1911.
The Doll, Stanley Paul, 1911.
The Desirable Alien, Chatto & Windus, 1913.
The Celebrity's Daughter, Stanley Paul, 1913.
The House Of Many Mirrors, Stanley Paul, 1915.
Their Lives, Stanley Paul, 1916.
The Last Ditch, Stanley Paul, 1918.
Their Hearts, Stanley Paul, 1921.
The Tiger Skin, Heinemann, 1924.
More Tales Of The Uneasy, Heinemann, 1925.
The Flurried Years, Hurst and Blackett, 1926.
I Have This to Say, Boni and Liveright, 1926.
The Wife of Rossetti, John Lane, 1932.
The Governess, by Mrs Alfred Hunt and Violet Hunt, Chatto & Windus,
  1912.
Zeppelin Nights: A London Entertainment, by Violet Hunt and Ford
  Madox Hueffer, John Lane, 1916.

INDEX

and effects, 106-108; Selsey, 108-109; resigns Receivership, 110; effects of publication of *The Governess*, 109-117; proceedings against *The Throne*, 111-117; meets Rebecca West, 112; death of mother, 113; Christmas at Farnham, 114; trial of *Throne*, 115-116; disgrace and exile, 116-121; return to South Lodge, 121; changes at South Lodge, 121-123; Germany with Mastermans, 124-125; Vorticists and *Blast!*, 125-127; guest of Mary Borden, 127-128; war and consequences, 128-134; publication of *The Good Soldier*, 131; distress at Ford's enlisting, 132; meets Frieda Lawrence, 132; alone in London, 133; visits Henry James, 136-137; quarrels with Ford, 137-139; meets Stella Bowen, 139; recurrence of syphilis, 141; dependence on Ford, 142; break with Ford, 142; concentration on writing, 143-151; party with Ford, 153; distress at Ford's abandonment, 152-155; response to Ford's writing, 156-157, 173-174; publication of *The Flurried Years*, 158; continuing friendships, 171; writes on Proust, 171; injunction by Elsie, 172; meets Virginia Woolf, 174; biography of Elizabeth Siddal, 175; work on Charles Howell, 182-183; loneliness and mental deterioration, xii, 183-186; visit of Pound, 184-185; removal of sculpture, 186; death, xi, 186; reputation, 187-188
appearance, 9-10, 36, 64, 107,

139, 154, 157, 185
personality, 17, 22, 28, 97, 119, 138, 151, 156-157, 168-170, 173-174, 178, 187
houses: South Lodge, xi, 68-69, 71-72, 76, 78, 84-85, 96, 101, 112, 119, 121-122, 125, 133, 137-138, 140-141, 151, 153, 163, 168-169, 183-187; The Knapp, Selsey, 123, 129, 131-132, 137, 139-141, 165; Tor Villas, 7, 20, 26, 33, 47, 186
as a writer, 39, 43-51, 61-63, 133-136, 156, 157, 158-170, 171-172, 175-182
influences on: Austen, 45, 50-51, 134; Browning, 32, 47, 167; Burne-Jones, 9, 175, 178-179; Crawfurd, 43; James, 40, 135-136, 167; Maugham, 49-50; Richardson, 50; Rossetti, 8, 32, 178-179; Ruskin, 20-25, 46-47, 166, 172, 181; Turner, 46; Wilde, 44-47, 136
on art and artists, 8, 11, 17, 22, 46, 61, 71, 118, 122, 125, 126, 144, 146, 161-164, 168-169, 175-182, 185
on education of girls, 18-19, 24, 148-149, 181
on marriage and divorce, 38, 50-51, 80, 98, 144, 145
on women's place in society, xii, 51, 80, 144, 146, 164-165, 169-170, 175-176, 178-181
works: *Affairs of the Heart*, 48; 'Alfred William Hunt, R.W.S. 1830-1896', 7; 'Arnold Bennett in Paris', 53; *The Celebrity at Home*, 49; *The Celebrity's Daughter*, 16, 115, 117, 134-135; *The*